An Ethics of Betrayal

An Ethics of Betrayal

The Politics of Otherness in Emergent
U.S. Literatures and Culture

CRYSTAL PARIKH

Fordham University Press
NEW YORK 2009

© 2009 Fordham University Press

All rights reserved. No part of this publication may be reproduced, stored in a retrieval system, or transmitted in any form or by any means—electronic, mechanical, photocopy, recording, or any other—except for brief quotations in printed reviews, without the prior permission of the publisher.

Fordham University Press has no responsibility for the persistence or accuracy of URLs for external or third-party Internet websites referred to in this publication and does not guarantee that any content on such websites is, or will remain, accurate or appropriate.

Library of Congress Cataloging-in-Publication Data

Parikh, Crystal.
   An ethics of betrayal : the politics of otherness in emergent U.S. literatures and culture / Crystal Parikh. — 1st ed.
      p. cm.
   Includes bibliographical references and index.
   ISBN 978-0-8232-3042-6 (cloth : alk. paper)
   ISBN 978-0-8232-3043-3 (pbk. : alk. paper)
   1. American literature—Minority authors—History and criticism—Theory, etc. 2. Betrayal in literature. 3. Ethics in literature. 4. Literature, Comparative. 5. Race relations in literature. I. Title.
   PS153.M56P37 2009
   810.9'3529—dc22

2009004718

Printed in the United States of America

11 10 09   5 4 3 2 1

First edition

A book in the American Literatures Initiative (ALI), a collaborative publishing project of NYU Press, Fordham University Press, Rutgers University Press, Temple University Press, and the University of Virginia Press. The Initiative is supported by The Andrew W. Mellon Foundation. For more information, please visit www.americanliteratures.org.

To Ila and Awanish Parikh

Contents

	Acknowledgments	ix
1	Introduction: An Ethics of Betrayal	1
2	Late Arrivals: An Ethics of Betrayal in Racial and National Formation	29
3	Accidents and Obligations: Minority Neoconservatives and U.S. Racial Discourse	64
4	Ethnic America Undercover: The Intellectual and Minority Discourse	96
5	The Passion: The Betrayals of Elián González and Wen Ho Lee	129
	Epilogue: The Traitors in Our Midst	160
	Notes	173
	Bibliography	219
	Index	237

Acknowledgments

My greatest pleasure in completing *An Ethics of Betrayal* comes in the opportunity I have to thank the many individuals who have seen me through the process of writing it. To begin, I have been deeply indebted to the intellectual challenges and generosity that Sangeeta Ray and Kandice Chuh offered me as a graduate student. They each introduced me to the questions that stirred and haunted me for years afterwards. They have also provided me with models of the responsible, committed scholar I have endeavored to become. Sangeeta once assured me that "the pleasure is in the critique," and this perspective has sustained my love of reading for quite some time. Also at the University of Maryland, I was fortunate to have had the guidance of exceptional teachers. I thank Orrin Wang, Martha Nell Smith, Bill Cohen, and Katie King for their particular contributions to my graduate education.

I am grateful for the friends and colleagues—many of whom work in areas quite distinct from my own—who have read, commented on, and helped me develop *An Ethics of Betrayal*. Vincent Cheng, Elaine Freedgood, and Corrinne Harol have been sources of insight and consolation for me, and they have each contributed to this project in ways that transformed it. I also thank Leslie Bow, Stuart Culver, Lisa Duggan, Adam Green, Philip Brian Harper, Martin Harries, Howard Horwitz, Jane Iwamura, Kimberly Lau, Alice Maurice, Viet Thanh Nguyen, Gary Okihiro, Minh-Ha Pham, Matthew Potolsky, Karen Shimakawa, Maeera Schreiber, Lok Siu, and Kathryn Stockton, for all that they have done to shepherd this book—and myself—along at different stages. I deeply regret that Gillian Brown passed away before I was able to share the outcome of this work with her; she remains for me a touchstone of integrity and compassion.

Although he might no longer remember, it was David Eng who suggested to me, many years ago, the concept of an "ethics of betrayal," and that formulation provided me a way to begin sorting through the heterogeneous dimensions of subjectivity, agency, responsibility, and consequences in U.S. ethnic studies that had been troubling me for some time. On the other end of the process, I thank Tina Chen and Daniel Kim, as well as Ricardo Ortíz, for their generous, enthusiastic engagement with what resulted. I have been the beneficiary of Helen Tartar's unflagging dedication to this project, and I am grateful to her for finding such an ideal home for *An Ethics of Betrayal* at Fordham University Press. I thank her, Tim Roberts, and Ruth Steinberg for their patience and for their extraordinary efficiency in bringing this book to print. An earlier version of Chapter 3 appeared in *Contemporary Literature*, 43, no. 2 (2002): 249–84. Parts of Chapter 4 were also previously published as an essay in *Racial (Trans)Formations: Latinos and Asians Remaking the United States*, ed. Nicholas De Genova (Duke University Press, 2006). The editorial advice that I received on these pieces was critical to the development of *An Ethics of Betrayal*.

There have been many gifted students, far too many for me to name, who have inspired and challenged me over the years that I worked on *An Ethics of Betrayal*. Nevertheless, I owe a special debt that I want to acknowledge to Andre Carrington, Miabi Chatterji, Stephanie Hsu, Rana Jaleel, Sabrina Lechter, and Roy Perez for the camaraderie and many kindnesses they have extended to me. I am also grateful for the institutional support that helped me to complete this book. This includes, at the University of Utah, a mini-grant from the College of Humanities as well as a Faculty Research Grant from the University Research Committee and at New York University, a Goddard Junior Faculty Fellowship and support from the Department of English Stein Fund. I thank the helpful staff members for aiding my research at the University of Miami's Cuban Collection at the Richter Library and the Asian American Collection at the Ethnic Studies Library of the University of California, Berkeley. I also thank Christopher Sánchez, who provided elegant translations for the numerous articles I located in these archives, as well as his genuine interest this project.

Of course, the years and effort it takes to write a book require a good deal of personal and emotional support, and I am extremely lucky to have generous friends who have provided me with it. Christine Cupaiuolo, Liz Deloughrey, Bernie Heidkamp, Keely McCarthy, Steve Newman, Cathy Romagnolo, and Geoffrey Schramm have given me more than they could possibly know. I am grateful to Nancy, David, and Emily Sobie for their encouragement and good cheer over the years. I am happy to have a chance to welcome Charlie Sobie, the newest of the Sobies, who arrived in time for me to acknowledge him here.

I have come to understand and appreciate anew the unconditional support my family has provided me and how it allows me do the work I do. I thank Sushrut, Ivonne, Kirin, and Arjun Parikh for providing me a place where I can rest and be charmed over and over again. I have dedicated this book to my parents, Awanish and Ila Parikh, whose loyalty to me never wavers and with whom all of my questions begin. I find it nearly impossible to put in words my gratitude and affection for Eric Sobie, who has not only been with me as I wrote and rewrote each page of this book, but who has built a life with me and has been my home for as long as it has mattered. Nikhil Sobie, my own precious third, reminds me each and every day what a gift my responsibility to an-other can be.

An Ethics of Betrayal

1 / Introduction: An Ethics of Betrayal

> *Treachery is more sweetly served by our dearest than by archstrangers we never see.*
>
> —CHANG-RAE LEE, *NATIVE SPEAKER*

In Dante's *Inferno*, as is famously known, the ninth circle of hell is reserved for the most loathsome of sinners, those given special trust and love who have proven themselves traitors to God, country, and family. Most impressively, Lucifer gnaws on the heads of Judas, Brutus, and Cassius and weeps as he struggles futilely to free himself from his own entrapment. In Dante's portrait, betrayal is a transgression in which crime provides its own punishment. Where traitor feeds upon traitors, betrayal exacts its own self-consuming vindication. Lucifer's flapping wings only produce cold winds, gusts of ignorance and impotence that further ensure he is trapped in the icy hell created by his own rebellion against God. *An Ethics of Betrayal* asks why and how, in a very different place and time than Dante's—the United States at the end of the twentieth century—this portrait of iniquitous betrayers remains a viable emblem of the relations between self and others, identity and difference, that undergird the charge of betrayal. This book investigates the structures of knowledge and feeling upon which betrayals depend, through which traitors are forged, and which these acts of betrayal transform.

In particular, *An Ethics of Betrayal* reads betrayals as performances of social difference in the context of Asian American and Latina/o racial formation and literary and cultural production. By adopting an ethical mode of inquiry to read what I describe below as "parables" of betrayal, this book asks what the possibilities and limitations of minority discourse are with respect to projects of democracy and social justice for "the Other." Betrayals, I contend, can perform a cultural critique of the social conditions by which the minority subject comes into being and of the possibilities for agency and transformation available to that subject once it has come into being. Betrayals channel these questions of being, agency, and change through constitutive, if contingent, relations of responsibility. *An Ethics of Betrayal* contends that it is only through such relations of responsibility that the emergence of minority subjectivity is actually possible. When the protagonist of Chang-rae Lee's novel *Native Speaker* (1995), Henry, surmises "in every betrayal dwells a self-betrayal, which brings you that much closer to a reckoning," he casts betrayal as neither a simple deception nor an easily committed or readily justified transgression.[1] Henry's further observation that "treachery is more sweetly served by our dearest" attests to how the force of injury and resulting bitterness that inheres in betrayal emanates from a privileged bond of intimacy, identification, or communion. In the exploitation of those closest and most dear, we turn the strength of our ties to others against those others, or they against us. Betrayals are only possible because of the inveterate attachments that the subject foregoes, in an act that evinces those attachments even as it violates them. Such betrayals are traumatic; they undo the binds between the self and those most intimate to the self. They enact ruptures that change one's life-world, ruptures from which there is no recovery. The "reckoning" attendant upon the act of betrayal counts the costs, to the self and to others, and a betrayal costs everyone dearly.

And yet, if there is no recovering oneself from the trauma of betrayal, there is nonetheless an "after" to the act, a new world of meanings and relations, brought into existence by betrayal, into which the subject is thrown. Thus, *An Ethics of Betrayal* asks whether traitors might offer a crucial and unique perspective on the complexities of belonging, assimilation, and exclusion in U.S. culture and politics. I argue that democratic politics and social justice cannot be conceived as, in Richard Rorty's words, a "larger loyalty," a broadening of the sphere of loyalty in order to build "a community of trust between ourselves and others," as benign as such an imperative might seem.[2] Because such an expansiveness recognizes the other only in its potential identification with, and assimilation to, the self, a "larger loyalty" obviates our obligation to the other "as Other," an obligation that precedes the self and makes the self possible. In adjoining ethical inquiry to a project of social justice, I would like to illuminate the conditions of betrayal inherent in the limited vocabularies, conflicted and contingent subject positions, crossed meanings, and heterogeneous intentions that prevent the "accomplishment" of justice and democracy in a full or timely manner. As I describe below, an ethical perspective understands that the futurity, *l'avenir*, of justice and democracy is founded in the subject's responsibility and responsiveness to the Other, involving all sorts of dissatisfaction, uncertainty, and even sacrifice, if the subject is to remain open to the possibilities of being.

An ethical betrayal, as I detail below, comprises the call of the Other and the reformulation of self-present identity that this call performs. The ethics of betrayal that concerns me in particular is the movement of alterity in American racial and national formation that I will examine in the following chapters. In these instances, betrayal is not a simple celebration of transgression, although transgression necessarily inheres in betrayals. Nor is it the institution of larger, more-encompassing, or even more "tolerant" communities of being (e.g., in this book, a rubric more inclusive than "Asian American," "Latino," "people of color," or "American"). Instead, justice and democracy proceed through the often traumatic and unanticipated ruptures that open, in Jacques Derrida's words, the "avenues" for the arrival of the Other. Accordingly, if the subject's responsibility to the Other necessitates a sacrifice of the self, a sacrifice that amounts to a betrayal of the self, this does not mean in turn that all betrayals can be conceived as ethical in and of themselves. Rather, I emphasize ethical *critique* as a mode for following the minority subject as it wrestles with the implications of its own existence, that is, with a subjectivity that is at once ex-centric to the dominant political and epistemological regimes of U.S. culture and society but also authorized in certain limited ways to speak by and to that culture and society. In this book, I will demonstrate that, as the minority subject confronts (and is confronted with) the conditions of its own existence, it engages in acts of betrayal. This subject continually and necessarily returns to founding moments, reckoning with the literal and symbolic violence at the heart of its own being, and it risks the self in order to call forth the others who haunt that being.[3] Thus, the ethico-politics I explore recognizes that the act of betrayal can simultaneously create and unmake selves in its orientations toward and obligations to the Other.

This is also a mode for reading cultural moments, social formations, and literary texts that, as part and parcel of the ethico-political project, faces up to the failures, responsibilities, and undoings of minority discourse. These failures, I should clarify, are not due to some shortcomings or flaws in individual visions that minority activists and agents propound. Rather, they are inevitable, structural incommensurabilities that plague social formations, juridico-political deliberation and agency, and cultural identities. This book draws extensively upon work in ethnic studies and critical race theory, along with feminist, queer, post-Marxist, and psychoanalytic theories. The analytical framework generated by this scholarship has proven crucial to understanding, in the site-specific context of the United States, how the "ideal" American is in part wrought through the deployment of racial and gender ideologies. Yet, a pitfall of this line of inquiry has too often been a seemingly facile celebration of transgression qua transgression. In such cases, critics have sometimes valued, above all else, any violation of normative subjectivity, without always considering the broader consequences and ongoing questions of responsibility that transgression and resistance entail. For example, for what injuries, to themselves and to others, can the minority subject be held accountable? By what means does one account for this responsibility? My analysis of betrayal in this book thus adds to extant criticism by foregrounding an ethical account of transgressions, especially as they reconfigure the cultural politics of minority discourse. *An Ethics of Betrayal* contends that we must account for the values that are established or undermined when antagonistic, or even traitorous, agents contest social identities and formations.

The Ethical Account

In reading betrayal in relation to an ethico-political project, I am concerned with an ethics that goes beyond the conventional notion of moral imperatives to which the normative subject is beholden. Instead, I adopt a post-Enlightenment conception of ethics as, in Emmanuel Levinas's terms, a "first philosophy." Ethical inquiry of this type positions ethics as a pre-ontological and irrecusable obligation to the Other, to which we are subject. For Levinas, responsibility *precedes* the notion of contracted commitments and ideas of community and arises from an unrepresentable "immemorial past."[4] This anachronistic and "anarchic" responsibility summons the subject from nowhere into a present time, bearing with it "the system of an immemorial freedom that is even older than being, or decisions, or deeds."[5] Levinas emphasizes a plurality of existence that otherness signifies, a plurality that is not a "multiplicity of existents" nor pure absence, but rather the stripping of the subject of its subjectivity, a stripping that participates in "existence" without "existents."[6] Traditional philosophy, in its adherence to the "very existing of the [singular] existent," guards a relation of the self to itself. In contrast, Levinas contends that thinking the Being (or the Heideggerian

Dasein) of being precipitates darkness, the impersonal and anonymous existence of "there is," as its own residue. The fundamental presence of absence against which existents or beings are forged or (again in Heideggerian terms) "thrown" issues forth from our very attempt to grasp being as Being.[7] Death, that which is "insurmountable," "inexorable," and "fundamentally incomprehensible," delimits ontology as a first philosophy, because death always exhausts "possible modes of meaning for thought."[8] Levinas replaces *Dasein* with the self's relationship to the Other by suggesting that death is not ultimately a test of authenticity or supreme virility, as in Heidegger's being-toward-death, but something absolutely unknowable and always in the future that nevertheless confronts subjectivity, marking the limit of the subject's virility. As Levinas contends, death stands not merely as the subject's not-being (present), but rather figures a relationship with the "impossibility of nothingness" and, accordingly, with "mystery" and with the future.[9] Located eternally in the future, death deserts every present, not because *we* evade death, but because death itself is ungraspable. If the "now," the present of self-presence, designates the mastery of the subject over (its own) existence, death in its futurity always ascribes the end of the subject's virility and heroism and proves the limits of idealism.[10]

Here, the assumption of being occurs only in and through the demand that the otherness of existence makes upon the subject, prior to which no self exists as self-presence. The possibility of the subject rests, in this account, "in passivity," in its subjection to the Other.[11] The openness to that demand, the responsiveness to and responsibility for the Other, are the irrevocable conditions of the self assuming itself, so that, as Judith Butler observes with respect to the Levinasian subject, "To claim the self-identity of the subject is thus an act of irresponsibility, an effort to close off one's fundamental vulnerability to the Other, the primary accusation that the Other bears."[12] The Other exists not as an alter ego but is in and of itself the condition of alterity, and being accedes to an intersubjectivity that is profoundly asymmetrical. Furthermore, the subject cannot return itself to the generalized existence of the Other, but it must also respond for "one's right to be," because Being forecloses the Other's existence: "My being-in-the-world or my 'place in the sun,' my being at home, have these not also been the usurpation of spaces belonging to the other man whom I have already oppressed or starved, or driven out into a third world? Are they not acts of repulsing, excluding, exiling, stripping, killing?"[13] Being, Levinas argues, entails a violence for which the subject is always responsible, despite its "intentional innocence."[14] The

Other, as a "neighbor" to self-presence, immanently obligates the subject to respond to that Other. The subject is enjoined to responsiveness and responsibility in its very right to be.

An ideal(ized) subject justifies itself by declaring the unconditional self-identity of its presence. In contrast, ethics as a first philosophy undermines the ontological priority of the subject with the overriding question it poses, that of whether "my being is justified, if the *Da* of my *Dasein* is not already the usurpation of somebody else's place."[15] "Responsibility" provides the "answer" to this crisis of selfhood, but it is not a reply that consoles the subject. Rather, it returns the subject "to its capacity to fear injustice more than death, to prefer to suffer than to commit injustice, and to prefer that which justifies being over that which assures it."[16] In order to delineate a methodology of ethical inquiry and to describe an ethico-political project for minority discourse, we might say that this concern with the modes of self-justification of being, and the undoing of it, distinguishes the "ethical turn" in critical theory, most thoroughly expounded by Derrida in a number of his later writings; I draw in particular from *The Gift of Death*, *Adieu to Emmanuel Levinas*, "Force of Law," *Specters of Marx*, and *Rogues*.

An Ethico-Political Project

The post-Enlightenment ethics of Levinas and Derrida characterizes a radically subjective interdependence between self and Other, an interdependence that precedes subjectivity and makes subjectivity possible. Responsibility toward the Other is therefore not "taken" by the self, but rather conditions the subject's very coming into being, a being that, as I have described above, must always attempt to justify itself to the Other.[17] However, in a move that complicates the relationship of the "highest passion" between the self and the Other, Derrida recasts the assertion of the singularity of Otherness that Levinas ascribes to God—the infinite Other—as an *infinitude* of alterity. In his formulation of "every other as every other" (*tout autre comme tout autre*), Derrida radicalizes the theological ground on which post-Enlightenment ethical critique emerges, by contending that duty to God (i.e., the single Other) is never sufficient, since every "other other" demands absolute responsibility from the subject.

Here, Derrida blurs not only the line between religion and ethics, but, even more so, the line between these orders of inquiry, based as they are on the duty to the *singular* Other, and those of law and politics, where adjudication *between* responsibilities to others ensues. In conceiving of "every other as every other," Derrida designates the unsustainability of the ethical relation as a *dyadic* responsibility between the subject and Other by evoking "the third." As he writes in *Adieu to Emmanuel Levinas*, the "interposition" of the third inaugurates the orders of justice in politics and law.[18] Because the third "arrives without waiting," it necessarily shuttles the subject into the realm of visibility, representability, thematization, and decidability (as in "before a court of justice"), necessarily into, that is, "places ethics should exceed."[19] Because this "third" is always already an other other that accompanies the Other's call to the subject, Derrida finds that questions of justice and politics attend Levinas's first philosophy of ethics at its very conception. Derrida describes this "thirdness" as creating a necessary "double bind" in the ethical relation. Because of the absolute responsibility that the ethical relationship demands, "pure and immediate ethics" suggests a "hypothesis of a violence," where the distinctions between "good and evil, love and hate, giving and taking, the desire to live and the death drive, the hospitable welcome and the egoistic or narcissistic closing up within oneself" become impossible to discern.[20] The third, Derrida suggests, protects against "the vertigo of ethical violence" by interrupting the "absolute unicity" of the self and Other. By mediating between demands of others, the juridico-political function called forth by the third breaks into the singular and exceptional ethical relation, bringing it into relation with all the *other* singular and exceptional relations to which the subject is responsible. Of course, this mediating role "violates in its turn, at least potentially, the purity of the ethical desire devoted to the unique."[21] The "terrible ineluctability of a double constraint" results from the absoluteness of the ethical bond and the necessary violation of that absolute bond by the necessary attention to other others.[22]

The third, the other other, then configures the relationship between the ethical and the juridico-political not as a teleological progression, but rather, I suggest, as "projects" of one another. In the "projection" of ethical responsibility onto legal and political orders, and vice versa, the dyadic encounter of the ethical relation forms the constitutive grounds and remains embedded in the multiple and competing claims of the political sphere. As such, juridico-political deliberation always "reverts" to the ethical, and the subject's asymmetrical relation of responsibility to the Other, such that the ethical always ruptures the political, rendering it continually unfinished and open.[23] Yet, if the ethical indexes the non-totalized and non-transcendent relation between the subject and the Other, then politics rewrites that relationship "to all the others, to the plurality of beings that make up the community."[24] For Derrida, justice and democracy are "to come," in the sense that they are always deferred onto the Otherness of the future. That which is to come impinges on self-presence. The future to come, paradoxically, does not wait and is always arriving, and its unknowability provides the time of the possibility of justice. In *Specters of Marx*, Derrida writes of this time, the "time of the other,'" as occurring "when 'things are going badly'" and "time [is] out of joint."[25] In contrast to Heidegger's sense that time-out-of-joint requires, as part of making right, a "proper jointure" that restores the fullness and self-sameness of presence in the present, Derrida argues that to "do" or "render" justice occurs in the moment of disjunction: "But with the other, is not this disjuncture, this dis-adjustment of the 'it's going badly' necessary for the good or at least the just, to be announced? Is not disjuncture the very possibility of the other?"[26]

Justice to come thus proves "not only a juridical or political concept," but "opens up for *l'avenir* the transformation, the recasting or refounding of law and politics."[27] The possibility for this transformative refounding of law and politics bespeaks the imperative to enter juridical and political battles, so as to prevent the idea of justice from being appropriated "by the most perverse calculation."[28] The idea of infinite justice continually "*requires* us to calculate," but at the same time, opens up those calculations to uncertainty. Thus, each "advance" in law or politics requires also that we "reinterpret the very foundations of law such as they had previously been calculated or delimited."[29] This return, made by and in the name of justice and democracy, which reinterprets the foundations of law, order, and governance, also provides, in *Specters of Marx* and in *Rogues*, the democratic politics of deconstruction. The method that this ethico-juridical orientation poses is never a simple reparation to an original state of being, but rather a *rearticulation of the very structure or conditions of the disjointure*.[30] Deconstructive justice illuminates that which cannot be gathered into "the One" as traces of both, that "which does not happen" and of "what would *happen otherwise*."[31] To seek out the Other, that which remains unintelligible and unintegrated to laws, norms, and representations, is to seek out the ethical possibility of justice to come and democracy to come.

"Democracy to come" then asks about the possibility of "living together," in such a way that undermines the positioning of the self-same as sovereign; it asks, "Must one live together only with one's like, with someone semblable?"[32] Derrida contrasts the structure of "the One," around which forms of "actual democracy" are realized and recognized, with democracy to come, "the truth of the other, heterogeneity, the heteronomic and the dissymmetric, disseminal multiplicity, the anonymous 'anyone,' the 'no matter who,' the indeterminate 'each one.'"³³ In the character of freedom that has become the basis for imagining and defining democracy (even beyond the more literal, etymological significance of the word to mean the "rule of the people"), he discerns the "suicidal" kernel at the heart of the concept of democracy. Taken in its most radical form, the freedom of democracy includes the freedom for the "enemies" of democracy to suspend or destroy democracy through the very channels of democracy itself, namely, those of egalitarian and majoritarian consensus.³⁴ Democracy's elemental freedom, which sustains its unpredictability and openness, means that "democracy is what it is only in the différance by which it defers itself and differs from itself."³⁵ Conceptually at least, democracy carries within itself the promise or threat that the presence of an "axial or univocal meaning" might destroy or "get carried away" with itself.³⁶

At the same time, the "to come" or futurity of democracy does not authorize a deferral of democratic politics; rather, Derrida contends, the injunction of democracy carries with it an urgency that cannot be postponed.³⁷ For this reason, he argues that thinking of différance *and* thinking the political, together, can amount to a democratic politics.³⁸ Where freedom entreats an openness to the most radical of possibilities, to the horizon of possibility (and not as "power, mastery, or force, or even as a faculty, as a possibility of the 'I can'" but rather as "incommensurability"), the possibility of democracy to come confounds the idea of democracy as the power of the people or the rule of the majority.³⁹ This critical advance toward the horizon of the idea of democracy, where the truth of the Other cannot be assimilated to the One, provides us with an opportunity to "know better what 'democracy' will have been able to signify, what it *ought*, in truth, to have meant."⁴⁰ "Democracy to come," like "justice to come," never indicates simply and only that ideal forms of democracy and justice do not and will never actually exist, but neither that one day they will be fully self-present. Rather, while these expressions do emphasize the ongoing deferral of democracy and justice in the material and historical practices of politics and law, they also yoke together the necessary survival of *desire* for democracy and justice and the obligation that "forces" the continual reemergence of democracy and justice in the "conditional grammar" of an "if there were."⁴¹

Derrida (reading Jean-Jacques Rousseau on democracy) contends that it is the *gap between* the impossible presence of democracy and justice and their flawed, finite actual forms (forms that exist nonetheless in the order of the possible) that provides the avenue of the Other's arrival. The "to come" sustains the unpredictable but assured movement of democracy and justice in the world.[42] It is precisely the urgency and imminence of (the demand for) democracy and justice that interrupts the idealization of these concepts as impossible: "This im-possible . . . is what is most undeniably real. And sensible. Like the other. Like the irreducible and nonappropriable différance of the other."[43] Thus, democracy to come and justice to come have what Derrida calls the structure of the promise, "the memory of that which carries the future, the to-come, here and now."[44] While these expressions "announce" nothing about the present or even about the certainty of a future present, in a constative sense, they continually and performatively enact "conviction" as to the possibilities of justice and democracy to come.

An Ethics of Betrayal

The non-assimilative encounter between self and Other is difficult to imagine precisely because it undermines the sovereignty of the subject who undertakes ethical responsibility. The ethical encounter as such always amounts to a "self-betrayal," one that inverts the formula, "In every betrayal dwells a self-betrayal," that Henry of *Native Speaker* describes. As a first philosophy, ethics is always an ethics of self-betrayal, an accountability to the Other that costs the self and those with whom the self identifies and is identified. The reckoning with the Other initiates the betrayal of the self. In an ethics of betrayal, then, the traitor cannot be reduced to the terms of deception, hypocrisy, or cynicism (although the act of betrayal might express elements of each or all of these), because all of these refer to a place of authentic self-presence from which the adequacy of (self-)representation might be evaluated. Instead, an ethical reading of betrayal discerns self-presence, the coherence of an autonomous, sovereign subject unto itself, as impossible.

The *OED* traces the earliest occurrences (in the thirteenth century) of the word *betray* as denoting "to give up, place in the power of an enemy" and "to expose to punishment," and *betrayal* as a "treacherous giving up to an enemy." In signifying both deceit and a perfidious complicity with an enemy, betrayal characterizes relationships that are, in the broadest sense, "political." Betrayal also registers its effects not only in collective, social, or structural registers, but in ways that are deeply intimate and affective, so much so that to betray has also meant "to seduce" and "to induce, through falsity, the surrender of a woman's chastity." Indeed, feminist critics and theorists in particular have recently offered sophisticated analyses of the themes and tropes of betrayal, often turning a critical eye toward the demands united in the figures of (as in Dante's conception) "God, country, and family," which continue to remain so deeply naturalized in social life as to seem intractable.

For example, works such as Leslie Bow's *Betrayal and Other Acts of Subversion*, Cherríe Moraga's *Loving in the War Years*, and Kamala Visweweran's essay "Betrayal" have theorized traitorous acts, arguing that betrayals define the bonds of loyalty while simultaneously marking off presumptions of innocence, boundaries of community, parameters of knowledge, and spaces of agency in which women, especially women of color, are situated. As Bow argues, betrayals can constitute a "subversion of repressive authority that depends on upholding strict borders between groups and individuals."[45] As a critical perspective, then, the labeling of the traitor, in which a subject is cast "as beyond the pale of an at times unspoken collective," illuminates "the fact that such affiliations have terms of admission, that they are neither natural nor, at times uncoerced."[46] As such, Bow locates betrayals, not only as subversions of such affiliations and authorities, but as rhetorical figurations through which women execute forms of "creative activism."[47] At the same time, Bow sounds a cautionary note, which we would do well to heed, about the consequences of multiple affiliations and the negotiation of difference. Despite critical innovations that accept identities as socially constructed, "the subject's struggle for self-definition is yet contained within ideological structures" that render the charge of betrayal enduringly meaningful in the first place.[48]

My own interest in understanding the work and effects of betrayal in American minority discourse originated in the ongoing vitality that the charge of "betrayal" retains for a range of subjects—male and female, queer and heterosexual, citizen and "alien"—in spite of the nominally postmodern sensibilities characteristic of contemporary cultural practices and social texts. In my initial analyses of scenes, tropes, and themes of betrayal, I concluded that betrayals manifest performances of certain kinds of difference, thereby making visible heterogeneous objects of loyalty, motives for violating such loyalties, and modes of violation. That is to say, I began with the *politics* of betrayal, and betrayal as a mode of political transgression by which the subject negotiated the heterogeneities of social formation. As serviceable as this thesis might be, and it is one to which I return repeatedly, it seemed unable to account for the remarkable ferocity that betrayals inspire and the special asperity with which charges of betrayal are leveled. Given that rebellion and transgression do not necessarily *always* meet with such intensely passionate responses, betrayal seemed to signal a crucial subset of such instances of social agency and decision making.

Acts of betrayal expose particular bonds—and they expose these bonds *as* particular and partial, not total—as they do damage to them. Indeed, these betrayals expose the bonds between subjects so as to damage them, thereby transposing those bonds, rendering them seemingly "false." However, an ethical inquiry, based on the Levinasian sense of the irrecusable, interminable responsibility to the Other, troubles the notion of "falseness" that betrayal conventionally evokes.[49] Instead, I argue, betrayals can open a future that is unimaginable and unintelligible from within the bonds of fidelity and identification. The traitor can never account for him- or herself according to the language that precedes betrayal; rather, betrayal is a moment of violent invention. From this perspective, betrayals are intersubjective, revealing to another or to, more generally and publicly, others, what had been thought to be a sacred or secret trust. *An Ethics of Betrayal* asks the political and social questions as to *whom* and *how* the traitor betrays: under what social, material, and historical conditions is betrayal possible? But it also asks the perhaps more difficult questions as to *why* the traitor betrays and *what* the betrayal makes possible, questions for which the traitor him- or herself is often unable to account, or to do so until too late. For if betrayals undo the bonds by which subjects know themselves in relation to others, they wreak havoc not only on the betrayed, but on the traitor as well.

Betrayals can rupture the subject's "being" and open it toward the Other. In these cases, the unintelligibility of betrayal points us to the limits of a generalized language that can account with finality for what the subject does and why it does so. Betrayal can intimate an-other knowledge, the knowledge of the Other, that is a nonknowledge, insofar as it can never be made transparent and communicable. This nonknowledge undermines self-presence, the subject's unified being that would foreclose the possibility of betrayal in the first place. By reading betrayal for the possibility of an ethico-political project, we keep alive, against a moralistic foreclosure, the possibility of the radical freedom that marks the subject's being-toward-the-Other. For example, in the following chapters, acts of betrayal repeatedly evoke "diaspora" as a conceptual space of otherness, preserved against the totalizing demands of both nationalist and minority discourses. At the same time, by linking ethical being with acts of betrayal and the figure of the traitor, my account of both ethics and politics insists upon the tremendous difficulty and strife that this orientation toward "justice to come" and" democracy to come" entails. The ethical relation with the Other who cannot be known and toward a future arrival that cannot be refused levies its toll in the present, and in the presence of the traitor.

The Politics of Otherness

The narratives I examine in this book represent the stakes and costs of betrayal, as well as the new possibilities that betrayals create. I contend that without considering the productive aspects of betrayal, we risk obscuring the difficult possibilities, the possibility of the Other, that betrayals can effect. Nevertheless, the political character of minority discourse makes readily apparent the injuries and losses that incur in and through betrayal. *An Ethics of Betrayal* is entirely concerned with acts, themes, scenes, and tropes of betrayal in minority discourse, where these stakes and costs are indeed very high. I would like to address this issue here in terms of the methodological encounter between ethnic studies/critical race theory and Continental philosophy. In other words, what are the implications for constructing a historical-material project out of a philosophical tradition that has, at its core, striven to abstract itself from the particularities of history, corporeality, and materiality? The tradition of Continental philosophy, which Levinasian ethics educes, has remained notoriously infelicitous to conversations about national formation and racial difference. As such, and especially with respect to the material histories and structural inequities through which race and nation are lived, critical race theorists and cultural critics of ethnic and American studies have approached Continental philosophy with understandable caution. Ethics has remained a largely inoperative term, lest it reintroduce, through a back door, the politics of "blaming the victim" which has long plagued racialized subjects.[50]

For Derrida, following Levinas, the ethical responsibility to the Other always precedes all the specific contextual, material, embodied, and social forms that it might take. Because it evinces "existence beyond existents," alterity as such is not associated with specific forms of social difference.[51] According to Levinas and Derrida, the constitutive ethical obligation is not to a positive other, but rather to an absence of being that is nonetheless not pure negation or void. In this light, it is a mistake to understand categories of social difference, such as race, gender, nation, or religion, as locations essentially inhabited by the Other, because at most they provide metaphors or thematizations of alterity. For Levinas, the responsibility to the Other always precedes the particular discourses through which we calculate otherness and derive meanings for it. As Sara Ahmed contends, to infer Levinasian ethics as being "on the side of the other," where the Other might be represented in, for example, the weak or the poor, presumes that Levinas thematizes the Other "as *some-thing* or *some-body* that one can be for."[52] By making the Other recognizable in the face of social others, we lose Levinas's insistence on the complete obscurity and alterity of Otherness.

However, given the genealogical tradition of classical and Continental philosophy that Levinasian ethics inherits, theorizing ethical obligation does not prove as simple as refusing to identify the Other with any particular bodies. Ahmed argues that the bind facing Levinasian ethics is that it both resists the thematization of otherness—we cannot and should not locate the Other as a representable form—while it also recognizes that the Other *has* already long been thematized in Western thought.[53] While Levinas might critique the "domestication" of otherness in particularlized morphologies, he also realizes that the Other is entrapped in this process by the imperatives of "thinking."[54] Thus, we find in Levinas's writing the contradiction that, although he maintains that the Other cannot be identified with or reduced to particular, intelligible tropes, he himself extends figures of the Other (e.g., the widow and the orphan).[55]

The persistent reiterations of these particular morphologies by which we think and speak of the Other carries with it a historicity that, if put under erasure, enacts symbolic or political violence against those particular others. The "abjection of alien forms," through which cultural productions continually imagine "close encounters" with the Other, confirms that the face-to-face has never been treated by philosophical tradition, political discourse, or popular culture as unrepresentable. Indeed, as I argue in the following sections, the "alien" in the United States has acquired a readily apparent morphology, that of the Asian and Latino. While ethical inquiry might aspire to preserve the encounter with the Other as unrepresentable, the historically specific cultural and political practices that attempt to represent, domesticate, or expel the Other all function to deny this unrepresentability.[56]

Thinking ethical responsibility through the mediated sociality of our encounters with otherness makes clear that, while one's responsibility is infinite and interminable, the imperative to respond takes place in material, determinate, and particular circumstances. One *must* respond, and response takes place in the realm of definitive, material action. However, this response does not exhaust responsibility. While thus offering a critical political perspective on the conditions and discourses that make the ethical encounter possible, we keep open the otherness of the Other that compels us to responsibility. As Ahmed concludes, the demands for justice to particular and embodied others challenge and rearticulate the systems and practices of distributive, calculated justice and representation. However, and this is the specifically *ethical* dimension of the political project that this book promotes, such redistribution cannot be consolidated as the Law or as a universal moral discourse. The opening for and openness to the unrepresentable Other attends the juridico-political project, while the latter insists that the ethical can never be withdrawn from the material, structural, and historical conditions by which otherness is encountered in the world. This ethics, Ahmed argues, "is not the forging of 'new' relations to the Other as an impossible figure, but the redressing of the constitutive violence which binds her to a given place."[57]

An Ethics of Betrayal attends to both sides of this question through its positing of an ethico-politics for minority discourse. My analyses in the following chapters asks how a subject already quite visibly not at home in the world, already a figure of the Other, the minority subject of U.S. racial and national discourses, attempts to find refuge, to make itself at home. What is the relationship between this figuration of otherness as racial and diasporic difference and the self-representations that the minority subject articulates on a multiracial and globalized terrain? Precisely how the minority subject seeks and how the minority subject *ought* to seek refuge is the crux of the ethical critique in this book. To the extent that this "ought" is always attenuated by the finite possibilities, heterogeneous discourses, and uneven resources available to the subject, I am describing the political character of this seeking refuge and of its extending hospitality to the Other. Because, as I have described above, the ethical and the political comprise one another's "projects," betrayal will mean that one's responsibilities to the Other cannot be neatly reconciled with one's responsibilities to other others.

As a study of racial and national formation, *An Ethics of Betrayal* explores the conditions from which narratives of race and ethnicity emerge and to which they respond. Because these conditions are heterogeneous and often conflicting with one another, there are also multiple possibilities for betrayal in minority formation. First, and perhaps the most visible form of betrayal, is the possibility that the minority subject undermines national unity through a treasonous act, often as an expression of "diasporic" loyalties. Second, minority subjects can betray other minority subjects, whether members of their own group or "people of color" more broadly, for example, through economic exploitation or in the political or cultural representations of "their own people." In these cases, ethical critique apprises the *possibility* of such traitorous acts as the grounds of emergent subjectivity that cannot be squared with the terms of a minority discourse of race and ethnicity.

In another significant variant, we might say that the nation betrays the minority subject by failing to uphold the promise of equal protection and treatment of all its citizens. In this instance, betrayal can only be described as unwittingly ethical, insofar as we must read for otherness *against* the foreclosure that the state attempts to accomplish. This particular version of betrayal provides the opportunity for a counter-discourse, as has been articulated in the politics of civil rights, against the accusations that nationalist discourse levels against minority subjects. However, insofar as this counter-discourse seeks to secure a unitary relationship of identity between the minority subject and the nation, ethical inquiry antagonizes the express political project of minority discourse. In this case, an ethical approach actually keeps alive the alienation ascribed to Asian Americans and Latina/os rather than denying it.

Nevertheless, it remains incumbent upon us to consider the state's construction of Asian Americans and Latina/os as alien others, which in turn secures appropriate, loyal citizenship as the grounds of political representation. Despite being the two fastest growing populations within the United States, Asian Americans and Latina/os have been racially marked by the cultural image of themselves as "forever foreign." The nation systematically denies them the trust, rights, and protection it purports to extend to all its subjects. In pairing Asian Americans and Latina/os and offering a comparative analysis of the representations of each, *An Ethics of Betrayal* argues that both groups have been plagued by images of alienness, treason, and duplicity. Yet, these representations also generate unexpected moments of responsibility and responsiveness to the Other. In the next section, I examine how the social and legal technologies of domestic racism, imperialist expansion, and exclusionary immigration policy subtended the nation's image of itself as a liberal, deracinated body politic. It is a history that haunts the nation and structures present-day Asian American and Latina/o alienation.

The Others of U. S. Racial Discourse

The postbellum nineteenth century proved a moment of significant rift in the nation's self-image. While the Fourteenth Amendment countered the earlier *Dred Scott* Supreme Court decision by incorporating African Americans as citizens, the arrival of immigrants from Europe, Mexico, and Asia, the westward expansion of the nation after the Mexican-American War, and expansion into the Pacific, the Caribbean, and Latin America following the Spanish-American War, all characterized the end of the nineteenth century as a moment of "national consolidation and imperial venture."[58] The reformist politics of Progressive Era social thinkers such as Jacob Riis proclaimed the incorporation of new immigrants into the nation to be vital to national interests. Yet they also maintained limits to this process. Reformers worked toward improvements in the material lives of nascent American citizens, but this mobility required the exclusion of those deemed racially incapable of citizenship.[59] Progressivism therefore tied political solidarity to a shared racial identity that constructed Americanism—and the democratic values ascribed to the subjects of nationalism—as a racial inheritance unavailable to inassimilable aliens.[60] This reformist program vacillated between a rhetoric of pluralist difference and the amalgamation of the melting pot. In both cases, however, it unflaggingly constructed racial limits to the liberal politics of incorporation.

Three interconnected events defined these limits with remarkable force. First, a series of legal decisions and policies culminated in the *Plessy v. Ferguson* decision, which legislated a particularized form of African American citizenship through its segregationist logic of "separate but equal." As Suzanne Oboler explains, the *Plessy* decision functioned simultaneously to enforce segregation for blacks and to "paradoxically . . . signal their partial political incorporation into the nation," a nation that could accordingly stabilize its public self-image as simultaneously democratic and white-only.[61] Second, the Spanish-American War, as Amy Kaplan has suggested, provided a cultural and political resolution to the domestic divisions and antagonisms of the Civil War and established "the birth of an empire," as it extended U. S. military and governmental hegemony into the Caribbean and the Pacific. Third, the consolidation of a comprehensive, national immigration policy, and the corresponding state apparatus to regulate and enforce that policy, produced by 1924, as Mae Ngai has demonstrated, the political and cultural image of the "illegal alien"—a "new legal and political subject" prohibited from attaining citizenship and barred from claiming rights.[62]

The *partial* incorporation of blacks into the nation that the *Plessy* decision enacted occurred against the materialized presence of the nation's *fully* other, the alien whose exclusion was secured through the management of empire and immigration. The U.S. frontier had always offered a symbolic space for the reconciliation of the ethnic and racial differences that plagued the modernizing nation, such that "marginal citizens" laid claim to full-fledged formal and cultural citizenship by "subduing others as aliens."[63] If, as Mark Weiner argues, modernization in the United States was forged through imperialist expansion, the meaning of national identity was determined through the racial, territorial, and economic discourses that empire conjoined. As Weiner explains, empire concentrated domestic wealth, necessitated the construction of a professional state apparatus, and created new market outlets for surplus capital. The concordant national narrative of progress activated specific forms of what Weiner refers to as racialized juridical discourse, which rationalized the government's break with the conventional practices of territorial incorporation that had been national policy since the Northwest Territory Ordinance of 1787.

In its adjudication of the Insular Cases, beginning in 1901 with *Downes v. Bidwell*, the Supreme Court called into question the status of native residents *as subjects* of the United States, but not as its (potential) citizens. It based this distinction on notions of civic identity and, consequently, ruled to withhold citizenship from these same subjects.[64] By characterizing the status of Puerto Rico (and other territorial possessions) as "unincorporated territory," and unincorporable without Congress's specifically acting to bring it into the nation, "the Court imagined a nightmare scenario" that inverted the terms of acquisition and colonization, whereby incorporation of Puerto Ricans, Filipinos, and other colonial subjects threatened to "undo [the nation's] sovereign government, dismember its body, enslave its citizens, and dissolve its familial bonds."[65] Kaplan explains that even the partial incorporation of African Americans as "more American than foreign immigrants" depended upon this logic: "they [could] only prove their national identity as imperial citizens."[66] In its representation of imperial encounter and domestic social relations, nationalist discourse cast the Asian/Pacific Islander and the Latin American as the inassimilable other, against whom *both* white and black citizenship was formulated. This national narrative of progressive modernity therefore occasioned specifically racializing effects, by attributing to particular, embodied others the status of alien otherness.

The nation's contemporary immigration policies further fortified the racial formation of the inassimilable alien in the twentieth century. Chicana/os, Puerto Ricans, and, eventually, all U. S. Latina/os were persistently racialized as the illegal immigrant.[67] The late nineteenth century also saw the progressive dispossession of Hispanos, those Mexicans who were incorporated as U. S. citizens after the U. S.–Mexico war by the Treaty of Guadalupe Hidalgo in 1848, from lands that had been, prior to that date, held communally.[68] The cyclical recruitment and deportation of agricultural workers by the United States further compounded the formation of Mexican and Mexican American workers alike as an alien wage labor force.[69] Consequently, although no law officially barred Mexican (or other Latin American) immigrants from entry into the U. S. and from citizenship, the increasingly intensified and publicized enforcement of immigration restrictions by the state throughout the twentieth century, such as the roundup and mass deportation to Mexico of these aliens and citizens alike, attested to Latinos' attenuated claims to citizenship rights.[70]

The similar recruitment, immigration, and later exclusions of Asian workers in the United States conceived of the Asian as an alien in the nation as well. While economic imperatives for cheap conditions of production drove the recruitment of Asian labor from 1850 to World War II, the various exclusions from citizenship rights, and ancillary alien land laws, assured that disenfranchised Asian ethnic groups would not themselves accumulate capital.[71] The cultural bars and legal prohibitions on the naturalization of Asians as American citizens eventuated in the multiple exclusion acts against Asians in the late nineteenth and early twentieth centuries. The internment of Japanese Americans during World War II demonstrated the effectiveness of this construction of the Asian in America. The relocation of 120,000 Japanese Americans, the majority of whom were U. S.-born citizens, from the West Coast to the nation's interior, and the various Supreme Court cases that upheld the state's interests and rationale for the internment (if not its constitutionality per se), broadly point to the cultural, legal, and political limits of the nation's imagined community.[72]

At the turn of the century, the conception of the usually excluded, and always ambivalent, Asian and Latina/o presence in national formation installed the black/white poles of U.S. racial discourse.[73] As Ngai discerns, by the mid-twentieth century, immigration policy and regulation had the effect of constructing not only a racialized image of the "illegal alien" as "impossible subjects," a caste whose social and economic presence always belies its cultural and political exclusion, but also a corresponding formation of the "alien citizen": birthright citizens who are nevertheless presumed foreign by national culture, and even at times by the state.[74] The extension of imperial and economic control over new territories and the alienation of *certain* others from national incorporation therefore also provided for a reformulated national imaginary under the conditions of capitalist modernity while keeping intact the color line so central to the continued function of the social order.[75] This alienation was accomplished through the interworkings of cultural and political representations of empire, legislated exclusion and restrictions, deportations, and social segregation.

At the same time, as Kaplan contends, with the "closing" of the frontier and territorial expansion, the twentieth century witnessed the redefinition of national power as an abstracted or disembodied one. The end of the Spanish-American War marked the entrance of the United States into "vaster yet less tangible networks of international markets and political influence" in the Caribbean and Asia-Pacific.[76] "Disembodiment" now came to characterize a cultural fantasy about the so-called "informal empire"—that "total control" might somehow be "disentangled from direct political annexation."[77] American expansionism in the Philippines, Cuba, and Puerto Rico thus responded to the socioeconomic and geopolitical complications posed to the nation by the closing of the frontier, even as it devised the nation's self-image as an exceptionally destined democracy.[78] The U.S.'s entrance onto the international stage of imperialism accordingly contrasted itself to both earlier European imperial enterprises *and* the contemporary anticolonial demands in Asia, the Pacific, the Caribbean, and Latin America.[79] If colonial insurgents in other regions compared their struggles to the U.S. War of Independence, such rhetoric was quickly dismissed in the United States.[80] The disavowal of these "other" democratic revolutions indeed grounded the exceptionalism of the nation's self-image.[81]

Thus, even as a progressive narrative of U.S. exceptionalism constructed the nation as the unique achievement of liberal democracy in the world, it not only could not resolve the fundamental contradiction of domestic racism and modernist claims of abstract equality, but profoundly deepened it. Modernity posed a generalized crisis for "all" subjects, who experienced the alienating, abstracting force of industrial capital and uncertainty as to what would replace the traditional cultural and political institutions, beliefs, and practices that anchored social order.[82] Assimilation to the liberal nation-state provided a compulsive ameliorative for the disruptions and anxieties that capitalist modernity engendered. Regardless of whether or not the nation *could* indeed resolve the crisis of modernity for its subject, the citizen as *normative* subject of the nation was, as David Palumbo-Liu points out, "still placed at the center of a modern teleology. Whichever way modernity was moving, that subjectivity was carried along in its flow."[83]

The position of the *raced* subject under modernity, in contrast, was notably tendentious, because "the psychic split for the racial subject threatened constantly to sidetrack and stall that particularly designated forward progress of racialized subjects: assimilation."[84] Racial otherness secured the normative subject of the body politic by marking the limits of incorporation.[85] The segregated presence of blacks, Asians, and Latina/os signaled the failures of racial integration that were attributed to their biological or, more recently, cultural difference. At the same time—and this is the complication that discursively *de*links Asians and Latina/os from African Americans in liberal discourses about ethnic assimilation in the late twentieth century—the specific racialization of Asians and Latina/os as *national* aliens, which continually puts under erasure their historical presence in the nation, construes "new" Asian and Latina/o immigrants (and their successive generations) as tabula rasa in U.S. racial discourse. The nation conceives itself to be innocent of any racial injury *to* Asian Americans and Latina/os (it has never betrayed the democratic promise it extends to them), and these latter subjects are conceived to be innocent of—in the varied senses that they are unconscious, ignorant, or "not guilty" of taking part in—the minority discourse that I explore in this book.

This "unmarked" innocence becomes, by the late twentieth century, the subject of the competing cultural politics of minoritarian discourse, neoliberal pluralism, and neoconservative nativism.[86] The genealogy of racial and national identities, as it has been received in the history of U.S. minority subjects, thus proves crucial to understanding the present-day disarticulation of Asian Americans and Latina/os from minority discourse that is framed as a black/white divide. *An Ethics of Betrayal* provides a comparative analysis of late-twentieth-century narratives of betrayal by and about Asian Americans and Latina/os. These "alien citizens," who simultaneously figure otherness to the nation and consolidate an emergent subjectivity through acts of (self-)representation galvanize an urgent ethico-political project for cultural criticism and U.S. ethnic studies.

An Ethics of Betrayal in Emergent U.S. Literature and Culture

As I have explained, racial minorities are both subjects and objects of betrayal in social relations. As such, both minority *and* hegemonic discourses significantly employ the figure of the traitor. *An Ethics of Betrayal* examines in detail different configurations of betrayal, and the relationships between these different forms, while insisting that betrayals from social positions of subordination are appreciably different from those enacted from positions of power. That is, such betrayals must be evaluated carefully and distinctly, in ethico-political terms, as to the gains they secure for minority subjects and the injuries they enact upon others.

Chapter 2 investigates betrayal as a matter of diasporic difference in racial and national formation. It reads paradigm shifts in U.S. ethnic studies and critical race theory to transnational and diaspora studies as an ethical betrayal of claims to citizenship and the formation of the minority American subject. By closely reading two Asian American works, Frank Chin's *The Chickencoop Chinaman* and Gish Jen's *Mona in the Promised Land*, which seem singularly concerned with claiming (Asian) American national identity, I argue that minority discourse remains responsible for the Other who has been foreclosed at its very inception. In their injunctions to think "other-wise," these narratives pose the ethico-political project as an interminable and irrecusable process that the texts, in conversation with one another, enact.

The question of diasporic difference remains at the forefront of the third chapter, which examines the assimilatory betrayals embodied by the Asian American model minority and by the *pocho* (the assimilated Mexican American). Chapter 3 examines Eric Liu's *The Accidental Asian* and Richard Rodriguez's *Hunger of Memory* and *Days of Obligation*, all of which have been widely accused of neoconservatism. I consider why cultural critics find these works so "objectionable," but also the works' notable appeal to other ethnic Americans. I also consider how, rather than securing the neoconservative politics they are meant to bolster, the texts' queer narrations of self cleave to a past that radically contests a hegemonic discourse of the nation as a deracinated and egalitarian public sphere. I conclude this chapter with a reading of Américo Paredes's short story "The Gringo," which returns to the nineteenth century, when the divisions between assimilatory whiteness and black separatism had yet to be consolidated. There, we see how the historical terms of American racialization will come inherently to throw into question the national allegiances of "alien citizens," rendering them always as potential "spies" and traitors who must prove their loyalty to the United States by being assimilated to the nation. In doing so, these subjects also always threaten to betray their "own people."

In Chapter 4, I consider narratives that actualize the metaphor of minority subjects as intelligence agents—racialized spies who are indeed "traitors" of their "own people." I begin with a stalemated issue that has faced U. S. ethnic studies since its inception, the divide between academic work and community experience. This division underpins charges that ethnic studies is out of touch and ineffective in producing change in the "real world" and that its practitioners exploit the community for professional advantage. To address this question, I turn to two spy narratives, Américo Paredes's *George Washington Gómez* and Chang-rae Lee's *Native Speaker*, both of which confront the anxiety that ethnic insiders might come to serve as traitorous informants against their community. The novels allegorize intellectual work, in this case, ethnic studies, as "intelligence work." They conceive of the institution as neither a space where one discovers an authentic racial identity, nor one that generates inadequate, second-order representations of racial identities that are essentially located elsewhere. Rather, the university serves as a crucial site, in conjunction and in conflict with other locations, for the making and unmaking of racial identifications. Further, I argue, the narratives theorize themselves *as* allegories of intellectual production and accordingly "invent" their necessary reader as the minority intellectual. By imagining the intellectual as an ethical subject of minority discourse, the novels delineate the responsibility to the Other that continually defers the authorization of the (minority) intellectual.

From the literary narratives of minority spies that I examine in the fourth chapter, Chapter 5 moves to a cultural narrative of international intrigue and to a potential case of literal espionage, the case of the Cuban child emigrant Elián González and that of Wen Ho Lee, the Chinese American physicist accused of spying on the United States. The ethics of betrayal in these cases, which were figured in the language of martyrdom, scapegoating, and treason, compels us to ask the difficult questions that a liberal discourse of minority subjectivity necessarily eschews. By taking seriously the claims of Cuban exiles against Castro and the possibility that Wen Ho Lee did in fact spy on the United States for the People's

Republic of China, I consider the "diasporic desire" that ethical critique manifests. The nation's seemingly anachronistic revival in both of these cases of the specter of Communism in a post-Cold War/New World Order—an anxiety irreconcilable to the prevalent stereotype of Asian Americans and Cuban Americans as model minorities—illustrates the anxieties about national self-image that plague the American subject. In both cases, hegemonic narratives sought to discipline what I characterize as the model minority's "diasporic desire," the intimate passion for something other than the "here and now" that the nation demands from its subjects. In particular, prevailing narratives attempted to smooth over the ruptures in national self-image wrought by transnationalism and global capitalism. From the openings or avenues for justice that an ethical inquiry into these narratives uncovers, I suggest, the subject of human rights emerges to make demands that cannot be registered in the national imaginary.

The Epilogue addresses the significance of an ethics of betrayal in the aftermath of the September 11 attacks, in the "war on terror." I describe the emergence of supranational discursive formations that articulate race, nation, class, and religion in ways that supplement, antagonize, and threaten the modern nation-state system. I also consider the way in which these formations rebound upon Americans, both "generic" and minority subjects, in the terms of loyalty and betrayal inaugurated by the nation and the state, as well as in the ongoing ethical responsibilities of the emergent subjects in the war on terror and of human rights.

Acts of Literature in Emergent U. S. Culture

Because it is primarily concerned with racial and national formations as they have determined the possibilities of selfhood for the modern subject, *An Ethics of Betrayal* adopts the operational terms of "minority discourse," "Asian American" and "Latina/o" formation, "ethnic America," and a host of other identity categories that have been central to the development of panethnic minority literary canons and historical archives. At the same time, by treating the individual narratives that I examine here as parables, that is, as exemplary and performative of an ethics of betrayal, I would contend that these texts always already betray the identity politics of representation that are so often attributed to them. I therefore cannot and do not intend to claim in any way that *An Ethics of Betrayal* provides "coverage" of emergent U. S. literature and culture, least of all with respect to panethnicity. In fact, as parables of betrayal, my objects of analysis actively undermine such a premise of representation.

A number of scholars in Asian American and Latina/o studies have detailed the pitfalls of panethnicity as a political and critical principle of organization, especially when foisted upon a broader constituency by intellectual or political leaders.[87] The normative construction of panethnic racial identities seriously risks conflation of very different and uneven historical and geopolitical conditions. As an organizing principle of representation, one largely determined by the state or hegemonic discourses, panethnicity restricts analysis to a comparative framework *between* different racial identities, thereby occluding other axes of relation by which we might read and engage minority formation. Forged in, as Kirsten Silva Gruesz describes it, "the crucible of proleptic anxiety," the construction of the minority subject is caught between the pressures of contemporaneity, where (re-)"present-ing" the minority subject risks either negating complex and contradictory pasts or engaging in a reifying historicism.[88] The fraught relationship of the minority subject to the past and future belies the internal hierarchies and stratifications that identity subsumes.

In this context, the "ideal projection" of such racial identities has been most effective in critical and academic discourses, and more dubiously so in other spaces. As such, the disciplinarity of panethnic formation tends to privilege the cultural critic's position as one free from the market pressures, state imperatives, and hegemonic discourses that condition the making of modern subjects.[89] Panethnicity can also provide a technology for a quiescent multiculturalism that anticipates and manages the coming multitudes of "others" that the nation encounters in its global ventures. It therefore proves as much an "enterprise" of the minority subject under global capital as an oppositional formation.[90] Thus, while cultural criticism might premise its own investments in panethnic identity as a commitment to a resistant or oppositional politics, it can miss the strategies of accommodation that racial categories provide subjects who negotiate transnational capital and the political economies of globalization. And yet, as Susan Koshy notes, the "fiction" of panethnic racial categories provides cultural critics a rubric that "we cannot not use," insofar as they do strategically address political needs for representation.[91] The membering of canons, archives, and body politics produces a sense of identity. But it also generates a contradiction between, on the one hand, the imperative to acknowledge conflicts, complicities, and heterogeneity, and on the other hand, the urgency of mobilizing representational forms of cultural politics.

In order, then, to avoid seeming as if I am prescriptively reducing a large and impressively heterogeneous body of cultural production, I would like to briefly characterize my own principle of selection in the following chapters according to what Derrida has described as "acts of literature," which lead us onto terrains and into worlds that might otherwise remain unimagined and inaccessible to us. As it works in a performative, inventive relation with material history, literature refers us to the "real world," but does so in order to generate "a new, supplementary world, a metaworld, a hyper-reality" that is "an irreplaceable addition to the already existing one."[92] Literature is certainly an "institution" that comes into being through material processes and has historical and geographical conditions and coordinates that determine its development.[93] And yet, as Derrida stresses, the "strangeness" of this institution "cannot simply be contained by our usual socio-economic-historical thought about such human construction."[94] Literature instead exists in a "suspended" relation to social realities, in a contingent and "innovative" relation to "settled modes of thought"—or, as I distinguish them, "discourse" (e.g., nationalist discourse or minority discourse). But literature is also a creation of something entirely new and heretofore unthought.[95] Literature crucially depends upon social discourse, the structures of thought and feeling that found social orders. But it also produces an experience of "an-other time" or a "time out of time" that is irreducible to the temporality and spatiality of "ordinary" discourses of social existence.[96]

Literature thus calls forth readings that move between rigorous, critical analyses of texts and an experience of the form as a kind of magical or mysterious encounter with the Other. This type of reading moves between the poles of "affirmation" and "analysis" and has been described by the critics from whom I am drawing here variously as "innovative," "aporetic," and "ethical."[97] On the one hand, the literary reading discerns the text as "radically situated," "written and read and re-read at particular times and places."[98] It attempts to account for the particular historical, material, semantic, and political conditions that make a text possible, and to evaluate how the literary work might be situated *in* the material world of the reader's existence. On the other hand, and all at once, it remains aware that literature keeps its secrets of an-other's time and place. The literary reading takes the text on its own terms, responding to the unconditional demand for the reader to give herself over to the alternative world *of* the literary imagination. *An Ethics of Betrayal* accordingly approaches its objects between these dual imperatives in order to delineate the sites, modes, and ethics of betrayal. The very tensions and unintelligibilities that literature harbors and to which the literary reading attends provide openings for justice and democracy—for, that is, the arrival of the Other "to come"—while discerning the social orders and discourses where this otherness will be encountered in its historical-political forms.[99]

As John Guillory explains in *Cultural Capital*, canon formation has conventionally taken place in academic and critical circles around the paradox of "difficulty," where the value of literature inheres in its complexity, and therefore inaccessibility, to potential readers. Difficulty requires study and interpretation, which secures a "difficult" work's place as an object of admiration by an elite class. It organizes literary criticism around the types of cultural capital that sustain the existence and value of the field and its purveyors. By approaching critical reading as an ethico-political practice, however, *An Ethics of Betrayal* implicitly already acknowledges the self-interest with which the critic selects (from) her archive, where choosing one literary or cultural narrative of betrayal always puts others under erasure, just as choosing to focus on a particular axis or mode of identification by which betrayal is enacted elides the other forms of betrayal that are always continually taking place.

It is not my wish here then to piece together anything like a canon for Asian American, Latina/o, or emergent U.S. literature. Instead the ethico-political project I theorize in this book recognizes the pitfalls of a cultural politics of representation, no matter how flexible and inclusive. Nevertheless, the mode of inquiry that drives this project also recognizes the very necessity of the politics of representation in which it participates. By describing and treating the texts I have chosen here as parables, and by restricting my readings to a very few cases, I hope to emphasize that I am not attempting "coverage" in any literary field. Rather, I have chosen works that, in my readings in these fields, struck me as articulating the historical-political themes of minority discourse with "lessons" about the Other. These narratives, I submit, provide examples of an ethico-political "pedagogy," such as I describe in Chapter 4, about the betrayals that the minority subject undergoes and enacts in its fraught loyalties and responsibilities to others.

Insofar as this principle inevitably constructs a representative narrative body, I would also claim for these texts a shared and profound concern with the stakes involved and debts incurred in such representation, a construction in which they are complicit. Derrida suggests that "every literary work 'betrays' the dream of a new institution of literature" that "invents" its reader, teaching him or her to read "*if s/he is willing.*"¹⁰⁰ As parables of betrayal for Asian American and Latina/o studies, as well as for American literature more generally, the narratives I consider in the following chapters often forego their loyalties to these fields and their constituent identities, in order to teach us about other possibilities for being. As parables of betrayal, these works invent their ethical subjects, their readers, on the difficult social and political terrain that we share with them.

2 / Late Arrivals: An Ethics of Betrayal in Racial and National Formation

Mona tries to imagine what it would be like to forget she's Chinese, which is easy and hard.

—MONA IN THE PROMISED LAND

During the past decade and a half, ethnic studies and American studies have begun to consider the disciplinary and epistemological relationship between their own objects and methodologies and those of diaspora studies, postcolonial studies, and area studies.[1] This question has been especially significant for Asian Americans and Latina/os in the United States, because the nation has constructed each of these groups as an "alien other," against whom to imagine itself.[2] Cultural critics working in ethnic studies have duly been confronted with the "both/and" impetus of the domestic and the global with respect to ethico-political action. In other words, if the work of ethnic studies is that of critique committed to social justice and democratic access, there can be no either/or between domestically racial and globally diasporic discourses. Both are needed to defend the citizenship rights of racial minorities—what amounts to a defense of minority claims to the nation—and at the same time to launch a critique of precisely that American imaginary and its global permutations and penetrations. This chapter considers how an ethics of betrayal opens minority discourse to this daunting challenge by allowing the ghosts of hard-won battles to return to haunt us in the name of the justice that the Other demands.

Can the recent paradigm shifts toward transnational and diaspora studies be *ethically* conceptualized as a "betrayal" of the original mission of the field? Do these changes, which critics have described as "denationalization," fail the project of democratic access for the minority subject?[3] Many of the warnings against positing diaspora as a central theme in

U.S. ethnic studies seem to characterize diaspora as an identity formation or political coalition that moves the subject (and thereby the critic) outside the nation.[4] Rather than attempting to reconcile the competing claims of the nation-state and its primary subject, the citizen, with those of diasporic migrants and exiles, I suggest that the gaps and fissures between the two offer avenues for an ethico-political project. As such, while we might welcome critical moves into diaspora and transnational studies, we should indeed understand these moves as necessary betrayals of (and by) the minority American subject.

Diaspora in Ethnic America

Broadly speaking, minority discourse in the United States since the 1960s has primarily been imagined in terms of nation-building. Organized around the dual poles of cultural nationalism and the civil rights movement, the "nation" to which the minority subject lays claims has been variously construed along a spectrum of separatist to assimilatory (i.e., "melting pot") desires. These claims have, nonetheless, been oriented around the articulation of a coherent national form for the minority subject. Of course, the cultural politics of these imaginaries has been shot through with tensions and anxieties of diaspora and transnational movements and exchange. Nevertheless, the locus for identification has been determined primarily by the singular form of national belonging. For example, the cultural nationalisms of the Asian American and Chicano movements drew their terms of resistance from anticolonial struggles, sharing with Third World nationalist movements and the black power movement in the United States the rhetoric of racial and ethnic unity that required political representation. However, in the context of a nationally bound discourse, and especially under the model of "internal colonialism," cultural nationalism largely *analogized* the situation of minority subjects in the U.S. to the position of colonial subjects around the globe.[5] Working in contest with the hegemonic nation-state, minority discourse has tended to invest in the national *form* from which minority subjects have been excluded.

Globalization complicates the oppositional projects of minority discourse. It has proven a powerful force that materially conditions the lives of people of color in the United States, often in ways that contest the ideological terms and political agendas generated by cultural nationalism.[6] Along with the older forms of diaspora (e.g., the more or less compulsory emigration of peoples from Africa, China, India, etc.) that the age of empire established, since the late-twentieth-century migrants have traversed the nation-bounded forms of domestic discourse from which minority formations emerge. As Arjun Appadurai puts it, when "money, commodities, and persons are involved in ceaselessly chasing each other around the world," the sovereign nation-state form becomes a casualty of globalization.[7] Global flows and exchanges create the circuits by which individuals move across the globe according to labor needs and consumer desires. The state's command of loyalty and compliance from subjects, extracted in the name of the nation, accordingly seems to waver and wane. Yet, national deterritorialization can simultaneously intensify investments in home–state culture and politics. Thus, globalization produces new "invented homelands," as "the nationalist genie, never perfectly contained in the bottle of the territorial state, is now itself diasporic . . . increasingly unrestrained by ideas of spatial boundary and territorial sovereignty."[8] Nevertheless, critics have warned against mistaking the transnational for the "postnational."[9] After all, the nation-state maintains a material and often overriding presence in everyday life, especially for people of color, migrants, and the poor. Thus, diasporas provide a perspective from which to examine the ideological valences of national sovereignty. But to avoid slipping into a facile celebration of globalization per se, we must continually ask how power enables and disables mobility and how mobility produces new systems of historically uneven "emplacedness."[10]

As has become well known in ethnic studies, reforms in U.S. immigration law and policy since 1965, in response to the mixed pressures of global capital, civil rights activism, and the Cold War political agenda, significantly transformed "America" by the end of the twentieth century. Demographic accounts of this reconstitution tell the story of millions of newly arrived migrants, documented and undocumented, political refugees and workers looking for economic opportunities under global restructuring.[11] The resulting, momentous increase in Asian American and Latina/o populations in the United States has meant that the number of people identified as minorities in the U.S. has grown substantially (i.e., more than 30 percent of the U.S. population are considered to be "persons of color").[12] Moreover, the terms "minority" and "person of color" are no longer synonymous with "African American," because, whereas in 1960 African Americans made up 96 percent of that population, they now amount to approximately 50 percent of racial minorities.[13]

Because the immigration reforms of 1965 were meant, in part, to facilitate the immigration of professional and white-collar workers, the class status of more recently arrived immigrants has become increasingly heterogeneous. At the same time, because public discourse around immigration and globalization casts these subjects in cultural and ethnic terms, it tends to evade the emergence of global class formations that reconfigure racial identities.[14] A number of those immigrants who according to domestic U.S. discourse would be considered racial minorities also belong to a cosmopolitan class of transnational elites. Having secured economic and cultural capital through globalized processes, many of these minority subjects remain *dis*articulated by U.S. minority discourse.[15] By recoding these processes as cultural traits (e.g., family values, the work ethic), hegemonic neoconservative discourse (and even many minority subjects themselves) produces representations of American "success stories" that occlude the unprecedented access to financial and cultural capital that facilitate immigrants' arrival to the United States in the first place. Moreover, the circulation of these cultural images elides representation of those "other" minority Americans—and people of color globally—whose participation in privilege has been tenuous at best, and more often, unimaginable.[16] The material circumstances of this emergent ethnic America, rooted as it is in globalization and characterized as substantially by diasporic ties to the homeland as to assimilatory desires to "claim America," both require and offer up terms for an ethico-political project of minority discourse. This project moves beyond and in tension with a nationally bounded civil rights discourse, even as it acknowledges the ongoing necessity of these latter agendas.

In Chapter 3 I will return to the historical-material implications of racial transformation and the emergence of an ethnic America that reconfigures extant versions of Asian American and Latina/o selfhood in the United States. Here, however, I would like to focus on the function diaspora plays in the *conceptual* formations of national and minority discourse, that is, in what David L. Eng describes as the "critical methodology" that diaspora provides.[17] As such, diaspora always already exists within the idea of the domestic, marking a fundamental repudiation that installs the division between the domestic and the foreign in national and minority discourses.[18] As a critical lens, diaspora offers more than a description of cultural politics and identity practices. It indicates a critical perspective from which the naturalized privilege of the nation can be rethought and "deformed" in and through minority discourse.[19] In terms of literary study, the diasporic perspective displaces minoritarian literature's status as a "minor ethnic province" of a national canon.

As such, it does more than produce a "global identity formation" and a "multiplier signifier" and does not simply incorporate increasingly "fresh immigrant subjectivities."[20] The ethics of betrayal that I will elicit in my readings below *cautions against* the celebration of polysemy that such a critical politics engenders, by asking about the stakes and costs of such an incorporation.[21]

This chapter will describe the unpredictable outcomes of thinking diaspora in national and minority discourses. Indeed, the historical-material outcomes themselves have hardly been singular; globalization and transnationalism have been the basis for both the consolidation of new economic hierarchies and exploitations and for a nascent counter-hegemony (as seen, for example, in the various protests in Seattle, Washington, D.C., Barcelona, Cancun, Genoa, and elsewhere in the past decade), as well as for alternative structures of feeling and belonging for minority subjects. As my reading of works by Frank Chin and Gish Jen in this chapter demonstrates, the most purposive approach to such changes might not be to think of the turn to diaspora in the nation as a "new" theoretical development. Nor might it be to expand the terms of minority discourse to assimilate the diasporic other. Rather, in what follows, I explain that, given the foreclosure of diasporic loyalties in the foundation of minority discourse, the seemingly "belated" arrival of the diasporic other, what amounts to its "return" to ethnic America, signals an ongoing ethico-political project of justice and freedom that minority discourse faces.

The Arrival of the (Asian) American Self

For many years now, Frank Chin's editorial and political writings have landed him at the center of an often heated debate about Asian American cultural nationalism's exclusion of women, gays and lesbians, and newly arrived Asian immigrants from its vision of panethnic racial unity. However, I want to suggest that *The Chickencoop Chinaman* constitutes a compelling work that proves much more ambivalent and uncertain about the contours and viability of the Asian American identity than some of Chin's political writings assert. Thus, I follow Daniel Y. Kim's suggestion that despite the controversy surrounding the author, there is a diagnostic acuity to Chin's production of "melancholic manhood" that affords us insight into the founding moments of minority American subjectivity.[22]

Chin's play, set contemporarily to its publication in 1981, recounts the arrival of a Chinese American documentary filmmaker, Tam Lum, in Pittsburgh; his reunion with a childhood friend, the Japanese American Kenji; and his meeting with Charley Popcorn, the man he believes is the father of the subject of his current film project, an African American boxer named "Ovaltine" Jack Dancer. Tam's film project and cultural fantasies double as a search for an originary father figure through whom he might conceive the Asian American experience.[23] A scene (which intercedes between Tam's arrival at Kenji's apartment and their meeting with Charley Popcorn) rooted in the history of the Old West and the character of the Lone Ranger deflates the possibility of one such authorizing figure. Tam's desire to see the masked figure of the Lone Ranger as a Chinese American in disguise is undermined with the materialization of the aging white cowboy hero, who "curses" Tam and Kenji as "honorary whites."[24] Tam's meeting with Charley Popcorn then weighs all the more heavily for the possibility of Asian American selfhood, because in the aging African American Tam hopes to locate "an aggressive antithesis of white authority."[25] Tam is therefore sorely disappointed in Popcorn's revelation that he is not the boxer's father and that most of what Ovaltine has told Tam about the older man is a fabrication.

Popcorn fails Tam not only because he represents "yet another unreliable legend," but, more importantly, because the older black man finds himself utterly unable to identify with Tam and Kenji, whom he views as complete aliens.[26] For example, in a comic exchange, Popcorn, who had been expecting to be interviewed by another black man, finds it practically impossible to reconcile Tam's claim that he is "American" with the Asian face he sees in front of him:

POPCORN: Isn't it strange, you're Chinese.

TAM: I'm a ... I'm an American citizen.

POPCORN: You don't talk like a Chinese, do ya? No, I don't thinks so ...

TAM: I was born here, Mr. Popcorn.

POPCORN: The way you talked, why, I took you for colored over the phone. But "Lum"? Why would a Chinese talk like a colored man?[27]

Popcorn is further perplexed by Kenji's presence, wondering whether Kenji is "Chinese too?" and admits to Tam and Kenji that he "don't like" Chinese, recalling that the Chinese waiters he'd known working in restaurants "treated us worse 'n white men treated us."[28] Frustrated, Tam declares to Kenji that Popcorn is "a bigot. He's nothin but a black white racist when it comes to yellow people."[29] Tam's hope for a reciprocal affiliation between Asian Americans and African Americans proves untenable, despite their common interests as racialized subjects.

Received by both blacks and whites as "forever foreign," the Asian American male characters envisage an alternative founding narrative for Asian American selfhood in the conclusion of *The Chickencoop Chinaman*. Kenji announces that he and Lee—a woman living with him and who is described in the play's cast of characters as a "possible Eurasian or Chinese American"—are having a baby, a claim that surprises Lee and is evidently a fantasy Kenji harbors for their future. This announcement, along with the narrative's energetic staging of a "Chinamans' Old West" that ends the play, foregrounds a particular discursive formation of Asian America. The story of the Asian American past, mythic in scope and tone, invokes a "grandmaw," played by Tam, who passes on to children the story of Asian American participation in the development of the American West during the nineteenth century. The two declarations, the announcement about the baby that is an avowal of the future and the story rooted in the past, suggest that Asian American claims to an American future will be also self-generative of an Asian American past. This continuous narrative consoles the Asian American when "blackness" fails to articulate Asian American selfhood.

Such a resolution though, relying as it does on an exacting positioning of women for its viability, belies the strict prohibitions on the immigration of Asian women during the nineteenth century, as well as the widespread prevalence of anti-miscegenation laws during this period that reformed Chinese American social organization into "bachelor societies." In the strategic production of the narrative, Tam must therefore both circumscribe and occupy, by performing in drag, the position of the feminine, privatized, and domestic other, that is, the grandmother, who tells the hidden story of the Asian American self. Tam's performance as grandmaw, and Kenji's speaking for Lee, also manage the otherwise palpably unjust displacement of the diasporic other of Asian America in the narrative's exposition. That is, the "arrival" of the Asian American self at the play's end evokes the dreamlike sequence that opens the play, in which Tam, on his incoming flight to Pittsburgh, is interrogated by the "Hong Kong Dream Girl."

In repeatedly claiming in this inaugural scene that Chinamen are made, crashed, stamped, anything, that is, but born, Tam's construction of Asian American selfhood entails a prerequisite "forgetting." This opening scene thus concludes:

> TAM: It's not right for a body to know his own origins, for it leaves the mother nothing secret to herself. I want to hear about you.
>
> GIRL: You sure have a way with words, but I'd like it better if you'd speak the mother tongue.[30]

Tam's exchange with the Hong Kong Dream Girl affirms that his access to the nation displaces the feminine *onto* the diasporic other and vice versa, *outside of* the play's discursive production of Asian America. We see in Tam's claim, "It's not right for a body to know his own origins, for it leaves the mother nothing secret to herself," a fundamental repudiation without which an Asian American body could not come into his own language and thereby "be right." A birth would mean, for Tam, the inheritance of a troubling history of otherness that entails responsibility, against the claims for self-emancipation and enfranchisement that are imagined at the play's end. Tam must therefore forget this dispossession of the other, symbolically and narratively reducing the lost mother to the Hong Kong Dream Girl and foreclosing her participation in the drama altogether.

Tam's predicament resonates closely with the "problem of historicity" that Jacques Derrida perceives as inexorably corrupting of self-present certitude.[31] The subject refuses to acknowledge his own historicity, because his being—and the freedom and self-knowledge that is the hallmark of that being—is suffused with contingency. Even as Tam struggles to articulate an (Asian) American self that specifies the history and experiences of the subjects that interest Chin, a structural forgetting predicates this materializing minority discourse. As Jinqi Ling suggests about the cultural work of Asian American nationalism generally, such displacement is the necessary effect of the historical parameters of the text's production, by which such work "constituted, for the first time since the mid-nineteenth century, a public claim on rights that Asian Americans were entitled to but denied historically."[32] The foreclosures effected by minority discourse are theoretically consonant with the more general exceptionalism that the nation attributes to itself. The play proper relegates its (diasporic) other to the fading, parenthetical margins of national belonging, hence my formulation of the "(Asian) American." And, of course, this is precisely the type of discursive move for which Chin has come under political and critical fire.

In liberal discourse, moral reason must separate itself from such historical conditions. But the ethico-political project that I have detailed in the introduction *submits itself* to these very contingencies and conditions of history. Diaspora thus proffers a specific possibility of ethical encounter, wherein the subject, seeking its own freedoms and rights according to the promises of the nation-state, never accomplishes the secreting of its own historicity. Chin rather self-consciously and *formally* remarks upon these historical pressures by inscribing the diegetic emergence of the (Asian) American self against the phantasmatic staging of the Hong Kong Dream Girl. The thematized fantasy of the Chinaman's creation, the founding of the self that so occupies minority discourse (and liberal discourse more broadly) institutes a synchronic social formation within and differentiated against the terms of American black/white racial discourse.

However, Tam's queerly transgendered performance of Asian American selfhood in grandmaw contains within it an implied gap between the synchronic formations of race and a diachronic relationship, which has been displaced to the exterior of the thematized symbolic order of the play and onto the feminine diasporic other. In order to install the Asian American subject in the structural relations of U.S. minority discourse, the writer foregoes and forecloses the possibility of the diachronic, diasporic past/other, and instead the self invents itself *ex nihilo* within American racial and national history. *The Chickencoop Chinaman* thus contemplates the fundamental repudiation, through which the subject comes into being and which remains unknowable for that subject. The foreclosure that Tam enacts, and by which Tam "arrives" (quite literally portrayed in the opening scene on an airplane) in America, reaches beyond the content of the "mother's secrets." It extends to the *presence* of the secrets themselves, so that the entire encounter with the Hong Kong Dream Girl and the mother's secrets is forgotten in the play's thematic drive toward a phallic father.

And yet, although such a foreclosure is the very condition for the possibility of social being, it also constitutes the space of ethical responsibility in the play. If Tam must shut out the Hong Kong Dream Girl's demands upon him, Chin's narrative seems unable to forsake the other entirely, installing her, instead, at the play's opening limits and reinvoking her gendered figuration of diaspora through his performance as Grandmaw.[33] The (Asian) American self has no memory of this lost mother to whom he remains fundamentally attached. Nevertheless, as a haunting fantasy of otherness, she forms the very channel through which (Asian) American selfhood discursively emerges. She stands as an incongruent remnant that the (Asian) American self must continually either reinscribe or repress in order to make sense of its own synchronic structure. But the intrepidly *ethical* character of the narrative recognizes that she harbors other possibilities for the future, so much so that it risks sacrificing Tam's manhood and masculine "dignity" to do her justice.

To further elucidate the relationship between an ethico-political project of minority discourse and the "mother's secrets," I suggest that reading *The Chickencoop Chinaman* alongside Gish Jen's novel *Mona in the Promised Land* manifests an ethical betrayal that seeks to do justice to the Other. In both of these texts, though, we should heed Rey Chow's caution against interpreting maternal tropology in the ethnic narrative as encoding the "truth" about ethnicity that requires liberation into authentic subjectivity. Chow suggests instead that we consider the particularly gendered implication that inheres in the metaphor of motherhood. In other words, to begin with, or to return to, the mother, rather than the phallic father, as a source of the subject's existence is to begin with or return to, not an origin, but rather the displacement, seriality, and relationality that femininity figures.[34] A liberal reading of realist minority discourse disavows the contemporaneity of these others in order to secure the subject's idealized version of its self, leaving us with the false choice of recuperating/liberating *or* forgetting/repressing the past from its otherness. In contrast, an ethics of betrayal takes the Asian mother as a "mute witness" of all that self-presence cannot contain and to which it nonetheless remains indebted.[35]

Read in dialogue with Chin's play, Jen's novel considers the implications of the *return* of the lost mother and of the lost mother who stubbornly remains present. To the extent that this particular staging of betrayal articulates the difference that sexual desire makes between female subjects and feminine others, we might say that *Mona in the Promised Land* brings a feminist ethics to bear on racial and national formation. However, the point here is not that the novel posits a new formation (e.g., of an "Asian (American) woman") against (Asian) American selfhood. Rather, Jen's novel allegorizes the responsibilities to and the secrets of the Other who interrupts the subject's progress to autonomous and sovereign selfhood, by posing a (m)other who is decidedly unrecuperable, unsentimental, unsympathetic, and indifferent to the project of (Asian) American selfhood. As such, it augurs an ethico-political project always immanent to the generic developmental narrative.

The Disparate Destinations of (Asian) American Arrival

Published in 1996 as a sequel to Jen's earlier novel *Typical American* (1991), *Mona in the Promised Land* was, like *Typical American*, immediately well-received by mainstream reviewers and literary critics for its humorous exploration of the two main stereotypes that have attended the Asian in America, those of the alien who is forever foreign and of the model minority.[36] Like *The Chickencoop Chinaman*, *Typical American* and *Mona in the Promised Land* both portray the "arrival" of the (Asian) American through and against these images derived from the black/white divide of American racial formation. I want to depart substantially from a more familiar reception of this narrative, one that celebrates Jen's depiction of hybrid and relational subjectivity as the privileged mode for this arrival. Instead, *Mona*, read in conjunction with Chin's play for an ethics of betrayal, evinces an ethico-political project that is both interminable and irrecusable.

Mona in the Promised Land is a novel about the adolescent daughter of Ralph Chang, the protagonist of *Typical American*, and his wife, Helen, and, among other things, Mona's decision to convert to Judaism. *Typical American*, I suggest, provides an important but "forgotten" prehistory to *Mona*. In other words, one need not have read *Typical American* in order to read *Mona*, despite the many allusions that Jen makes in *Mona* to the first novel, a point which I elaborate in detail below. Set in the fictional town of the largely Jewish Scarshill, New York, during the 1960s, *Mona* is located at a crucial historic crossroads in Asian American formation. Ralph and Helen's immigration in *Typical American* occurs between the periods of the late-nineteenth- and early-twentieth-century immigration of Asian labor and the 1965 immigration reforms. Along with Ralph's sister Theresa, Helen and Ralph represent some of the first of the Cold War refugees entering the United States during the second half of the twentieth century.

Moreover, the novel opens in 1968, a year that has accrued mythic status in American historiography, with the assassinations of Martin Luther King Jr. and Robert F. Kennedy, the election of Richard Nixon as president, and the escalation of the war in Vietnam after the Tet offensive. Thus, from its outset, Mona's developmental narrative is conjoined to that of the nation's fall from "innocence," and *Mona* embodies the possibility and difficulty of the articulation of both Asian America and America more generically at this juncture.[37] The uncertain position that the Asian occupies in the United States is readily outlined in the novel's opening chapter, where Jen describes the Changs' move to Scarshill. Declaring that "they're the New Jews, after all, a model minority and Great American Success. They know they belong in the promised land," the third person narrator then equivocates: "Or do they? In fact, it's only 1968; the blushing dawn of ethnic awareness has yet to pink up their inky suburban night. They have an idea about the blacks because of poor Martin Luther King. More distantly perceived is that the Jews have become The Jews, on account of the Six Day War; much less that they, the Changs, are The New Jews."[38] And yet, despite their still tenuous claim to this "promised land," the Changs quickly learn that life in Scarshill will be easier than it has been in the past; in Scarshill, "they're not so much accepted as embraced."[39] While the central joke of the novel, Mona's conversion to Judaism, turns on the incongruities in the *religious* and *racial* coupling of the Chinese and the Jewish, Mona's conversion seems quite sensible through the social logic of *diaspora* and *class* that align the Chinese and Jewish American.

As Susan Stanford Friedman has pointed out, a familiar linear story of young adult love, rebellion, and initiation structures the narrative. However, questions of social difference generate the novel's movement and conflicts.[40] In the character of Mona, the narrative continually asserts an open-ended and reconciliatory vision of national belonging. For example, when Helen and Mona argue about Mona's adoption of Judaism (and to some extent, Jewishness), Mona insists that "Jewish is American," and, furthermore, "American means being whatever you want, and I happened to pick being Jewish."[41] Likewise, she explains to her Japanese middle-school boyfriend, Sherman Matsumoto, that one can "switch" one's identity to American: "Everybody who's born here is American, and also some people who convert from what they were before. You could become American."[42] To be American, from Mona's perspective, refers to the *process* rather than the *content* of identity, since "American means being whatever you want." Given such an amorphous definition, we might surmise, the only way to betray America is to refuse this "becoming," to refuse to "let go" what one once was in order to enter into the *becoming* that is American.

Yet, Helen and Sherman both point to how the unyielding corporeality of race as well as sexual identities demarcate the limits of this American "freedom." Helen presses Mona, conjecturing as to whether Mona will "want to be black" and "want to be a boy instead of a girl."[43] Likewise, Sherman crudely draws caricatures of the "American" ("something that looks like John Wayne), "Jewish" ("something that looks like the Wicked Witch of the West, only male), "Japanese" ("a fair rendition of himself"), and "Chinese" ("another fair rendition of himself").⁴⁴ Sherman also avers that "Atomic bomb dropped on only one people.... The Japanese do not forget."⁴⁵ An altercation ensues between Helen and Sherman over his drawing of the Japanese flag in a gesture of national affiliation:

> When Helen comes in, her face is so red that with the white wall behind her, she looks a bit like the Japanese flag herself.... She crumples up the paper. She hisses at Sherman, *"This is U.S. of A., do you hear me!"*
> Sherman hears her.... Mona, on the other hand, is stymied.... How can two people who don't really speak English understand each other better than she can understand them?⁴⁶

In Helen and Sherman we witness the deep-rootedness of historical memory, and the historicity of the material bodies that populate ethnic America, that refuse both incorporation into a panethnic social order of Asian American formation and accession to the multiculturalism of a hegemonic nation. Although, when reminded of the catastrophic implications of Japanese nationalism for the Chinese, Helen insists that "*This is U.S. of A,*" the novel suggests that the more characteristically American response is Mona's, an absolute ignorance about the burden of history that structures the animosity of this scene. To be American is to have nothing to do with the pasts to which Sherman's drawings and Helen's anger testify. To be American is to let them go, to forget, or better yet, not to ever have known.

Of course the question that looms large behind this formulation of the process of national becoming is that of whiteness. That the particular racial heritage of whiteness escapes this intransigence is an issue I take up in detail in Chapter 3. For now, however, I would like to emphasize the way in which this configuration of national becoming and racial and ethnic conscription bears upon the Changs' status as Americans and as American minorities. During one of her many conversations with Rabbi Horowitz, the young, hip rabbi of the local temple, Mona considers her parents' aversion to being labeled as a "minority," because "they say they were never a minority when they were in China, why should they be a minority here."⁴⁷ When Rabbi Horowitz suggests that "your parents want to be Wasps. They are the only ones who do not have to make themselves heard ... because they do the hearing," Mona agrees:

> "I said, we are a minority, like it or not, and if you want to know how to be a minority, there's nobody better at it than the Jews. I

said it's our job to ask questions now. We can't just accept everything the way they did in China. We can't just go along."

"And what did she say then?"

"She said that as soon as the Communists leave she is going to take me back to Shanghai, where I won't have so much to say."[48]

Although Rabbi Horowit'z reference to "Wasps" critically acknowledges that national belonging has always been formed against the often invisible, but hegemonic, standards of whiteness, the construal of Helen in this scene nevertheless forecloses diaspora as a possible avenue of identification. Even though Helen herself is reported to speak according to the time and space of a diasporic affiliation and return ("to Shanghai"), Mona and Rabbi Horowitz fail to countenance this other language, assimilating Helen instead to the dichotomized terms of whiteness ("Wasps") and blackness ("minorities"), whether Helen "likes it or not." Helen's diasporic desire does not dissipate, though, but returns in the most significant of ways by the novel's end, as I discuss further below.

In addition to being an identity that can only be known in a domestic context and in relation to others, minority subjectivity, as Mona describes it, rests in vocal, oppositional, pre-scripted activities such as rioting, or "just march[ing] in parades and protest[ing]," or writing letters. Mona's assertion that "there's nobody better at [being a minority] than the Jews" explicitly conjoins Jewish and Asian American minoritarianisms. This discourse values oppositionality over assimilation. Moreover, because Mona leaves unspoken the very historical conditions of minority subjectivity out of which Jewish counter-hegemonic formation arises, she appeals to a privileged outspokenness that need not even take to the streets, as it were. Elsewhere in the novel Mona *does* demonstrate her familiarity with both the Judaic religious tradition and the histories of Jewish dispossession and displacement. Yet, this scene remains intriguing, as Mona attempts to articulate her parents' identity, not through shared material histories, but through the formal class and social privilege of protest for protest's sake.

Implicit too in her contention that "Jews are the best kind of minorities" is that there are "worse" types of minorities, those who do take to the streets to riot, march, and protest—namely, African Americans. Coupled with Rabbi Horowitz's remark that her parents aspire to be "Wasps," Mona's comments unwittingly make evident the elision of class hierarchy in this conceptualization of minority politics. Ralph and

Helen's wish to distance themselves from minority politics, most visible in their minds as African American collectivity, and to align themselves with Wasps, is symptomatic of their class position, where "it's all a matter of manners" and to some extent "jewelry."[49] Mona implicitly realizes this when she appeals to them with a "smarter" version of minority politics in the model of Jewish Americans. Indeed, Helen does eventually begin to show interest in Judaism and Jewishness, and begins to accept Mona's conversion, largely as a reaction to the threat of being identified with African Americans.[50]

In portraying the workplace hierarchies and politics at the Pancake House that the Changs own, Jen incorporates into the developmental narrative of (Asian) American selfhood the various economic strategies—and their rationalization according to imperatives of cultural affiliation—that undergird the "success story" of the Asian entrepreneur. Jen briefly recounts a fight between two Chinese employees, Cedric and Fernando, which leads to the Changs having to fire Fernando. She depicts the workplace hierarchies between the waiters from Hong Kong and the restaurant's various dishwashers. Moreover, we learn that Mona and Callie work in the restaurant out of familial obligation and that Ralph treats all of the restaurant staff "like far-flung family, buying them glasses and dentures and shoes, but also expecting them to run errands, or help fix the furnace at home."[51] Although at first seemingly tangential, a mere backdrop to the narrative of Mona's romantic and familial crises, the Pancake House proves eventually to be pivotal in the ethical betrayals that the novel enacts. As the site for emergent "social action" on the part of Mona and her friends, the Pancake House stands at the intersection of the familial and the public, the personal and the political of Mona's subjectivity.

Although Mona attributes Ralph's and Helen's elitist attitudes to their Chineseness, she soon comes to realize that her Jewish American friends are also keenly aware of and motivated by the hierarchies of socioeconomic mobility, what Mona's best friend Barbara describes as being "aware what set you're talking to." If Ralph and Helen's social snobberies accord with the class structure of Scarshill, it also becomes clear that for Mona's parents, the certainties of class privilege and cultural knowledge they enjoyed in China do not translate readily across national borders: "The trouble is that here in America, they often can't tell what set they're talking to. And they're not sure what set we are, either."[52] From this point on, the narrative traces Mona's politicization, as she comes to grapple with the various "undemocratic," "un-American" exclusions that structure the lives of those around her, whether to their benefit or to their derogation. At the same time, Jen evokes the historical memories and structural inequities—both national and extra-national—that make the conception of a freely chosen American identity impossible. The most bitter of these include the Nanking Massacre of the Chinese by the Japanese, the U.S. atomic bombing of Japan, American slavery and segregation, and the Holocaust.

The racial, ethnic, and class hierarchies against which Mona chafes precipitate the many conflicts around which the narrative revolves. Mona's dispute with Helen over her conversion and the conflicts at the Pancake House prove to be only two of these. The novel actually opens with Mona's awkward eighth-grade romance with Sherman, who, prior to returning to Japan, suggests, but then abandons, the possibility that he might marry her when they are sixteen, if she "switches" to Japanese. Sherman is later, in high school, replaced as Mona's boyfriend by Seth, a well-read Jewish hippie who becomes a source of romantic and sexual tension between Mona and Barbara. The text also narrates the tensions between Ralph and the African American workers, including the black cook Alfred, whom Mona, Seth, and Barbara befriend. Mona's relationship with her parents, and especially to Helen, is further mediated through the character of her older sister Callie, who, as the less favored of the two daughters, competes against Mona for their affection and attention, often by betraying Mona's confidences (Callie, for example, informs Helen about Mona's conversion). And while this catalogue is hardly exhaustive of all the conflicts that take place throughout the novel, the ultimate crisis that proves both most profoundly formative and resolutely insurmountable for Mona is Helen's discovery of Mona's sexual relationship with Seth and the damage it wreaks upon the mother-daughter relationship.

The romantic comedy of Mona's enduring love for Sherman, further encouraged by the mysterious phone calls that she receives over the years from a shy but contemplative person claiming to be Sherman, ends when Seth reveals himself to be the caller. Mona's discovery of Seth-as-Sherman should, as the novel metanarratively points out, mark the traditional end of the comedy: "You know," [Seth] says, "this is the big recognition scene. If we were in a Shakespeare play, this would be the happy ending."[53] But this scene of anagnorisis pointedly does not end Jen's novel. Instead, Helen's discovery of Mona's sexual activities lead to her avowed rejection of Mona at the novel's end. Mona's sexual relationship registers in a thoroughly different, even tragic, valence when read from Helen's point of view as an act of betrayal. Whereas the recognition scene between Mona and Seth seems to suggest the coincidence between the self and the beloved that satisfies both sexual and narrative drives, Helen's discovery of that desire inaugurates a rereading of this scene in another, tragic—and, I will contend, ethical—direction.

Mona's awakened sexual desire, which Jen earlier describes as being like "a whole self inside the self that she knows, someone sharing her skin," initiates this ultimate betrayal in a novel full of many potential and actual betrayals; it leads to the story's end of family fragmentation.[54] Helen's discovery of Seth and Mona stands as a climactic point in the more fragmented and marginalized movement of this "other self" emplotted within the narrative. A first incident takes place during Mona and Sherman's farewell as his family prepares to return to Japan. In this scene, Sherman's contemptuous disdain for an undone button on Mona's blouse, a sign of her sexual forwardness, leads him to judo-flip her off her feet: "Two swift moves, and she went sprawling through the late afternoon, a flailing confusion of soft human parts such as had no idea where the ground was."[55] A second instance occurs when Mona is attacked by a masked car thief whom she comes upon in her family's driveway. After Seth manages to frighten off the attacker, the two keep the incident a secret from her family, a bond that begins their romantic and sexual relationship. In both cases, physical and epistemic violence accompanies Mona's encounters with sexual desire, a violence that seems jarringly at odds with the otherwise comedic and lighthearted tone of the novel.

The disparate destinations to which the narrative leads, the comic resolution of the romantic mystery, and the tragic fracturing of familial attachments by sexual desire dovetail into one another. The novel's ending is decidedly not comic, with Helen symbolically refusing to recognize Mona as her daughter: "'Who is this?' [Helen] says. . . . 'Is this my daughter?' Helen returns to her bedroom; and this time she doesn't even close the door, she doesn't have to. For it's as if this is what she's seen with her glasses off, operating on inner sight—that this disturbance can be trusted to leave by herself. Finally she's big enough not to need to be told."[56] The devastation that Helen's discovery wreaks on the relationship between Helen and Mona completely overshadows all of the other conflicts in the novel and cannot be predicted before it occurs. This is not to argue that this crisis is not situated and circumscribed by the multiple categories of identification and difference that the narrative lays out. Certainly, this final and most significant betrayal is made possible only through the wide network of relations that the novel constructs around and through Mona—Ralph and Helen, Seth, Barbara, Sherman, Callie, and Alfred.[57] But, none of these relations, nor the tensions and conflicts that they produce, is "about" or anticipates the rupture that proceeds from Helen's coming upon Mona under the covers with Seth, nor can they compensate for the loss that Mona undergoes. This loss that Mona suffers, Helen's beratement and abandonment of her daughter, displaces the narrative of racial and national formation with one of sexual desire and transgression. The trajectory of the novel has, prior to this point, moved according to the imperatives of (Asian) American selfhood, so that Mona's betrayal of her family seems to revolve primarily around racial and ethnic rebellion. Yet, the seemingly secondary and "forgotten" narrative of her sexual relationship with Seth generates the ultimate crisis that rends Mona's relationship with Helen (but pointedly not, as we learn in the Epilogue, with Ralph), ending the novel with the irreparable rupture between the two.

Yet, the two narratives—of the racial and ethnic skirmishes in which the Changs are caught and of Mona's sexual life—are never as functionally separate as my characterization here might initially suggest. Indeed, I want to posit that, insofar as *Mona* tracks the arrival of (Asian) American selfhood, Helen, as the symbolic face of China in the novel, must *necessarily* be lost to Mona, as the Hong Kong Dream Girl must be lost to Tam, if Mona is to come into "her own" self. To that end also, sexual desire and gendered transgression in the novel's closing serve to dramatize "dual affiliation as a matter of gender role expectation, with sexuality serving as the mediator between opposing cultural dictates."[58] The sexual and gendered inflections of this betrayal especially accord with the American ethos of freedom that the young Mona had professed to both Sherman and her mother.[59] Mona manifests her nominal freedom, her autonomy as an individual apart from her mother and as an (Asian) American apart from China, expressly as a sexual liberation.

The rupture here thus seems to mark a final turning away of Mona and Helen from one another. But, as Derrida asserts, and as we found to be the case in *The Chickencoop Chinaman*, "history never effaces what it buries; it always keeps within itself the secret of whatever it encrypts, the secret of its secret."[60] *Mona* considers the ethical implications of such a "secret history" for the (Asian) American identity of freedom and freedom of identity that Mona seems to have achieved. Because, unlike the Hong Kong Dream Girl, the loss of Helen is not technically a *fore*closure, but the tragic *end* to the comic narrative: the rupture subordinates the novel's thematic concern with the arrival of the (Asian) American self.

The ending instead *foregrounds* the loss of the Other as the cost of (Asian) American selfhood. It is this responsibility to the Other, I contend, that makes *Mona* a novel not primarily about identity and subjectivity, but rather, about an ethics of betrayal that concerns alterity, to which I turn my attention here.

What Mona Wants

In *Mona*, the novel's formal or proper ending is succeeded by an epilogue that depicts a melancholic Mona, "some years later," who seems to have lost most of her youthful naiveté as an adult. Mona contemplates, as Callie accuses, whether she "might be the death of her mother," and writes letters to Helen but "does not hear back, and wonders."[61] In this future present, we see that Mona has come to her subjectivity in and through her guilt as traitor, and she remains in a suspended relation to that guilt. Having lived without her mother for some time, melancholia here seems to preserve the supposedly relinquished, and formerly loved, object, and to preserve love itself, as a haunting remainder of guilt: "Melancholia rifts the subject, marking a limit to what it can accommodate."[62] As a traitor, Mona's character also makes visible the irony of desire, that, even as desire constitutes the very grounds for Mona's be(com)ing (Asian) American, also threatens to undermine that selfhood. Unlike Tam, she is not completely unaware of what she has forsaken for her freedom, but she is also unable to make reparations for the betrayal, since the betrayal has made an entire other future possible. From this perspective, Mona remains responsible to her mother, although she cannot rationally or fully articulate what this responsibility means. Instead, as a subject who neither excuses her act of betrayal nor transcends it, she has become subject *to* a desire that cannot be justified; she has been made by this desire and has been made responsible for it. The ethics of betrayal implicates Mona in a responsible agency, one that takes the guise of a patient receptiveness in the novel's epilogue.

Mona *is* eventually reunited with Helen at the end of this epilogue, that is, at an end after the end. After having lived with Seth and having borne a daughter, Io, with him, Mona has decided to legitimate their relationship through marriage. The epilogue closes with Helen's surprise appearance as Mona dresses for the wedding: "Helen exclaims as Mona turns, adjusting her illusion veil . . . the way she's crying, anyone would think that Helen is the person Mona's taking in sickness or in health—is it really her mother, so tiny? The way Mona's crying, anyone would think that she's being taken too—finally!—for better or for worse. Until death do us part, she thinks, and rushes forward, just as Io falls down."[63] In Friedman's reading of this ending, a cultural politics of hybridity resolves family fragmentation: "The restitution of the social and familial order is intercultural. . . . The mother-daughter plot overwhelms the marriage plot as Mona and Helen embrace with a clapping baby Io at their side. As a product of cultural and biological mixing, Io signifies the new American, the future."[64] But if the epilogue offers up hybridity as the solution to the crises and losses of the past, it also ironizes this particular model of compensation, for example, when Mona unenthusiastically muses about changing her name (as well as Seth's and Io's) to "Changowitz."[65] In contrast, I suggest that the epilogue seeks to do justice, not by assimilating the diasporic other to a hybridized (Asian) America.[66] Instead, it reconceives justice as the arrival of the Other on her own terms, an arrival that is "late" and inexplicable in its coming.

The arrival of this Other returns us to the movement of desire that traverses the narrative. As I note above, in the novel proper, Mona experiences desire not as a "selfish," internal truth, but as an external demand, as an "other self" existing just at the limits of interiority, even sharing her skin. Indeed, the final betrayal of the novel radically reorganizes the interiority and exteriority of Mona's being, installing, with its fallout, the new boundaries of familial and cultural belonging and exclusion. Mona has followed desire regardless of other loyalties and mandates. Helen's discovery of Mona's sexual relationship with Seth indexes the intersection between the subject's *desire for* the Other and its *responsibility to* the Other. That is, the betrayal manifests Mona's responsiveness to the desire *of the other* as it *moves in her self*. In this structure of desire and responsiveness, Seth stands as a placeholder for the Other—first for Sherman, but, even more radically in the epilogue, for desire itself: "Mona wishes that she could open a door and discover, not Sherman turned into Seth, but—to her utter stupefaction and relief—Sherman turned into a woman."[67] Who is this "other woman" that Mona wants?[68] She is Helen, certainly, but not, as I will explain below, the Helen (she thought) she knew.

In light of her enduring desire, we might contend that Mona's character in this epilogue allegorizes the trace of the treacherous desire that enacts (Asian) American selfhood. The desiring Mona of the epilogue offers a heuristic mechanism by which to read the proximity of the Other at the heart of subjectivity, her betrayal having undone and re-created subjects and others, exteriority and interiority, in its wake. In the terms of post-

Enlightenment ethics, this type of "eschatological desire" provides a modality of subjectivity that relates the self to the Other while maintaining the Other's infinite alterity. Desire thus affirms the separation of the self and Other but also provides the language that makes this separation intelligible, bridging the gap between the Other and what the self wants.[69] For Levinas, it is not a void in self-presence, but rather the infinity of existence, its plenitude and excessiveness, that constitutes desire. Desire responds to the infinitude of otherness that exceeds self-presence, and so desire itself cannot be fulfilled or satisfied while preserving the self. Thus, the subject's desire is always also a desire to "free itself of itself."[70] The paradox of desire and agency defines the struggle at the heart of betrayal: desire, the compulsion of an-other order, provides the conditions for the subject to respond, but only in such a way as to undermine self-presence. Mona thus stands in the epilogue as an indeterminate remainder from the betrayal—suspended, ambivalent, and uncertain as to what she wants, with whom to identify, and of what she has forsaken. As a desiring trace of existence, the subject experiences the Other's proximity, the "other-in-me," that disrupts the subject from gathering itself into being. In the epilogue, then, Mona is like the walking wounded, turning her most intimate and abjected attachments inside out. To this end, her act of betrayal opens onto the time, space, and language of the Other. And yet, even if Mona cannot know what acting upon her sexual desire will have meant beforehand, and although she is subject *to* that desire and thus obligated to act upon it, she nonetheless is held responsible for and must live with the consequences of that act.

I would like to argue, then, for a reading of the novel's end(s), in which the "end" does not in fact signal a resolution per se. Rather, *Mona* manifests an abiding concern with the Other that cycles the (Asian) American back into an interminable project of ethical responsibility. Mona's reunion with Helen constitutes a moment of recognition and forgiveness proffered as part of the inexhaustible ethico-political project of justice. If liberal discourses of minority formation cannot tolerate the failures of self that ground the desiring subject's being and agency, the radical potential of ethical betrayal is precisely to "remember" continually those others who block the subject's achievement of self-presence. The agency of the ethical subject as such "may well consist in opposing and transforming the social terms by which it [i.e., the agent itself] is spawned."[71] Furthermore, Mona's betrayal countenances the definitiveness of the intersection between material history and ethical agency. While eschatological desire for the Other may be "essentially objectless" (because it registers the infinite existence of the Other), it manifests itself in historical time so that it is subjectively experienced by social and material bodies.[72] *Mona* theorizes this juncture of the ethical and historical-material in the haunted temporalities of irony and prolepsis that pervade the bildungsroman. In its constant evocation of other times and spaces, the novel postulates a return to origins that Derrida has described as "hauntology," where one learns to live with and respond to ghosts in order to do justice to the past and encounter the future as open to the Other.

Hauntology

Mona, the character—unknowingly—and *Mona*, the novel—more consciously—are haunted by Western literary history, with the eerie possibilities of, in Hortense Spillers's words, "a self-generated phantasm that bites back." Perhaps the most haunted structure in the novel is the Gugelsteins' enormous new home. For example, when surveying the mansion for the first time, Mona and Barbara explore what the Gugelsteins had been told was a "real-life entrance for the Underground Railroad."[73] As they descend into the cellar of the house, Mona contemplates, "Now this is the heart of darkness." "But before she can remember who wrote that story, much less what *The horror! The horror!* in it was, she bangs into some kind of metal rack," and she discovers, much to Barbara's delight, that the "Underground Railroad" is in fact a wine cellar.[74] The allusion to *Heart of Darkness* in *Mona* marks slavery and colonialism as the necessary, but repressed, horror that haunts Mona's trek of (self-)exploration and discovery and the Gugelsteins' social and economic mobility, both of which emblematize a broader history of national development.

The narrative's intertextuality intensifies, as Friedman has so convincingly and insightfully argued, in its citation of that "classic" American novel about youthful freedom and race relations, *Huckleberry Finn*. Mona, Seth, and Barbara decide to hide Alfred, who has been evicted from his apartment by his girlfriend, in the Gugelstein house, which has been vacated for the summer by everyone except Barbara and her cousin Evie. In the course of this effort, they replay the most crucial dynamics of Twain's novel, Huck's struggle to "free" Jim (whom, we recall, has already been granted his freedom by Miss Watson, unbeknownst to himself and Huck). In rigging an elaborate system of entrance and exit for Alfred through the underground tunnel system in order to avoid Alfred's detection by Evie and Barbara's neighbors, Mona, Barbara, and Seth congratulate themselves on their generosity toward Alfred. Alfred lives in the servants' quarters, in a room fully furnished from a previous tenant, where "there is a definite atmosphere, as Seth observes, of unplanned departure."[75] If the house itself feels haunted, Alfred takes up residence in it like a ghost.

Pointedly though, and unlike Jim's character in Twain's novel, Alfred intervenes in Mona and her friends' attempts to "help" him, in ways that indicate his own agency and desires, which cannot be readily reduced to those of his benefactors. He begins to resent the constraints upon him in the home and begins wandering around the house—playing the radio, watching TV—and risks having Evie catch him out. Even more acutely subversive, Mona, Barbara, and Seth later learn that in fact Alfred and Evie have not only been acquainted for a number of weeks, but have begun a sexual relationship and conspired to keep it a secret. As Mona concludes, "You didn't want to be in someone else's experiment."[76] After Mona, Barbara, and Seth discover Alfred and Evie's relationship, the experiment at "Camp Gugelstein" expands to include a number of Alfred's friends, an African American "mod squad" whose company Mona and her friends come to enjoy, especially during conversations regarding racial and cultural issues.[77]

The entire arrangement ultimately devolves, however, with two conflicts, the theft of a silver flask from the Gugelstein home and the Gugelsteins' discovery of Alfred and Evie's relationship. Resentful at the implication that one of them might have stolen the flask, Alfred and his friends leave the Gugelstein home. The end of the experiment in social action proves "devastating," especially to Seth, who, in surmising that, "They considered me a racist bastard, and I considered them my friends," begins to realize that the deeply structural inequities of racial difference cannot be easily surmounted by sentimental good will.[78] In Mrs. Gugelstein's discovery of the photographs Evie has taken of Camp Gugelstein, Jen carefully plots the violent historical implications of these inequities. In addition to the pictures of Alfred and Evie in bed together, Mrs. Gugelstein finds that, "There are also pictures of the gang hanging out, and the gang getting down, and the gang having a good old time, and every one of these is perfectly focused, with lovely detail. If your aunt were so inclined, she could hang every one of them."[79] This final sentence, with its ambiguous antecedent for "them," which could refer to the photographs but possibly also to Alfred and the other members of "the gang," closes out the haunted Part Two of the novel tellingly. Calling to mind the lynchings that have pervaded American history—mob "justice" against black men accused of sexually assaulting white women—*Mona* keeps alive the phantasm of racial violence that haunts the self-righteousness of white indignity against so-called black incursion.

At this point, the narratives of Mona's family tensions and of her political exploration of identity intersect: the Changs fire Alfred from the Pancake House for his part in the scandal. Jen ties the intimation of lynching at the end of the previous section of the novel to the opening of this next section through a simile. While Alfred explains to Mona that "Somebody's going to take the heat, it's got to be the Negroes, right? Who else gets burnt up and keeps walking?" his jacket, which he dangles on his finger, "swings in front of him like a hanged man."[80] Coincidentally, Barbara's father is fired from his position at a brokerage house as a scapegoat in a scandal for which another broker was responsible, proving, as Barbara observes, "that Gugelstein was never how you spelled Popularity to begin with."[81] The still tenuous inclusion of the Jewish family in the American dream is further punctuated when we learn that the Gugelsteins never actually owned the home, but leased it with an option to buy.[82]

Although Barbara's father is unable to sue, because he is unable to prove any discrimination, Alfred has more success in initiating a lawsuit, because Mona had confided, as part of a "camp rap session" that her parents' preference for the Chinese Cedric over Alfred was indeed racially and ethnically biased. Like Huck following the moral code of his heart, Mona runs away from Scarshill when Helen berates her for having betrayed her family in this confidence, with Helen warning her that, "Once you leave this house you can never come back."[83] At Grand Central Station, as she begins her adventure, she senses the openness of the future as tied to her innocence: "Before she sees herself in perspective, she feels, quite unexpectedly, as though she stands in the Garden of Eden . . . not even that she is standing in, but as though she is herself the Garden of Eden. . . . She feels as though she stands at the pointy start of time. Behind her, no history. Before her—everything."[84] Yet if Mona's optimism and perception of herself as innocent embodies the American ideal she professes throughout the novel, Helen's voice quickly intervenes in the fantasy: "How arrogant! *As if you have no mother! As if you came out of thin air!*"[85] This scene thus resembles nothing so much as the closing pages of another American "classic," *The Great Gatsby*, where the vision of the unfettered future that Gatsby (the apotheosis of being "whatever you want") shares with the Dutch sailors forever recedes into a past (im)possibility.

This type of ironic intertextual distance between the narrator and reader on the one hand, and a naive but kindhearted protagonist on the other hand, pervades the novel. But if we accept that *Mona* owes this strategy of ironic comment about American naiveté to Twain's novel, we should then also take into account Stacey Margolis's argument that *Huckleberry Finn* is a novel "about the limits of intention, in which your effects on other people rather than your feelings about them define what you have done and, more important, what you can be held accountable for."[86] *Huckleberry Finn* attempts, as Margolis writes, "to imagine accountability even in the absence of malice."[87] Divorcing "collectivity from experience" and extending corporate responsibility to a national level, Twain's novel holds individuals responsible "not simply for harms [they] have caused but also for harms committed in [their] name"[88] Margolis's incisive analysis of both the narrative and the controversies surrounding *Huckleberry Finn* discerns a model of impersonal responsibility that supplements an "intentional model" by taking responsibility for the "unpredictable effects of individual action."[89] Twain's novel, she demonstrates, takes its ethical urgency from the post-Reconstructionist problem: how does the nation account and compensate for the many harms of slavery? To this end, *Huckleberry Finn* attempts "to think about the problem of American racism in structural rather than personal terms," thereby shifting attention from "belief to practice, from intentions to effects."[90]

Mona in the Promised Land inherits this ethico-political question from *Huckleberry Finn* and, I suggest, projects it into a post–Civil Rights context. The question of what is owed to the racial *others* of the nation remains, as it has been for civil rights discourse, an ongoing concern for *Mona*, insofar as the injuries to these others are ongoing and unredressed. It provides the impetus to Mona, Barbara, and Seth's "comparative-tragedy project" in which they rank the various injustices of American history, and "though it's a tough decision, they finally, generously agree: The Chinese revolution and the Holocaust notwithstanding, by and large, in present-day America . . . it's generally an advantage to look more like Archie Bunker than like Malcolm X."[91] They house Alfred as a form of "social action," an attempt to "undo the harm done" by bringing the political to their personal lives.[92] Nonetheless, "spiritual connection among disparate individuals," like the bonds of solidarity that Mona, Barbara, and Seth try to forge with Alfred's friends, prove insufficient.[93]

In the final pages of the novel, then, Mona finally begins to recognize the extent to which her family's discussions about whether "to be or not to be" minorities impinges on the racial formations already in place. Pointedly, Mona's education in the legal and historical realities of race culminates in (the threat of) juridical action, what has proven to be the arena *par excellence* for the politics of civil rights. Against the more affective bonds that Mona, Seth, and Barbara have attempted to consolidate in their social experiment of Camp Gugelstein, Alfred's lawsuit evokes the liberal state's limited recognition of racial identities as injured plaintiffs. This construction of racial difference thereby generates the reverse discourse of identity politics to which a public form of minority discourse attaches itself. Even more to the point, the conditions surrounding Alfred's lawsuit embody the model of collective responsibility that the novel inherits from *Huckleberry Finn*. In a remarkable way, the Changs are made to stand in for the injuries that *all* of Scarshill, and even more broadly, the nation, inflict upon Alfred. As Helen observes, "Our trouble is that we are in the middle.... Alfred is mad; he would like to sue your friend Barbara's family. But he cannot sue them, so he sue us."[94] Ralph and Helen's individual discrimination against Alfred proves to be "circumstantial" of a much broader constellation of social forces at work in the community. The Changs might sincerely be ignorant of the law and their transgression of it, but they are nonetheless responsible to Alfred.

Mona's effort to repair relations between Alfred and her parents comports with this responsibility as well. Mona herself, upon returning from her stay with Callie and after her mother's discovery of her relationship with Seth, hides out with Seth in the Gugelsteins' now empty house. During their stay, they discover that Fernando, the Chinese cook whom Ralph fired and who cursed the Pancake House, is the burglar who stole the flask from the Gugelstein home. She delivers the news to Alfred that he has been absolved of any part in the theft, and in return he agrees to drop the lawsuit. Despite this trade-off, Jen punctuates the ongoing need for the civil rights politics that Alfred's lawsuit represented. When Mona learns that Alfred's friend Luther, "the Race Man," who had encouraged Alfred to bring the suit against the Changs, was "beat just about dead" at a protest, Mona's "heart blows open."[95] In light of this evidence of ongoing violence against African Americans, Alfred's decision to forego the lawsuit is an act of notable generosity, one that more than returns the gift of the flask which Mona and Seth present him with. Mona's heart blown open not only recognizes, as Margolis contends with respect to Twain, "the poverty of treating racial justice as a question of sentiment ... instead of as a question of structure," but also suggests the affective unpredictability by which realigned social identities and coalitions return to that same form of justice.⁹⁶

And yet, if Mona's gesture of giving the flask means to suture the relations between Alfred, herself, her parents, Seth, and the Gugelsteins, Helen rejects this offer of reconciliation. The narrative logic for Helen's refusal, as I have already made clear, follows because it is not the lawsuit, nor Mona's part in it, that stands as the ultimate betrayal in the novel, although it is an important one. Nonetheless, this "secondary" betrayal does have undeniable and unalterable consequences for Ralph and Helen's future, despite Mona's attempts to undo it. Insofar as the lawsuit inscribes Ralph and Helen as politically and juridically represent*able* subjects, the state incorporates their presence, obviating their liminal and ambivalent participation (as immigrant, middlemen minorities) in the nation.⁹⁷ In her journey to (Asian) American selfhood, Mona thus takes her parents along for the ride. And, we should also note, to the extent that the modern state *has* come to incorporate various axes of difference (e.g., gender, class, religion, race, etc.), this capacity for representation is neither static nor one-directional. One can imagine that the injuries and inequities to which Ralph and Helen have been subject (catalogued in *Typical American*) might themselves become matters of juridico-political action, which minority discourse engages.

But another radical departure at the novel's end overshadows this shared journey into (Asian) American selfhood, since, as Rabbi Horowitz, now a counselor at Harvard-Radcliffe, observes to Mona, to leave "Fort Chang" is to "betray" it.⁹⁸ This is the departure that Helen enforces, as she waits out Mona, the "disturbance" who "can be trusted to leave by herself." Here it becomes crucial in our analysis to delink Helen from Ralph. If Ralph does indeed forgive Mona and submit, albeit with some bemusement, to being incorporated by the nation, Helen embodies an elemental difference in this submission to, or achievement of, (Asian) American selfhood. As the final chapter, titled "Discoveries," begins, "already [Mona] knows . . . symmetry will elude them; . . . [she and Seth] discuss coincidence, and pattern, and the sorts of synchronicities such as are no more than you can expect from novels, but that in real life do give you the heebie-jeebies."⁹⁹ Thus, while critics have commented at length about *Mona*'s thematics of the relationality and hybridity of (Asian) American identity, I contend that the novel's (in)conclusion, its proleptic relations to its epilogue, and its status as a sequel subordinate this concern with the self-presence of the (Asian) American. Instead, the novel prioritizes the obligation to others that makes subjectivity possible in the first place.

In this regard, Helen's repudiation of Mona at the novel's end dissolves the ties that bind Mona to her mother, but rather than propelling her into autonomy, the opening of the epilogue suggests that Mona's subjectivity founders. Nor does this threat of subjective *dissolution* amount to an *absolution* of the subject's responsibility. Rather, it resignifies and redistributes responsibility, a transformation that, as I discuss below, projects the ethical obligation onto *political* relations. For now, though, I propose that, in its specific concern with (Asian) American formation, *Mona in the Promised Land* asserts that treating diasporic difference as a matter of sentimental nostalgia for the "motherland" will never compensate for the epistemic and material violence the other undergoes in "our name." Against a narrative drive for symmetry and resolution, then, the end of the final chapter and the epilogue countenances the "an-economic" condition of justice, a possibility that is engendered not in the felicitous resolution of narrative crises, but in the suspension of such a resolution. If the flask symbolizes justice as a gift that does not (desire to) receive anything in return—"[Mona] would have liked to apologize [to Alfred] without receiving anything in return"—Helen's refusal to accord Mona any recognition sets the stage for a gift that is to come, gesturing to a time and place beyond the novel's close.[100]

Other Times and Places

The formal aspect of loss supercedes Mona's reconciliation with Alfred at the novel's end. Loss, as we find in the epilogue, structures the circulation of desire that sustains the (Asian) American subject, whose very existence is anchored in the traitorous departure from her mother. If the foreclosure of the mother, as Chin portrays it, enacts the originary violence of the subject's arrival, the epilogue to *Mona* formally enacts the haunting (and hauntology) that foreclosure occasions. But this haunting is not a matter only for the future that the epilogue makes present. Returning one last time to the critical work of irony in *Mona*, we might ask what role irony plays in the novel's epilogue, especially with respect to the hybridity that the final pages propose. If, as Friedman herself has shown, the novel proper is shot through with the irony of a naive, albeit clever and likeable, protagonist who knows not what she does, perhaps it might be too hasty to attribute a finality to the epilogue in its relation to the novel proper. As Paul de Man suggests, irony reveals a non-organic temporality that "relates to its source only in terms of distance and difference and allows for no end, for no totality."[101] Derrida further observes that, while irony presents itself publicly (in literature, etc.), it simultaneously depends upon differing forms of knowledge between its objects and its subject.[102] Irony therefore creates a "nonpublic public within the public," where "the difference between the public and the nonpublic remains an indecidable limit."[103] As such, irony's evocation of and dependence upon other times and places calls us to read the novel and epilogue according to a disjunctive temporality and spatiality, specifically, I contend, according to the past and future that prolepsis and sequentiality generate.

Throughout *Mona*, there occurs a proleptic "breaking in" of a future narrative perspective on the events that are being presently portrayed. We find prolepsis, for example, in the opening sections I have quoted: "In another ten years, there'll be so many Orientals they'll turn in to Asians," or, in relation to Mona's attraction to Sherman, "And later in life, she will catalog the ways in which the Chinese and the Japanese are as opposite as their geographies."[104] Perhaps most significantly, the novel metanarratively reflects upon the effective role of prolepsis when Mona decides to have sex with Seth for the first time:

> This is what she thinks later: there are moments when the zippy narrative of your life lets up, and swampy reflection sinks in. There are moments when you begin to feel ending. . . . There are moments when the inexorable shrinking of the days makes you miss people who have not left you—people like Barbara, Alfred, Seth.
> It as if you have come unmoored from your present—as if you are floating out in the floodplain of your future. So that, out of a sort of nostalgia, you might decide yes. All right. It's time.[105]

This technique, of course, illustrates the retroactive construction of identity through memory and narrative. And yet, except in this instance, prolepsis in *Mona* reflects mostly upon moments that seem, in the end, to be incidental rather than pivotal ones. In a narrative that is expressly about Mona's political and sexual emergence or arrival, it is therefore in its *formal occurrence*, rather than its *referential content*, by which prolepsis generates its most significant and ethical effects. That is to say, prolepsis formally gestures to a future to come, whose possibility always provides an ethical counterpoint to the knowing self-presence of the narrative. As the grammar of a time in which we cannot live, prolepsis evokes a future anterior that is always genuinely literary. We are compelled to read these proleptic incidents back into the epilogue, then, not to arrive at some truth about Mona or Helen; rather, they institute an ethical agency that keeps the narrative open, even after its end.

We might take the epilogue along the lines of an epigraph, which Derrida describes as a speaking from beyond the grave.[106] Beyond the tragic ending of non-recognition that ends the developmental narrative, the epilogue moves to a distant time and differential place, particulars that hold only a parenthetical place in the novel proper. The epilogue engages the arrival of the Other, in this other time and place. The "anachrony" of otherness, where the seeming continuities of self-presence break apart and things are "going badly," constitutes the very possibility of justice, for the arrival of the other.[107] In its depiction of Mona's melancholia, the epilogue also counters any attempt to *mourn* the past in order to detach from it. The epilogue stages the failure of encrypting the past by mourning it, demonstrating instead that the future will always instead carry with it the otherness of this past.

This failure of encryption intensifies when Mona discovers that Helen herself had, as her Aunt Theresa intimates, "secrets"—a history of which Mona never knew and whose actual content is not revealed here. This intimation of a secret history returns us to Jen's first novel, *Typical American*. Do we (and perhaps Mona too) need to read that novel in order to know Helen's secrets and consequently set things right? Yes and no. We do learn there about Helen's extramarital affair (as well as Theresa's affair with a married man) and the violent repercussions she suffers as a result. Yet Helen remains as inaccessible in *Typical American* as she does in *Mona*; we are never privy to her perspective and know almost nothing about her motives, except what we surmise from her actions. In both novels, then, Helen is portrayed as a forceful, yet removed, figure whose very presence and metonymic affiliations with China interrupt and reorganize, first Ralph's, and then Mona's, development as fully formed American subjects.

Mona's failure to grasp Helen's "secret of the secrets" in the novel proper reflects the forgetfulness incumbent upon a generative narrative of the subject's emergence. This unknowable past determines, from the outset, the horizon of possibilities for Mona and the possibilities of her narrative. For *Mona*, *Typical American* and the secrets contained therein stage an immemorial past through which the Other comes to contest and rift the grounds of (Asian) American selfhood. As a sequel, *Mona in the Promised Land*, and its subject, the (Asian) American Mona, depends upon but, in order to stand as an autonomous text, also severs itself from, the familial history of *Typical American*. However, an ethics of betrayal uncovers the possibility of an "other" articulation that remains to be made, between the emergent subject of Helen's secrets and Mona's "other self"—an articulation of sexual desire that violates the injunctions of chastity and fidelity in both novels. This articulation of desire remains then to haunt the narrative as a trace of an alternative future for (Asian) America. This "other" articulation, the narrative suggests, remains just at the limits of representability and haunts the narrative's portrait of democratic politics, social justice, and racial formation.

Secrets of the Other

The arrival of the Other, as Derrida suggests, occurs in a time and place that differs from, and defers, the present. It marks the "beyond" of repression and interrupts the "distributive justice" of an economy of vengeance that repression installs. As such, desire opens the "possibility of a step beyond repression."[108] While the formal relation between the epilogue and the novel proper in *Mona* offers a parable of this "beyond" (which, we should remember, exceeds all thematization), the possibility of this articulation of justice to come and democracy to come remains lodged in the temporal present of the narrative. Indeed, the very scene of Mona's betrayal, where Helen comes upon Mona under the covers with Seth, proffers the hope of an opening onto an alternative future. When Ralph and Helen come to retrieve Mona from Callie's dorm room, Mona hides behind a half-naked Seth under a pile of bedding. But Helen's discovery of Mona's secret sexual life becomes apparent: "When Mona looks out the window, she knows what her mother knows. For Helen has always taught Mona to walk properly. Helen has always taught Mona never to drag her feet, especially in a place where people might look down on you. But there Helen is, shuffling as if she doesn't care who sees . . . her head is bent."[109] Embedded in this scene of Helen's disappointment and Mona's guilt and betrayal, the text also offers a short-circuit to another reading. Mona sees that the belt from her mother's raincoat, a raincoat Helen prized and "intended to wear . . . for the rest of her life," because of its fit and quality, has come undone and drags behind her: "There is the belt, dangling, getting full of mud. Mona hopes her parents have parked nearby; otherwise, she's afraid, that belt's as good as lost."[110] Mona cannot reconcile the dangling belt to the Helen that she knows. Although a small visual detail in this scene, the belt, affiliated with, but not integrated to, the portrait of Helen that Mona knows, comes to bear the weight of the impending break between mother and daughter.

The trailing belt that Mona spots as a poignant emblem of her mother's disappointment inscribes the disciplining of Helen's own desire in *Typical American*, although Mona cannot know of this history, which supplements her own relation to Helen. In other words, if Mona knows what it is that Helen knows about Mona's desire, this series of acknowledgments remains open because Mona does not, indeed cannot, know of Helen's own secret desire. The trailing belt that leaves things open stands as a metonym of desire, an object that "speaks to" the undone button and the hanging jacket of earlier scenes, all figuring the proximity between desire, violence, betrayal, and rupture or change in the novel. These objects suggest that there might be an-other way to read Helen's final refusal to recognize Mona, a reading that might unleash the alterity that Mona necessarily fails to recognize. This other unspoken and incommunicable order (which must thus be designated by a series of mute objects) drives the ethical character of *Mona*. As she moves through the heart of betrayal, from adolescence to womanhood (specifically, as I elaborate above, becoming a woman who wants another woman), Mona emerges with a sense of a responsibility that she bears but that she can never fully realize.

The seemingly minor character of Theresa, who Jen describes earlier as the "subject of a whole other book," provides a specific focal point for an ethical reading of betrayal in this respect. Theresa sympathizes with Mona in her estrangement from Helen, has access to knowledge that Mona does not, and possesses her own history of sexual transgression. In many ways, Theresa proves a potentially "ideal" reader of *Typical American* and *Mona*, keeping the appropriate distance from their subjects and politically sensitive to the overdetermined racial, ethnic, and national dynamics of the narratives' situations. However, she notably never exposes Helen's secrets to Mona. She does not give Mona the ammunition by which Mona might reduce Helen's disappointment and anger to the terms of hypocrisy or assimilate them into self-same identification. Instead, as an *ethical* foil, Theresa orients us and Mona toward a respect of the secret.[111] The revelation that the epilogue makes, then, is not of the truth as an object of knowledge. Mona never learns of the "contents" of Helen's secrets, but comes to respect the secret as the trace of the Other's alterity that grounds her own being.

The recognition between Mona and Helen grapples with and at the limits of representation. Mona cannot consciously articulate a narrative of secrets without foregoing her mother's arrival/return. Instead, her recognition of and respect for the secret of secrets brings her to the appointed time and place of the ethical reckoning she wants to make, but which is ultimately possible only through Helen's arrival—generous and unaccountable, like an act of grace. Helen's arrival at Mona's wedding is inexplicable (especially since she did not visit Mona after Io's birth, which, one might assume, would be the expected scene of reconciliation). As Derrida insists, and the epilogue dramatizes, "One does not make the other come, one lets it come by preparing for its coming."[112] If, not unlike *The Chickencoop Chinaman*, *Mona in the Promised Land* has allegorized the arrival or invention of the (Asian) American self, the epilogue offers a parable about the arrival of the Other. It refers us to a time and place where the exhausting search for identity through an economy of the same might be suspended so that something *different*— unexpected and unaccountable—might take place. Thus, even the pace of the epilogue—more deliberative, contemplative, and patient—reflects the difficult reorientation of the self toward the encounter that is to come, that cannot be calculated or programmed, but only awaited, welcomed, and witnessed. Helen's forgiveness comes *despite* all of Mona's failures, not because of anything Mona has done to ameliorate them. Her arrival and forgiveness initiates a reversal of the subjectivity that saturates the novel proper, wherein Helen becomes the *agent* rather than an object in Mona's narrative. Or, perhaps more radically, Helen's arrival and forgiveness suspend the relation between the self and the Other, inscribing the ambivalence from which justice arrives and which enables the ethical reorientation of subjects and others.

In the specific discursive terms of the novel, the epilogue suspends the relations between racial and diasporic difference, victim and oppressor, injured and injurer. As significant as they are to the political projects of civil rights and diasporic allegiances, these distinctions provide no ready anchors by which to calculate, evaluate, and judge, once and for all, the ethical positions of each of the narrative's characters. There is no final balancing of the scales, nor synthesis, such as those upon which liberal discourses of rights and justice so stridently pin their hopes. *Mona in the Promised Land* stages an ethics of betrayal, where forgiveness and justice, while unconditional, nevertheless cannot be tied to the sovereignty of the subject. The (Asian) American self risks everything by placing herself in relation to the other. As an "act of literature" the narrative generates a sense of plenitude, such as in the hybridity that Friedman delineates, only by self-consciously marking the necessary structure of loss, in the process establishing a new relation between the subject and herself. It brings us to the question of justice as an interminable, incalculable, and, most significantly, *irrefutable* process, a process of re-membering history as if anew.[113]

In light of this structure of secret loss, forgiveness, and justice at the novel's end—or more precisely, *after* the novel has ended, in the epilogue—what do we make of the relation between responsibility and freedom? In Io, Jen inscribes a figure of witnessing whose presence authorizes the responsibility that culminates in Helen's return. That is to say, she witnesses ethical responsibility *as* agency; to "truly see" and represent one's self here means facing a past and future otherness that invade, contradict, and forestall the present and self-presence. As such, Io also ironizes the possibility of witness, as she stands by childishly celebrating that which she does not and will never fully comprehend. Mona's innocence is displaced from the novel proper onto Io; the latter remains unaware of the foregoing histories of trauma and loss that make her existence possible. In this sense, and in contrast to Theresa's position as the ethical reader, Io's witness is akin to that of the naive reader who too easily identifies with Mona's (Asian) American self, her utopian visions of America, and her narrative of rebellion and search for autonomy.

And yet, this *is* a scene of witnessing. We might say that Io is precious, as Jen writes her, her presence delightful and cherished. Mona feels her responsibility to Io to be as weighty and absolute as, and thus perhaps conflictive with, the one she harbors for Helen: "For how could she leave Io out—bright Io."[114] The introduction of Io in the epilogue, this third element in the otherwise dyadic relationship of Mona and Helen, renders the ethics of betrayal that the novel enacts as an ethico-*political* project. That is, it moves from the ethical relationship between self and Other, to the mediated relations of the political. If betrayal seems to emplot duplicity in the subject's relation to other others, the epilogue moves us from *duplicity* to a *duality*, or even, *multiplicity* of loyalties that attend betrayal. This move to multiplicity corresponds to the projection of the ethical onto the political. The histories passed onto Mona are riddled with the impossible choices, haunted by every other who is lost and who demands responsiveness and responsibility. Io's naive witnessing of the violence inherent in the "foundation" of (Asian) American selfhood comes too late for Mona and too early for Io, but it nevertheless comes; we might say, it necessarily must come, and that is also the novel's consolation.

Io figures the utopian promises of (Asian) American subjectivity that cannot be easily dismissed, and thus cautions against reading the subject's deconstructive ethical encounter as a suicidal nihilism. Rather, the forgetfulness of betrayal, which enables the possibility of freedom and agency, exists in a necessarily troubled relation with the remembering and returns to origin that an ethical betrayal effects. Both respond to the historical pressures of belonging and exclusion that cross cut minority subjectivity and racial and national otherness. Io's presence in the epilogue reorients us to the subject positions and relations that the narrative has heretofore generated, because she both is a product, or "consequence," of those relations and she supplements them, signifying Mona's experience of a radical freedom Derrida characterizes as elemental of democracy to come. Instead of the jealously guarded, self-possessed property of liberal discourse, the radically democratic freedom, which we witness in the return of Helen and the conception of Io, exists always in a future conditional tense. It is a "freedom to come" in a dual sense: it maintains the possibility that the other might come, without any coercion or predilection on the part of the self, and it is the continual deferral of that arrival that alleviates the unbearable weight of the utopian promise. Io cautions us against closing off the novel at the epilogue and therefore closing out what Judith Butler describes as the "difficult future terrain of community."[115]

In positing the (return of the) diasporic other, my readings of *The Chickencoop Chinaman* and *Mona in the Promised Land* in this chapter thus extend a possibility of theorizing race and ethnicity out of the rarefied polarities of victim and oppressor, injured and injurer. As I explore in the following chapters, racial formation and minority discourse are rife with the possibilities of betrayal for a host of structural reasons. These include, but are not limited to, the fragility of panethnicity as a salient mode for articulating racial identity; the predominant dichotomy of whiteness and blackness in organizing the terms and conditions of minority subjectivity in the U.S.; the disparate histories of economic and cultural dispossession of certain groups at certain moments in the U.S.; and a national discourse that recodes and circulates class differences as authentic markers of minoritarian subjectivity. Minority discourse provides the possibilities of affiliation and coalition-building but also of intense conflict, pervasive hostility, and traumatic betrayal. As *The Chickencoop Chinaman* and *Mona in the Promised Land* both demonstrate, to arrive as a raced subject in America is to enter onto a terrain at once exhilarating and dangerous in its complexities and potentialities.

3 / Accidents and Obligations: Minority Neoconservatives and U. S. Racial Discourse

> *The trauma of American race relations, as with all trauma, is that there is, really, no language for talking about what happens between communities of color, for talking about how racialization happens between people of color.*
> —TRAISE YAMAMOTO, "AN APOLOGY TO ALTHEA CONNOR"

> *Racial order imprisons modern subjects under the control of classifying schemas always delimiting possibilities. It thus splits selves and subjects between the "can" and "ought," between possibility and impossibility, requirement and liberty.*
> —DAVID THEO GOLDBERG, THE RACIAL STATE

Because U. S. racial formations have been structured as the relations between a dominant center and raced margins, one of the most troubling questions that has attended the emergence of minority discourse is the resilience of assimilation as a viable model for cultural, political, and economic access within the United States. As has been extensively documented and recounted in ethnic studies, during the 1960s and 1970s, influenced by the dual political projects of the civil rights and black nationalist movements, Asian Americans and Chicana/os began considering their own positions within the nation and developing an oppositional cultural politics that interrogated hegemonic discourses. Cultural nationalism was interested in resisting the debilitating stereotypes that dogged racial minorities by insisting upon Asian American and Chicano self-representation. It began the important work of recovering and reconstructing the histories and images available for these groups. Upon the heels of the civil rights movement, which demanded full citizenship rights for people of color, cultural nationalist activists strove to ensure that integration would not necessitate assimilation, that is, a loss of the specific cultural and social practices that define minority racial identities. Thus, the formation of "Asian American" and "Chicano" as overtly politicized identity categories was much indebted to the civil rights and black nationalist movements, both of which centered on the color line as the primary axis of difference within the nation.

Nonetheless, another, more conciliatory assemblage of ethnic identity has surfaced alongside of these self-consciously minoritarian forms. Even by the mid-1960s, social scientists and journalists were beginning to refer to Asian Americans—who had only begun to identify, and be identified, according to this panethnic rubric—as a "model minority," that is, a "relatively quiescent minority."[1] Such commentators argued that, especially in the face of African American social protest, the educational and occupational accomplishments of Asian Americans attested to the viability of the "American dream." In the context of a putatively democratic United States that guarantees freedom to its citizens, *all* of its citizens, labor and self-discipline result in the material and ideological rewards of belonging.

Likewise, already in 1959, José Antonio Villarreals published his novel, *Pocho*, a bildungsroman about Richard Rubio, the son of a Mexican Revolutionary who settles in California, and Richard's struggle between emulating his father's loyalty to a Mexican identity and the impulse to assimilate to a hegemonic Anglo-American society. In Richard's father, Juan Rubio, Villarreals posits a Mexican heritage that was once heroic, albeit brutally hypermasculine, but that is regressive and stalled as a contemporary cultural politics. Richard therefore adopts the assimilatory Mexican American identity of the *pocho*. Concurrently, during the 1960s the term "Hispanic" was instituted to refer to a wide range of peoples from Spanish-speaking countries. Many cultural critics infer an assimilatory bent to the label, which has been described as a "pro-white" cover, because it indexes a European, rather than an indigenous history, and has even been applied by the state to include European immigrants from Spain.[2]

The nation's hegemonic incorporation of minority subjects, and the attempt to "pass" as "generic" citizens by subjects who have been racially excluded from whiteness, supplement and often constrain the politics of resistance that an oppositional minority discourse promotes. The modes of assimilation available to minority subjects have proliferated in the past three decades, so that ethnic Americans need not give up their cultural affiliations and attachments to achieve a modicum of political or economic mobility. The constructions of the Asian American model minority and the Hispanic *pocho* maintain extant cultural differences while foregoing an oppositional politics. In sum, the discursive politics of racial representation have become even more complex and fractured with the emergence and the consolidation of these specific figures of assimilation, the "model minority" and the *pocho*, figures that I examine at length in this chapter.

With this context in mind, I offer below readings of Richard Rodriguez's *Hunger of Memory: The Education of Richard Rodriguez* (1982) and *Days of Obligation: An Argument with My Mexican Father* (1992), as well as Eric Liu's *Accidental Asian: Notes of a Native Speaker* (1998), all of which have been widely characterized and criticized by scholars and activists as tracts of neoconservative assimilation. Much of this criticism takes the authors to task for the political arguments they forward and the experiential grounds upon which these arguments are based, apprehending an implicit betrayal of the very minority subjects that the authors claim to represent. Indeed, as I discuss below, Liu and Rodriguez are themselves quite conscious of (and even promote) this reception of themselves as "race traitors." Although a few critics, whose work I cite below, have attended to the formal and literary dimensions of these three texts, for the most part the harshest evaluations have been ones that treat them as singularly political tracts advocating assimilation.

In contrast, in this chapter I explore these texts as works of New Journalism, a genre that became especially visible beginning in the late 1960s and early 1970s, disseminated by writers such as Tom Wolfe, Norman Mailer, Terry Southern, and Truman Capote. This is a genre that traversed the boundary between the novel or literary autobiography, on one hand, and journalism, on the other hand, to produce reports of social realities that, as one observer describes it, were "virtually antiofficial, impressionist, nonfactual, totally personal account[s] of a happening."[3] As it was associated with the nascent neoliberalism of the period and was usually conscious of various contemporary social movements, New Journalism constructed and infused a particular version of (white) masculine subjectivity.[4] Although there are some notable exceptions of women writing in the genre (for example, Joan Didion), much of the force of New Journalism revolved around the (de)construction of American masculinity under the cultural, political, and military upheavals of late modernity, and in some instances (as in the case of Mailer) it took the author himself as the hero who navigates the terrain of national and global transformation.

I suggest that both Rodriguez and Liu characteristically adopt the generic mode of New Journalism, thinking and writing through the personal insofar as it offers insight into the social and political, and vice versa. As such, these authors move across the borders of several genres: those of conventional autobiography that designates overtly political questions as beyond its purview; those of traditional journalism that seems to shun the personal for the sake of objectivity; and those of political rhetoric motivated by specific policy and legislative agendas. Rodriguez, employed as a contributing editor for *Harper's* magazine and a commentator on public television's *MacNeil/Lehrer News Hour*, and Liu, a speechwriter under the Clinton-Gore administration, clearly lay claim to the machinery of both mass media and Beltway politics. But it is the conjunction of and mutual investments *between* the personal, the political, and "the facts," that I take as my subject, as it provides the body of evidence, indeed, the body *as* evidence, that makes possible the rhetorical stances that the texts assume.

I contend that, like the other New Journalists whose works often explicitly and unabashedly forwarded a cultural politics, usually of neoliberal nationalism, *Hunger of Memory*, *Days of Obligation*, and *The Accidental Asian* might be most productively read not as unmediated, ethnographic reports of the experience of minority subjects, nor simply as opportunistic political maneuvering by overly ambitious professionals. Rather, by approaching these texts as parables of betrayal, we might comprehend the potent appeal they extend to both minority subjects and white Americans. In this chapter, I argue that the assimilatory betrayals of the minority neoconservative—the model minority and the *pocho*— must be read as betrayals compelled by the structural configurations of race, ethnicity, class, and diaspora in late-twentieth-century America. Moreover, these narratives, although deeply invested in the historical and discursive formations of the nation-state, remain open to the ethical "accidents" of betrayal that defer their closing, thus wresting them open to the otherness—and to the obligations to otherness—that such an encounter poses.

Toward this end, I distinguish between two dimensions of the texts, one of which I will refer to as the "rhetorical," that is, the overt political arguments made by Liu and Rodriguez regarding racial and ethnic politics; and the other, which I shall call the "narrative," by which I mean the discursive constructions of the protagonists, Eric Liu and Richard Rodriguez, who constitute the texts' rhetorical agents. The narratives are the resultant textual productions of selves embodying the inherent contradictions of race, nation, class, and gender, even as they might struggle to surmount these contradictions in order to assert a coherent, linear, and generic story of the neoconservative minority subject's existence. In my discussion, the "narrative" thus refers to the stories of self that the texts offer, ones told through personalized tropes and images of family, education, and romance. This dimension, I suggest, might be distinguished from the more generalized claims and discussions about the national good, the body politic, governmental policy, and social welfare, although the latter remain firmly authorized and bolstered by the former. The "rhetorical," in this sense, refers to the efforts at political persuasion that Rodriguez and Liu attempt, drawing on their own authority as assimilated minority subjects.

By reading these two dimensions of the texts against one another, my priority is not to "demystify" or "correct" the authors' political claims by referring them to an empirical state of lived social relations by which to verify or delegitimate such claims. Rather, my reading concerns itself with understanding the extent to which such claims fundamentally, if contingently, depend upon the *narrative* production of a peculiar and conflicted subject: the traitorous minority neoconservative. But, perhaps more significantly, it seeks to draw out the desiring subject, and its others, produced in the contradictions and at the limits of such a narration of self. For the reader engaging an ethics of betrayal, texts like *Hunger of Memory, Days of Obligation,* and *Accidental Asian* must be taken beyond a prescriptive juridico-political program. Such an ethical reading, which might seem potentially to pose a betrayal to the primary and conventional political commitments of ethnic studies and minority discourse, leads us to surprising moments of responsibility embedded in *any* narrative of national belonging. I conclude by turning to Américo Paredes's short story "The Gringo," and its re-creation of the historically formative nineteenth-century moment from which late-twentieth-century demands for assimilation originate. As Jinqi Ling reminds us, literary texts do not "simply live out the results prescribed for them," because the material constraints of their discursive production render a text's significance and effects historically contingent and unpredictable.[5] Together, the readings of these three authors draw out the ways in which the narrative productions of neoconservative discourse can betray the authors' rhetorical intentions, haunted as they are by the history of forgotten others.

Assimilating Appeals

In one of the moments that best characterize the assimilatory rhetoric of *The Accidental Asian*, Eric Liu voices doubt about the extent to which committing oneself to an Asian American past excludes one from an American history. As he explains, while it occurs to him "that nothing becomes universal unless it is first particular," and although he is reminded, in a conversation with writer Shawn Wong, "not to forget history... Asian American history: the trials of people before my time, whose estrangement from the mainstream years ago made possible my entry into the mainstream today," Liu cannot also help but wonder, "Should I stop with Asian American stories? Should I even begin there?"[6] He describes how, as a speechwriter for President Clinton, he participated directly in the narrative fashioning of the nation. He recalls one of his most noteworthy memorial speeches, an address for the fiftieth-anniversary tribute to D-Day veterans delivered in Normandy: "On the day of that address, in the presence of the old veterans who still lived, my memory-envy eased a bit. Welling in my eyes, catching in my throat, was a *nation's* memory, a public history: something that, I, too, could claim."[7]

In *Days of Obligation*, Rodriguez makes, with even more vehemence, a similar argument about the need for a unified national history: "Teachers and educational bureaucrats bleat in chorus: we are a nation of immigrants. The best that immigrants bring to America is diversity. American education should respect diversity, celebrate diversity. Thus the dilemma of our national diversity becomes (with a little choke on logic) the resolution to itself. But diversity is a liquid noun. Diversity admits everything, stands for nothing."[8] He describes multiculturalism as a condescending evangelicalism, "the worst sort of missionary spirit" in the American character.[9] Wondering whether anyone attempted to "protect the white middle-class student of yore from the ironies of history," Rodriguez declares, "America is not a tale for sentimentalists." He asks: "If I am a newcomer to your country, why teach me about my ancestors? I need to know about seventeenth-century Puritans in order to make sense of the rebellion I notice everywhere in the American city. Teach me about mad British kings so I will understand the American penchant for iconoclasm. Then teach me about cowboys and Indians; I should know that tragedies created the country that will create me."[10] Obviously, logical flaws and factual errors pervade Rodriguez's and Liu's assessment of ethnic studies and revisionary historiography.[11] But these errors prove neither the most interesting nor most significant sites for an ethical inquiry into the cultural politics of minority neoconservatism that these works adduce.

Rodriguez's and Liu's arguments hold a wide appeal, not only for the hegemonic nation and neoconservatives, but often for minority subjects as well.[12] Certainly these two writers are by no means alone in their desire to be free of the restrictive categories of "minority author" or "ethnic literature."[13] However, Rodriguez and Liu heighten their own disavowal of the category by rhetorically thematizing it and grounding it in autobiographical narratives of minoritarian subjectivity. How does someone who abdicates, or desires to abdicate, the burden of racial representation not only speak from the position of a racial and ethnic minority, but, as Rosaura Sánchez writes of Rodriguez, come to be "tapped by mainstream media as if he were the official representative of the very population that he views in the text with disdain"?[14] In other words, how do Liu and Rodriguez, who describe minority discourse as a "self defense" based in "the myth of victimization" and deployed by "professional minorities," nonetheless harness the ethos and pathos of minority subjectivity toward their own rhetorical ends as effectively as they do?[15]

The appeals of this rhetoric demand close attention to the narratives of self that sustain them. Writing in the specific tradition of New Journalism, Rodriguez and Liu construct their own "personal mythos," where their own "experience, and traits, values, and ideals influence interaction with the nonfictional subject and determine [the] work's ultimate vision."[16] As "writers of hybrid factual/fictional forms," both authors use this personal mythos to overdetermine "the subjects to which they are repeatedly drawn, and the facets of a subject upon which they repeatedly focus."[17] By referencing this literary tradition, my goal is not to widen the scope of that genre in order to incorporate Rodriguez and Liu (although such an end is certainly possible), but rather to understand what happens to the generic production of national subjects in literature when racialized subjects run up against the limits of conventional generic forms—here, nonfiction prose—in their claims to the nation.[18] I submit that a complex narration of self as failure allows Rodriguez and Liu to speak *to* and *as* "accidental" minority subjects while always relinquishing any obligation to speak *for* these subjects. In their yearning to be the "generic" American citizen, they must use the neoconservative rhetoric of their texts to continually renounce the obligation to represent minority subjects. Yet, circumscribed as they are by the history of racial formation in the United States, a complete transcendence of or abstraction from racialized subjectivity remains impossible.

In the cases of Liu and Rodriguez, this contradiction results in a complex narration that is constructed through and butts up against figures of fatherhood and those of various diasporas—African, Jewish, Asian, Mexican, and Latin American. It is only through this narrative construction of self as failure, as failed man and failed diasporic subject, that both writers can argue for a privatized ethnic life that need not disturb nor be disturbed by a purportedly race-blind public sphere. Thus, although neither Liu nor Rodriguez can in good faith deny instances of exclusion and marginalization in the United States, when their own doubts about the fait accompli of equitable representation and functional meritocracy do erupt, these doubts can be couched as deeply personal and private moments, a temporary unruliness in their selves to be disciplined by the masculine, American father they have idealized for and of themselves. Ultimately, however, the narrative ground that sustains such a neoconservative rhetoric proves to be actually a quite shaky and contradictory symbolic economy that elicits other histories and other futures.

Betrayals of a Class Apart: Delinking Race, Class, and Ethnicity

For both Rodriguez and Liu, assimilation constitutes an alienation from the intimate space of personal and familial attachment, an alienation readily characterized as a betrayal. In *Hunger of Memory*, by way of describing his own narrative as a "middle class pastoral," Rodriguez aligns his editor's appeal to him for more "ethnicity," with "more Grandma." For Rodriguez, "Grandma" provides an apt symbol of a private space where the ethnic, Spanish-speaking self keeps alive Mexican customs, familial relations, and religious practices. In his narrative, which he considers in large part to be a "history of my schooling," Rodriguez describes the construction of a very different self, a public Richard who speaks English and has assimilated to the civic and political life of the hegemonic nation. As in many accounts of minority discourse, language comes to bear the weight of assimilation; Spanish is a language of the home, and English the language of the gringo world. English becomes a sign of public belonging.[19] In contrast, Richard's grandmother—"stern," suspicious, and "ancient"—symbolizes the private, ethnic subject left behind in his quest for the public self: "A mysterious woman to me, my only living grandparent. A woman of Mexico. . . . My one relative who spoke no word of English. She had no interest in *gringo* society. She remained completely aloof from the public."[20]

In this narration of self, Rodriguez depicts the gendered split between the private and public realms of belonging as *symmetrical*; his grandmother's alienation from America parallels Richard's participation in it and his corresponding alienation from Mexican ethnicity. He describes the reproaches both his grandmother and other Mexicans level at him for his inability to speak Spanish fluently. "*Pocho*" comes to connote, in both *Hunger of Memory* and *Days of Obligation*, this loss: "*Pocho* then they called me. Sometimes playfully, teasingly, using the tender diminutive—*mi pochito*. Sometimes not so playfully, mockingly, *Pocho*. (A Spanish dictionary defines that word as an adjective meaning 'colorless' or 'bland.' But I heard it as a noun, naming the Mexican-American who, in becoming an American, forgets his native society)."[21] Because Spanish circulates as the language of insidership among Mexican Americans, Rodriguez surmises that by learning English he has violated a bond of intimacy: "I felt that I had somehow committed a sin of betrayal by learning English."[22]

As with the figure of the grandmother, the maternal also functions as the central trope for the Mexican diaspora in *Days of Obligation*. In the context of "Mexico, mad mother," Rodriguez emphasizes the linguistic distinction between the two forms of Spanish second-person address, *tú* and *Usted*. According to Rodriguez, the distinction marks not only the split condition of private and public existence but, further, that of authenticity and inauthenticity: "In Mexico, one is most oneself in private. The very existence of *tú* must undermine the realm of *usted*."[23] In contrast, he continues, "in America, one is most oneself in public."[24] Thus, in the Mexican context—which Rodriguez characterizes throughout *Days of Obligation* as oriented toward the past, the material, and the tragic—the self is originally and primarily rooted in the familial and the intimate. In both texts, then, the public and the private are rendered completely separate, and the separation of the two languages both symptomatizes and maintains this division. Moreover, this split comes to stand in for the *international* relationship between the two nations. Because in Mexico politics and public life more generally, he contends, is a kind of drag "archtransvestite, a tragic buffoon," Rodriguez implicitly posits the U.S.'s comprador relation as providing Mexico with the chivalric protection that it cannot muster for itself.[25]

Thus, Rodriguez does not consider this division as necessarily unjust or unwelcome; he understands himself as having the "right," and the obligation, to speak the public language of "*los gringos*."[26] He further describes the "unsentimental teachers" who anglicize his name and insist to his parents that their children learn English. When the family ceases speaking Spanish in the home, an ever growing silence between Richard and his parents ensues.[27] As Henry Staten argues, the dichotomized structure of identity in the narrative results from Rodriguez's fetishistic attachment to a familial intimacy "that is the object of his hunger of memory."[28] While Richard emerges as a "public man" alienated from the privatized, ethnicized family, he never fully severs himself from the desire for intimacy. Instead, the self rediscovers lost intimacy "in a new, reflective, articulate inwardness" where "in the sanctuary of mourning memory, lost intimacy is sealed off from the possibility of defilement."[29] Rodriguez at once compensates for the loss of the ethnic other and holds that other apart at a safe distance in and through his writing.

But perhaps more telling than Rodriguez's romantic rhetoric is how his model of assimilation fails him when confronted with the racial difference of the minoritized, yet undeniably American, presence of blackness. A brief incident related in *Hunger of Memory*, a "non-encounter" where Richard overhears black teenagers on a bus speaking neither about nor to him, inspires both annoyance and envy. Whereas he claims that in his daily life, "I rush past the sounds of voices attending only to the words addressed to me," so that he claims to be able to divorce the meaning of the words spoken from the voices and faces that utter them, with these young African Americans, "I do not take their presence for granted, I listen to the sounds of their voices."[30] He continues: "Of all the accented versions of English I hear in a day, I hear theirs most intently. They are *the* sounds of the outsider. They annoy me for being loud—so self-sufficient and unconcerned by my presence. Yet for the same reason they seem to me glamorous. (A romantic gesture against public acceptance.) Listening to their shouted laughter, I realize my own quiet. Their voices enclose my isolation. I feel envious, envious of their brazen intimacy."[31] In Rodriguez's absorptive America, the meaning of English words remains constant, despite the heterogeneity of the speakers' voices and bodies. But racially marked "black English" erupts onto this scene in a decidedly different way.

Why the special attention to the voices of these young Americans? In the brief but authoritative parenthetical remark, Rodriguez attempts to contain his unruly attraction to these subjects, casting it as a residual but ultimately empty sentiment tied to his former, private, Spanish-speaking and consequently minority self. Yet, the wish to discipline this attraction notwithstanding, we note that these "outsiders" *are* indeed American, the language they speak, unlike the Spanish that he feels alienates Latina/os from a public American identity, is not a language entirely other than English, but rather is a reconstruction of a "standard" English that embodies the very history of racial inequality in the United States that Richard wishes to transcend.

Rodriguez must "warn" himself away from the envy of their "brazen intimacy." Despite his willingness to believe that "black English is a complex and intricate version of English," he insists that it is as much a language for the private as Spanish is, because "what makes black English inappropriate in classrooms is not something *in* the language. It is rather what lower-class speakers make of it . . . it reenforces feelings of public separateness."[32] He claims that there should be no need to distinguish between the different accents of the "deep baritone" of a business associate, the mumbling of the "crazy man who sells me a newspaper every night," the questions from a Japanese tourist, the words of an Eastern European in "a neighborhood delicatessen," "the Texas accent of the telephone operator," or the "Mississippi accent of the man who lives in the apartment below me."[33] For Rodriguez, differences in class, region, ethnicity, and nation are negated by the equalizing effect of the English language. Black English extends a singularly powerful grip on the writer, though, because it attests to an existence that is at once minoritarian and American. By attributing this difference to the class of its speakers—the "public" he so highly prizes is never white, but only "middle-class," in contrast to the black youth, who are primarily "lower-class"—Rodriguez attempts to separate out race and class, arguing against the reduction of one to the other. The signifying chain that Rodriguez adopts naturalizes the continuities between American, middle class, and racelessness, so that anyone can become a public, middle-class American, and by doing so, leave behind his or her foreign, racialized, *or* lower-class self. The "or" in the second half of this equation is crucial. In *Hunger of Memory*, Rodriguez can imagine no alternative genealogies between these modes of outsidership. Thus, he can imagine no national identity other than one consolidated through the betrayal of assimilation.

A black vernacular, as it has been symbolically reinvested by minority discourse, profoundly troubles this model of national identity, however, because it *can* and *does* articulate a social presence other than, and in contestation with, the naturalized version of assimilation and ethnic identity that structures this notion of the public and private. Not only do these minority subjects represent themselves "loudly" (pointedly in contrast with the polite, hushed tones of middle-class manners), they are "annoying" because they cannot be reconciled to the deracinated national identity to which Rodriguez attributes his own narrative of selfhood, displaced and dispossessed from ethnic intimacy. In this narrative episode, the abstraction upon which Richard's public self depends comes up against the limits of a deracinated national imaginary, one unable to account for the embodied presence of black difference. At the same time, however, the "non-encounter" indicates the extent to which minority discourse cannot account for the diasporic difference of the resident alien—they are "unconcerned by my presence"—a disinterestedness and *dis*articulation that mobilizes Rodriguez's resentment and a sense of outsidership from the autonomy of black subjectivity.

The disarticulation of the Mexican American from black separatism, which comes through in *Hunger of Memory* in such slippages of attraction and annoyance, receives much more explicit treatment in *Days of Obligation*. In arguing that Chicano nationalism based much of its own activism on a "rough" analogy to African American experience that elided racial and historical differences, Rodriguez writes: "Black Americans had suffered relentless segregation and mistreatment, but blacks had been implicated in the public life of this country from the beginning. Oceans separated the black slave from any possibility of rescue or restoration. From the symbiosis of oppressor and the oppressed, blacks took a hard realism. They acquired the language of the white man, though they inflected it with refusal. And because racism fell upon all blacks, regardless of class, a bond developed between the poor and the bourgeoisie, thence the possibility of a leadership class able to speak for the entire group."[34] In contrast, he asserts, "Mexican Americans of the generation of the sixties had no myth of themselves as Americans."[35] In *Days of Obligation*, then, Rodriguez seems more willing to acknowledge why black history cannot be reconciled to his abstracted public sphere. Despite his neoconservative politics, he is unable to deny the history of racial hierarchy and violence in the United States. As descendents of slaves forcibly relocated in North America and denied almost all connection with native African cultures, African Americans had no choice but to see themselves as Americans. At the same time, the legacy of slavery and segregation cemented a specific form of African American cultural belonging in the nation. Thus, Rodriguez seems more willing to allow for a competing African American public discourse and politics rooted in the collectively based, *structural* experiences of slavery and segregation.

But the black/white poles of racialization remain firmly entrenched here, as they do in *Hunger of Memory*. For Rodriguez, then, one participates in American public life *either* as a disembodied, deracinated citizen *or* in the mode of embodied blackness. But precisely because of the historical and racial specificity of the latter, Rodriguez declares it disingenuous and inauthentic for Mexican Americans to adopt the rhetoric of black separatism. Rodriguez's texts provide a useful point of engagement for Liu's *The Accidental Asian*, not the least because Rodriguez himself acknowledges the extent to which Asian American presence has helped anchor a sense of himself in the black/white terrain of U.S. racial discourse: "When black and white America argued, I felt I was overhearing some family quarrel that didn't include me. Korean and Chinese and Japanese faces in Sacramento rescued me from the simplicities of black and white America."[36]

On a rhetorical level, Liu seems in many ways more forthcoming than Rodriguez. For example, he acknowledges that the discursive and material formation of "America" has been deeply rooted in the construction of whiteness, something that Rodriguez seems loath to admit except implicitly and begrudgingly, in reference to black experience. Indeed, Liu describes himself as "an assimilist in recovery," willing—as he was not before—to "play" the Asian American activist in public venues, in particular to protest ongoing racial discrimination. Yet Liu's adoption of an Asian American identity in *The Accidental Asian* is persistently shot through with hesitancy, especially because, he contends, "more than ever before, Asian Americans are only as isolated as they want to be. They—we—do not face the levels of discrimination and hatred that demand an enclave mentality, particularly among the second generation, which, after all, provides most of the leadership for the nation-race. The choice to invent and sustain a pan-Asian identity is just that: a choice, not an imperative."[37] Liu's skittish use of first-person and third-person pronouns here and throughout his text indicates his own rhetorical uncertainty about aligning himself too closely with minoritarian identity politics and, furthermore, uncertainty over the identity and identifications of his audience. Liu senses that Asian American activists and critics refuse to see the changes that the nation itself has endured: "The meaning of 'America' has undergone a revolution in the twenty-nine years I have been alive, a revolution of color, class, and culture. Yet the vocabulary of 'assimilation' has remained fixed all this time: fixed in whiteness, which is our metonym for power; and fixed in shame, which is what the colored are expected to feel for embracing the power."[38] From the perspective of minority discourse, assimilation, including Liu's own assimilation, can only be perceived as a betrayal ("the assimilist is a traitor to his kind, to his class, to his own family") when, in fact, he contends, "assimilation" might merely register the *accidental* intersection of race and class.[39]

These observations lead Liu to a number of conclusions about his own position as an Asian American activist (i.e., he has been called upon by national news media to represent Asian Americans) and as a racialized ethnic subject. Rodriguez contends that the panethnic formation of

"Hispanic" is a "complete political fiction."⁴⁰ Likewise, Liu argues that Asian Americanness is *only* a public role that is played, rather than an identity that is personally embodied: "The private side, the realm of close friendships formed through race, I have entered only lately."⁴¹ The dearth of personal, affective relations underpins his reluctance to *be* an Asian American rather than, as he puts it, "play one on television." Liu's portrait of Asian Americans echoes Rodriguez's, highlighting the disarticulation of this group from both black and white collectivity: "Something Professional Asian Americans sometimes overlook is that they are not honorary blacks either. African Americans created the template for minority politics in this country. . . . Asian Americans haven't the moral purchase that blacks have upon our politics."⁴² Thus, Liu, like Rodriguez, stipulates that a double failure vexes Asian American cultural politics: panethnic organizing effects an evacuation of a meaningful private realm of ethnic belonging *and* it is unable, ultimately, to intervene significantly in the public life of the nation.

Liu moreover insists that assimilation is not merely a loss, but rather that there is something to be gained in its process.⁴³ In Liu's words, "When I identify with white people who wield economic and political power, it is not for their whiteness but for their power."⁴⁴ Liu, like Rodriguez, thus delinks racial and ethnic formation from class formation. As Renny Christopher argues about Rodriguez's work, both these writers not only take class as a serious analytical category, but class provides the primary, if not determinant, factor in these narratives of self.⁴⁵ Both Rodriguez and Liu construe whiteness as an epiphenomenal sign of hegemonic mobility, whereas class is "really" what matters, to whites and non-whites alike. As Rodriguez writes in *Hunger of Memory*, his own interest in racial difference was rooted in "the connection between dark skin and poverty. . . . I considered the great victims of racism to be those who were poor and forced to do menial work."⁴⁶ As an adult, then, Rodriguez's own dark complexion comes to signify, not the condition of *los pobres*, but rather "a mark of leisure and wealth": "Have I been skiing? In the Swiss Alps? Have I just returned from a Caribbean vacation?"⁴⁷ Rodriguez represents racial difference as a symptom of the more deeply rooted divisions of class that occupy his narratives, such that "complexion" is always (to be) read (or not) as race according to the social divisions of class hierarchy. Rodriguez's claims here suggest that, for many minority subjects, the struggle to "be white" (i.e., to assimilate) in a post-segregationist, post–civil rights moment, in fact indexes a desire to become "unraced" altogether, holding on to only those ethnic traits considered superfluous, "merely" multicultural, and thus non-threatening to the hegemonic nation.

If Rodriguez and Liu seem at best ambivalent about, and at worst too happily celebratory, of class mobility as the solution to social division, Christopher reminds us that an individual, personal attitude will not ultimately mitigate the structural problems of alienation and affective "homelessness" that socioeconomic hierarchy creates.[48] Nevertheless, in our ethical reading of betrayal, a reading that runs counter to the rhetorical politics promoted by their authors, these narratives reveal openings for different discourses such that "we remember that mobility for individuals does not create social justice for all."[49] In the next section, I describe how, in refusing a minoritarian racial identity, the *pocho* or model minority attempts to share in the material privileges of white normativity, before then turning to the others who must be negated for this assimilatory subject to come into being.

Betraying Class: The Ideological Formation of Race and Ethnicity

As numerous critical race theorists have argued, large-scale social and political transformations took place in racial discourse during the last quarter of the twentieth century (the "post–civil rights" era). The state moved from explicitly using racial distinctions for discriminatory purposes to maintaining them in order primarily to enforce and promote *anti*-discrimination laws and policies, thereby reaffirming the "reality" of race, albeit toward reformist ends.[50] The terrain of racial politics and representation has grown increasingly complex, partially as a result of the social movements of the 1960s. Prior to the civil rights movement, the framework of racial discourse in the United States was predominantly unified, if rigidly hierarchical. It has since become increasingly difficult to contend that race even "matters" in discussions about social and political justice.[51] In this context, neoconservatives using the language of civil rights denounce affirmative action and other entitlements for racial minorities, in part by embracing the figure of the model minority or *pocho*. This political logic holds that *certain* minority subjects, because of their adherence to cultural values that emphasize the family, education, a work ethic, etc., and "natural" talents, deservedly advance in U.S. society.[52]

Neoconservatives employ images of Asian American or "Hispanic" successes and seek out minority neoconservatives to support their social and economic agendas, denying altogether the continued existence of racial hierarchies and promoting a "color-blind" politics of individualism and ethnic pluralism. In their conformity to hegemonic standards and structures of success, minority neoconservatives ideologically affirm the validity of "the American dream." Although, as I have explained in Chapter 1, Asian Americans and Latina/os remain marked as "forever foreign" in the United States, images of Asian American and Latina/o familial, religious, and labor practice also function against African American claims to enfranchisement and reparations, so that the *pocho* or model minority is set against other people of color.[53] The minority subject's adoption of neoconservative politics takes place against this heterogeneous and contradictory set of cultural and political representations.

Moreover, the construction of race and ethnicity in the United States, and in particular the way that race and ethnicity provide two distinct but overlapping modes of identification, facilitates neoconservative identity for minority subjects. Although many Asian Americans and Latina/os readily claim an ethnic identity for themselves, they occupy a collectively ambivalent social position in the United States with respect to race.[54] The "ethnicity paradigm" offers an appealing precedent for neoconservative cultural politics: "What the neoconservatives oppose is . . . not racial equality but racial collectivity."[55] Like this broader neoconservative bloc, minority neoconservatives represent themselves "as simultaneously opposed both to discrimination and to anti-discrimination measures based on 'group rights' principles."[56] The minority neoconservative can at once take pride in his or her ethnic "heritage" and disparage "discrimination," while denying that racism is a systemic and institutional problem.[57]

Minority neoconservatism and its disavowal of racial identity troubles cultural critics who continue to believe that a collective identity could tenuously link racial minorities to a politics of radical democracy. As a constituency, minority neoconservatives exceed the oppositional politics of cultural nationalism. These conflicted discourses of minority formation mean that a platform of racial unity does not guarantee the transcendence of class, ethnic, and political differences, and these conflicts also drive the rhetoric of Rodriguez's and Liu's texts.[58] Perhaps even more significant than class differences is, as Viet Thanh Nguyen points out with specific reference to Asian Americans, the "ideological heterogeneity"—the diverse political orientations toward assimilation, economic mobility, and liberal individualism—that inheres in ethnic America and its cultural politics.[59] If ideological reductionism enables the radical thought and politics of ethnic studies, it also poses a "fundamental problem," because it compels racial identity to be an entirely "resistant" one.[60] Thus, the acquiescence of many Asian Americans and Hispanics to the very structures that uphold social hierarchy delimits the collective consciousness of race-based social movements.[61] From the perspective of the model minority and the *pocho*, we see that middle- and upper-class status can no longer be interpreted according to the conventional terms of whiteness, because whiteness itself is currently undergoing a transformation that benefits *some* Asian Americans and Latina/os.[62] The face of middle- and upper-class America has become increasingly diverse. This does not mean that Asian Americans and Latina/os do not experience discrimination, but that minority subjects are themselves also implicated in racism. Without taking into account this shifting terrain of U.S. racial discourse, Asian Americans and Latinos will (be) continually shuttle(d) back and forth between identifying as white, and thus assimilated to and implicated in existing power structures, or as black, and thus marginalized victims of and resisting agents against systematic racism.[63]

If Rodriguez and Liu argue that Asian Americans and Latina/os cannot claim a "moral purchase" on American national life, this is precisely because the racial dispossession of these subjects was, as we saw in Chapter 1, carried out *as alienation*. The point here is not to reserve their own share of "moral purchase" for Asians and Latina/os and therefore equate, much less prioritize, the history of racialized exclusion and alienation over that of bondage, segregation, racial violence, and second-class citizenship to which African Americans have been subjected. Rather, it is to probe what Traise Yamamoto so eloquently describes as "the trauma of American race relations" and the absence of a "language for talking about what happens between communities of color, for talking about how racialization happens between people of color." As I have been arguing heretofore, the conditions that constitute ethnic America complicate any polarized theory of race relations, where Asians and Latinos become white simply because they cannot be black.

Caught in the binds that liberal discourse, cultural nationalism, and civil rights have all found(ed) between whiteness, citizenship, and middle-class status, minority discourse grapples with how it is that minority "insiders" achieve their apparently normative positions. The figure of the assimilated minority subject antagonizes *both* nativist discourses of national belonging *and* minority discourse's representations of the raced subject marked by injury and resistance. Might we locate in the model minority and the *pocho* the possibility for an ethical critique of the ideological terms of race, ethnicity, class, and nation, through which assimilatory betrayals are enacted? Further, can we find in these betrayals openings onto other possibilities for forging political identities and alliances? In the following sections, I suggest that the contradictory strategies of the narrative production of self in *Hunger of Memory, Days of Obligation*, and *The Accidental Asian* mark the limits of liberal, neoconservative, and separatist discourses and point to alternative terrains of minority formation in America.

Demanding Mothers and Failing Fathers: Diasporic Longings and Disappointments

If neoconservatism upholds the national imaginary of an abstracted public sphere, Liu and Rodriguez nevertheless face the demands of the diasporic others who might forestall their accession in the hegemonic nation. Both authors enact two contradictory and alternating narrative strategies in response to the diasporic parent who will not allow for a "freedom of choice" that is also, as Liu describes it, a freedom from "the burden of history."[64] First, when faced with the embodiment of a specific history, the authors depict themselves as failed men in the diaspora, a feminizing identification that hastens their entrance into America, by engulfing and dissolving the masculine figures of remembrance proffered in their fathers. Second, and in tension with this first narrative strategy, the authors depict anything that stubbornly refuses to be entirely penetrated—namely, in both these texts, the father—as un-American. In this second narrative strategy, then, Rodriguez and Liu do not deny their fathers' masculinity per se, but rather, render those masculinities illegible in America. While these conflicting narratives of self are constructed somewhat differently in each text, both figure and displace diaspora through gendered and sexual representations. Rodriguez, although an openly gay Mexican American man, rarely overtly refers to his own sexual identity in his writing, but does grapple with received notions of the *macho* and of Mexican masculinity. Liu, a heterosexual man married to a white woman, is nevertheless well aware of the prevailing images of Asian American men as emasculated, and sometimes entirely asexual, even as he denies the relevance of these images to his own familial and romantic attachments.[65]

Both Rodriguez and Liu regard—and resent—Mexico and China, respectively, as demanding mothers who make diasporic claims on their "children" despite the traversals of migration. As Rodriguez writes, "A true mother, Mexico would not distinguish among her children.... Mexico was not interested in passports; Mexico was interested in blood. No matter how far away you moved, you were still related to her."[66] The *pocho* thus figures as the disobedient child: "The Mexican American who forgets his true mother is a *pocho*, a person of no address, a child of no proper idiom."[67] Mexico's feminine charms—whether maternal or sexual—hold little appeal for Richard, as he makes clear in his portrait of a Mexican nightclub scene where a "goddessy woman" sings what Rodriguez thinks of as Mexico's de facto anthem, "*Vete pero no me olvides*" (Leave me but don't forget me).[68] Unable to emulate his father's enduring loyalty to Mexico, Richard first tries to put off her advances, and then sings along with her in a desperate attempt to be rid of the embarrassment she poses to him: "I sing to her of my undying love and of rural pleasures. *Tú. Tú.* The ruby pendant. *Tú.* The lemon tree. The song of the dove. Breathed through the nose. Perched on the lips. Anything to make her go away."[69]

If "Grandma," "mother Mexico," and the nightclub diva represent for Richard the diasporic affiliation that he both betrays in his failures as a man and must leave behind in order to achieve public American manhood, Liu similarly aligns his maternal grandmother's residence in New York's Chinatown with the enduring ethnic difference that subtends his own movement into public American life. Despite acknowledging the racist history of segregation and anti-Asian violence that has created Chinatown as an ethnic enclave, he nonetheless surmises that, "In some respects Chinatown today is as far removed from public life, as confined to the unlit realm of secrets, as it was in the last century."[70] While deployed perhaps with less rancor than Rodriguez's, Liu's rhetoric shares with *Hunger of Memory* and *Days of Obligation* a schematics of the private and public, femininity and masculinity, diaspora/ethnicity and nation, the ahistorical Third World/Latin America/Asia and the progressive West/U.S. *The Accidental Asian* makes clear that these dichotomies are not Liu's own invention, and he despairs throughout the text that such a reductive perspective pervades American politics and culture. Yet, as is also evident, especially in "Fear of a Yellow Planet," he has little interest in challenging the construction of these binaries and imagining alternative forms of affiliation. Rather, Liu chooses sides and affirms his own national loyalty to an America that is ultimately so penetrative that it "*synthesizes* the many cultures it welcomes": "I'm not sure I would want to be a middleman, a mediator, in disputes political or commercial.... That I belong to no side. Such are the perils of a go-between identity: moral agnosticism, self-imposed exile. What I would want to be is, oh, say, the U. S. ambassador to China. Now, that's a role I'd relish: representing my nation, its interests, its values."[71]

As in "The Chinatown Idea"—where Eric as a child is relieved to return late at night, after an awkward, accidental run-in with his grandmother in Chinatown, to his family's "own safe enclave" in the suburbs, and forces himself to stay awake long enough to take a shower—the adult Liu resists the claims of the Chinese diaspora, "this vision of a borderless Chinese tribe."[72] He instead calls upon America to rise above a nativist image of itself as a white, European nation that will prevail against the encroaching "idea" of China, by assimilating the new waves of Asian immigrants to the nation's abstract, globalized ideals.[73] Eric cleanses his body, and his rhetoric, of any mark of racial and diasporic particularity. This move resembles remarkably the opening scene of Rodriguez's *Days of Obligation*, which depicts Richard as an American tourist in Mexico, vomiting, as Sánchez explains, in "an effort to purge out of the body that which is perceived as alien to the body: Mexico and its discourses."[74] Moreover, because Rodriguez's narrative is structured from the outset as a backwards movement in time through memory, this abjection can also be read as a repudiation of the later moment where he acquiesces to the nightclub singer's demand for intimate recognition. Both Richard and Eric chafe and rebel against what Patricia P. Chu terms "the maternal principle" of the diasporic mother who "retard[s] the American socialization" of her children.[75]

Despite their rejection of the claim that feminine diaspora makes on them, the authors must still negotiate the models of manhood that their fathers provide them. Liu does so in the opening and closing of *The Accidental Asian*, in which, I contend, he "outs" his father as an Asian body and then constructs himself as an orphan and a point of origin in his own narrative of American manhood. In "Song for My Father," Liu describes with admiration what he sees as his father's "fluency" in "American small talk," his ability to play a "public role" in white environments, such as at neighborhood parties: "On those occasions he was the social dynamo: outgoing, loud, backslapping, playful. In conversation, he had a bantam energy and a penchant for running jokes that simultaneously charmed his guests and kept them from getting too personal. . . . I'd never seen a Chinese immigrant of his generation behave so exuberantly with white folks."[76]

In contrast to this public American face—comic, optimistic, exuberant—that his father performed at such moments, Liu also reveals that his father had a private self that was more pensive and (to draw again on Rodriguez's schematics) tragic, marked by a "deep and silent current of existential sadness."[77] For Eric, this melancholy finds its symbolic vehicle in his father's disease, kidney failure that was a result of medication he had taken as a child in China: "His body was no longer capable of cleansing itself. His blood was choking on its own pollutant."[78] Liu describes the secrecy surrounding his father's disease as the "warp and woof of our family life," and realizes that for himself, the Chinese American son, this secrecy took on the figurative dimension of racial and ethnic signification: "I had my own set of reasons for going along with the family charade: as a Chinese boy in an American world, I wanted generally to project a *normal* image, to cloak any handicap, real or imagined."[79]

In light of this *closeting* of the Asian father's diseased body, and the positioning of the Asian father's body as the disease threatening generic Americanness, "Song for My Father," for all the tenderness it shows Baba (as Liu refers to his father) nevertheless performs an outing of his father's secret self. In revealing Baba's diseased/Asian body, Eric distances himself from that racialized self, which otherwise would be his "natural" inheritance from his father. Liu describes himself as "failing" to live up to the inheritance his father left him: "Where my father seemed to have an endless reserve of inner strength and self-knowledge, I have but an echoing well," a vacuum that a turn to Chinese identity cannot fulfill and that, without his father, seems to leave him orphaned and disoriented.[80] It is striking, then, that "Notes of a Native Speaker," the chapter that immediately follows "Song for My Father," begins with a description of "some of the ways you could say I am 'white.'"[81] This narrative turn suggests that Eric's neoconservatism is the product of a failure that takes root in the father's private self. Because the father fails at assimilation, that is, he can never seamlessly tie his private self to his public American one, he remains unknowable, and the son is left without a model of masculinity he can live up to. Whiteness fills this vacuum.

This narrative outing of the father as a failed model of manhood comes to bolster the rhetorical dimension of Liu's text. In the concluding essays of *The Accidental Asian*, "New Jews" and "Blood Vows," Liu ponders what his own "memory-envy" of American Jewish collectivity (envy for the sense of a shared history in Jewish America that is unavailable, Liu contends, for Asian America) will signify to his future children, especially considering that he has married a white woman of Scottish and Jewish heritage. Although he will want his father to be "knowable" to his children, Liu describes his own upbringing as based on "the absence of history's command": *"the original generation."* As he says, "This is not some ancient touchstone; it is me. I am the first in my family to be born American."[82] He imagines choosing "never to burden [his children] with the weight of history, the very history that had made them possible," a decision that transmits to them a *freedom of choice*.[83]

Because he cannot "remember" his father's language, a lament that resounds throughout *The Accidental Asian*, Eric eventually, in the final essay, "Blood Vows," transfers his identification from his father, who leaves Eric an impossible inheritance, to his mother, who seems to promote more willingly such a loss of memory. Likewise, at the end of *Hunger of Memory*, it is Richard's father who serves as the repository of silence (despite his mother's petition to her son not to "tell the *gringos*" the intimate details of their family's life). The narrative closes as Richard and his siblings depart from their parents' home after a Christmas celebration: "I take [the coat] to my father and place it on him.... He turns. He asks if I am going home now too. It is, I realize, the only thing he has said to me all evening."[84] Richard's father embodies the ideal Mexican man, as described by Rodriguez's mother; he is "the three F's," "feo, fuerte, y formal" (ugly, strong, and formal).[85] Mexican (im)migrants, who are "men without women ... Mexicans without Mexico," as Rodriguez describes them, are unable to reconcile themselves to the outspoken exuberance of public Americanness, beholden instead as *machos* to "mother Mexico": "Machismo in Mexican Spanish is more akin to the Latin *gravitas*. The male is serious. The male provides. The Mexican male never abandons those who depend upon him. The male remembers."[86] His own inability to be "formal" like his father identifies him more closely with his mother; "my attachment to words made me like her."[87]

His identification with his mother becomes especially pronounced in *Hunger of Memory*'s primary scene of queerness, which Rodriguez describes as his "first conscious experience of sexual excitement," a swimming excursion with his parents that he portrays as inseparable from his growing consciousness of his dark-skinned complexion. Standing alongside his mother watching his father in the pool, Richard finds himself identifying with her and her desire for his father: "A nervous excitement encircled my stomach as I saw my mother's eyes follow my father's figure curving into the water."[88] The shared pleasure quickly turns to one of "shame and sexual inferiority" as the child is reminded by his mother to cover his shoulders in order to prevent himself from tanning more darkly than he already was: "I felt my dark skin made me unattractive to women."[89] Rodriguez continues on to describe his increasing "disgust" with his body as he grows into an overweight adolescent. *Hunger of Memory* is thus fraught with this insecurity and instability. The dark skin "divorces" Richard from the intimacy of women, and even from his own body. At the same time, it aligns him with the *braceros*, who throughout both *Hunger of Memory* and *Days of Obligation* stand for an authentic Mexican identity from which Richard has become alienated. Rodriguez describes his own distance and overwhelming envy for the *braceros'* "physical lives, their freedom to violate the taboo of the sun."[90] Yet, he recognizes too that the *braceros* are also *los pobres*, "the poor, the pitiful, the powerless ones" who "worked very hard for very little money."[91]

The ambivalences that mark Richard's gender, sexual, racial, and class identifications culminate in his description of his final summer after undergraduate studies, spent working at a construction site. Rodriguez finds that he is not excluded from the world of the (racially undetermined) construction workers who, in their diversity of interests and education, he discerns to be "middle-class Americans."[92] In contrast, when encountering the temporary Mexican contract workers whom the contractor occasionally hires, he becomes aware of the complete alterity that these "aliens" exhibit: "I was sad for the Mexicans. Depressed by their vulnerability. Angry at myself. The adventure of the summer seemed suddenly ludicrous. I would not shorten the distance I felt from *los pobres* with a few weeks of physical labor. I would not become like them. They were different from me."[93] As Staten explains, these complicated representations fissure Richard's sense of self between his father and *los pobres*: "There is a Chicano Richard identified (immediately through his dark skin and mediately through his father's subalternity) with the abjection of the poor Mexican, and there is a Mexican American Richard who is the heir of his father's sense of distinction and focus on upward mobility."[94]

The resolution to this crisis comes in his recognition of the *braceros'* alienation, which seems to release Richard from the Mexican ideal of manhood. The narrative moves from a concern with the Mexican's body under the conditions of hard labor, to that of the narrator's body as a source of pleasure, "worked out," pumped up, and decked out in the "symbols of leisure and wealth" of the dandy—"reassuring reminders of public success."[95] Richard's body and its accoutrements provide a metonym for the public voice, "able to defend my interests, to unionize, to petition, to speak up—to challenge and demand," that he has acquired, one that remains resolutely inaccessible for the *bracero*: "They lack a public identity. They remain profoundly alien. Persons apart. People lacking a union obviously, people without grounds."[96] At the same time, however, he becomes detached from his father as well. Against the optimism that the nation proffers the son, Rodriguez describes his father as "mild and manly," a "Mexican in California" who knows that "tragedy wins," a model of masculinity that Richard still cannot perform.[97] Thus, in *Days of Obligation*, Rodriguez describes his father (and the Indian in Richard himself) as ultimately "disappearing" into America, and, as he writes in *Hunger of Memory*, his mother comes to stand as "the public voice of the family."[98]

Negation and Absorption

The treatment of fathers in Rodriguez's and Liu's narratives, as men attached and loyal to the diaspora, secures their American sons' repudiation of them. Unlike the *foreclosure* of the diasporic (m)other that I have described in the previous chapter, however, the forgetfulness of these narratives take the form of what Ali Behdad describes as the historical "amnesia" of *negation*. As Behdad explains, while the process of foreclosure allows the self no conscious access to the other, in negation "one may acknowledge an event" on the condition that the subject "either denies its significance or refuses to take responsibility for it."[99] Negation aptly characterizes Liu's depiction of the "shock of arrival" in America as a "relentless" forgetting, and his portrait of "American life [that] is neither monoculturalism nor multiculturalism; it is *omniculturalism*."[100] Likewise, in *Days of Obligation*, Rodriguez describes America as a place where memory is erased; history begins anew, which he emblematizes in a diner waitress who, in "one complete gesture" wipes away the remnants of past diners. As in Behdad's account of historical amnesia, where disavowal is "accompanied by a supplementary act of acknowledgement," negation in these narratives predicates absorption into the nation, ensuring a sense of cultural "innocence" for its subjects, who need not take responsibility for the racial other.[101]

In describing the more personal terms by which their own assimilation has taken place, the two narratives diverge, but both displace responsibility for assimilation. While Eric vaguely, in a passive voice, "finds" himself to be "the bearer of a strange new status, white by acclamation" (the most remarkable tribulation in the process, he suggests, is managing his "Chinese hair" to accord with the "standards of cool"), Rodriguez attributes his incorporation to a very specific institution, the Catholic Church. Indeed, in his two texts we discover that ultimately there are only two identities that Rodriguez is really willing to claim unreservedly for himself, that of "American" and that of "Catholic." Especially by the very rhetorical schematics that he has himself set up, to claim both these names at once is a contradiction, since, for the most part, Rodriguez thinks of America as a rather Protestant, specifically Puritan, concept, that precludes—in its imagining of itself as stridently masculine, individualist, and as "not really existing"—the communal, feminine, embodiedness of Catholicism (the Catholicism, e.g., as represented by the Mexican Virgen de Guadalupe).[102]

At the same time, though, it is important to note that Catholicism never functions only as a private affiliation for Richard. As he explains in *Hunger of Memory*: "I grew up a Catholic at home and at school, in private and in public."[103] In other words, Catholicism (in particular, the church life that the Irish Catholic nuns who oversaw his early years of schooling embodied) mediates the child's progress from the private, intimate affiliations of family life to the public world of the nation: "As a Catholic schoolboy, I was educated a middle-class American."[104] In his description of himself as a devout Catholic, Rodriguez acknowledges: "The Catholic Church assumes it is the nature of men and women to fail.... Catholicism is all-forgiving."[105] This tolerance of failure grounds assimilation in America, which Rodriguez describes as "irresistible." Assimilation has "nothing to do with choosing," a reality, he claims, of which immigrants are unaware, but which, "for the child of immigrant parents comes like a slap: America exists."[106] He contends, "When I was a boy who spoke Spanish, I saw America whole. I realized that there was a culture here because I lived apart from it. I didn't like America. Then I entered the culture. I entered the culture as you did, by going to school. I became Americanized. I ended up believing in choices as much as any of you do."[107]

While immigrant parents demand their children's loyalty to the homeland, Rodriguez asserts that the child is *forced* to betray them, even against his inclinations otherwise.[108] As the passageway between the public and private, masculine and feminine, Mexican and American, the "a universal language" of Latin bears a special significance in uniting Rodriguez to a communal experience, one that has elsewhere receded from him as he undergoes his Americanization.[109] In both texts, then, Rodriguez mourns the loss of the Church's communal authority (this loss is symbolized most resolutely for him in the transition from the Latin Mass to multiple Masses held in both English and immigrant vernaculars). Rodriguez surmises that the Church risks becoming irrelevant to American life, relegated to the world of impoverished, immigrant grandparents, while a publicly aggressive Protestant evangelicalism takes it place.

Thus, although posed as a collection of loosely related essays (and although Rodriguez claims that, "Despite the quantities of novels I have read, I find I do not believe in sudden shifts, revolutions of plot, reformation"), *Days of Obligation* does follow a narrative structure of rising conflict, denouement, and resolution, culminating in the central chapters of "The Missions" and "The Head of Joaquín Murrieta."[110] In these chapters, Rodriguez aligns his own "Catholic nostalgia" (e.g., his fascination with the ritual and transcendent rather than historical value of the California missions) with California's Spanish–Mexican past and pits them against an Anglo-Protestant spirit of advancement, best displayed for the author in the style and spirit of the city of Los Angeles. Once again, Rodriguez relegates his "nostalgia" and Mexicanness to a private space of ethnic femininity. He identifies himself with the wife of Joseph Alioto, a former mayor of San Francisco, whose disappearance, while she toured the California missions, caused a media stir. He then implicates himself, seemingly against his own inclinations, in the search for the head of Joaquín Murrieta, floating in a jar as a symbol of California's past, where "a good man [was] made monstrous." In both cases, Rodriguez asserts the need for the past to be and remain buried, quite literally in the cases of the missions and Murrieta's head.

In *Hunger of Memory*, Rodriguez writes "I became a man by becoming a public man," resolving the conflicts of diversity and gendered confusion by quarantining ethnic difference to the private sphere.[111] The chapters in the latter half of *Days of Obligation*, "Sand" and "Asians," accordingly usher in some of Rodriguez's most insistent rhetoric regarding a unified public self and language.[112] The progressive narrative, founded on the rigid binary structure of private and public, then moves with seemingly unassailable logic beyond the United States, tracing the growth of "the Protestant spirit" in Latin America. Rodriguez does not associate the spread of evangelical Protestantism in the Americas with the neo-imperialist incursions of U.S. corporate and military institutions. However, the aggressive penetration of the former clearly parallels those of the latter, and Rodriguez's rhetoric maps an Americanization that moves expansively outward, a synthesizing spirit that dissolves differences well beyond the literal borders of the republic.

Failing to Forget

As a paradigmatic American and Catholic and as a child of immigrants, Rodriguez locates himself at a privileged position to see the "whole," his Whitmanesque voice absorbs all the parts, even the contradictions and his failures, to be a man, to be Indian, to be Mexican. In so doing, he names himself as "American." This receptiveness is what Randy Rodríguez has quite persuasively described as Rodriguez's queer aesthetic, his willingness to play *la chingada* against masculinist, heterosexist modes of oppositional minority discourse. In his analysis of this queer aesthetic, Randy Rodríguez demonstrates that *Hunger of Memory* inscribes a submerged strategy of identification.[113] Unable to take up the mantle of Chicano nationalism, Richard's "soft assimilationist narrative" renders him everything that the masculinist politics of Chicano discourse abjects, including a neoconservative purveyor of cultural literacy and assimilation. As Randy Rodríguez contends, Rodriguez provides an "alternative landscape of gender and sexual transgression and transformation" by "crossing the border into the landscape of forbidden possibilities in queer 'America.'"[114]

Indeed, the queer receptiveness, which rhetorically Rodriguez initially attributes to Mexicanness, and prior to that, to Indianness, ironically provides the terra firma for the masculinized, public American self. America is founded, not on individual heroic accomplishment, but rather, on a *failure* of self that his narratives represent. Rodriguez is able to forward a neoconservative rhetoric precisely because he offers up his very body as the sign of absorption and receptiveness, as queer and as Catholic. This narrative of sacrifice calls the public, masculine Richard into a relation of responsibility for the other Richard whose loss founds the American self.[115] An ethical reading of *Hunger of Memory* thus holds us responsible to the other who is never explicitly identified as gay, but who occupies a queer space in the narrative of assimilative education.

The narrative of *Days of Obligation* notably does not end with an assertion of Richard as the fully formed man, but rather returns to the uncertain desires and identifications of the child. Two male figures haunt the final chapter of the text, "Nothing Lasts a Hundred Years": Richard's father and his Uncle Raj, a Catholic immigrant from India who Rodriguez suspects was a Communist sympathizer. The opening lines of the chapter wonder "Where's Papa?" and the closing section ends with, first, a moving, erotically charged recollection of Raj and, second, his father's enduring perspective of his Mexican homeland:

> One summer, my uncle was beautiful. His skin was darker than Mexico. His skin wore shade. It was blue. It was black. When I was seven years old, my girl cousins threw me into the lake at Lodi and, with several islands to choose from, I swam toward the island of my uncle. His eyes were black and so wide with surprise they reflected the humor of the water. His nipples were blue and wet black fur dripped down his front and floated in the water at his waist. . . .
>
> In Mexico my father had the freedom of the doves. He summoned the dawn. Each morning at five-thirty, my father would climb the forty steps of the church tower to pull the ropes that loosened the tongues of the two fat bells. My father was the village orphan and it was his duty and his love and his mischief to wake the village, to watch it stir: the pious old ladies bending toward mass; the young men off to the fields; the eternal sea.[116]

Raj and Richard's father embody the disavowed others that Rodriguez's narrative is unable to integrate but also apparently unwilling to expel completely. Richard instead cleaves to these men, at the risk of his American manhood. In Behdad's terms, we might read these images as symptoms that plague the American self, traces of negation's inadequacy.[117]

Richard's queerly loving return to his father and Uncle Raj refracts Liu's wish to "unburden" his future progeny from his father's "inheritance." The memories of the fathers contest the claims for national inclusion and enfranchisement that Rodriguez and Liu imagine. On the one hand, for both writers, their fathers' refusals to enter fully into the realm of public Americanness leave Richard and Eric dispossessed of viable models of manhood; Richard and Eric turn to the American imaginary to locate sources of a "true," that is, readily intelligible, manhood. On the other hand, Richard and Eric (unlike their fathers) are failed men in the diaspora, unable to direct their filial and sexual loves to the proper objects; they are American because they allow themselves to be penetrated by and assimilated to the nation. It thus ultimately becomes impossible to know who the "real men" in these narratives are. This confusion provides the neoconservative subject the avenue to come into being, but it also continually threatens to unravel that self. As monuments of a history that remains lodged within the subject's bodily memory, the fathers gesture toward an alternative futurity, a democracy to come where the diasporic other is not erased or consumed by the nation. Indexed by the gendered ambivalences of desire at the limits of narratives meant to secure generic self-presence, these others confound the certitude of that being. Liu and Rodriguez are haunted by the(ir) raced bodies that stand at the site of contradiction from which the nation imagines its own assimilating inclusiveness. If Liu and Rodriguez were to attempt rhetorically to absorb these haunting others, they would risk exposing the discontinuities that a progressive narrative of assimilatory nationalism seeks to cover over.

How does this queer, ethical concern for diasporic others impinge on these authors' vision of the nation? Staten suggests that Rodriguez's critiques of racial and class formation are too often overshadowed by his adherence to the "to-be-or-not-to-be of identity talk."[118] In contrast, Staten calls for "some other language than that of simple identity."[119] To this end, a language of *obligation* (to draw from the title of Rodriguez's second book) articulates race, class, and nation in a discourse, not simply of identity, power, and mobility, but of social *justice* and returns to the negated history of Asian and Latino presence that I have sketched in Chapter 1. To conclude my analysis of minority neoconservatism and the betrayals of assimilation here, I move to a short story by Américo Paredes, the historical fiction of "The Gringo." "The Gringo" links late-twentieth-century demands for assimilation, wherein whiteness stands as the generic sign of national belonging, to this earlier historical moment, when such a symbolic economy of race and nation had only just begun to emerge. In returning to this foundational moment, with whose consequences we continue to live today, Paredes's story reterritorializes the racial terrain of nation that Rodriguez and Liu have assumed.

Paredes, like Rodriguez and Liu, is a writer working at the intersections of multiple genres and disciplines. Having made substantial contributions to Chicana/o cultural studies as an ethnographer and social historian, Paredes is probably best known for his crucial recovery of borderland *corridos* in the 1950s and 1960s.[120] If New Journalism provides an avenue for the generic production of the minority neoconservative in that it attempts to negate the raced body in its very telling, Paredes's historical fiction articulates an ongoing ethical responsibility to the racial and national others who encroach upon these narratives. Written in the early 1950s, published in 1994 (as part of the collection *The Hammon and the Beans and Other Stories*), and set in 1846 at the beginning of the Mexican-American War, Paredes's story surveys the emergent racial landscape of the late nineteenth century as it comes to determine that of the late-twentieth-century nation.[121] Written precisely at the moment when the unified image of the hegemonic nation, exceptional in its promise of a deracinated public sphere, begins to unravel with the onset of the civil rights movement, Paredes's composition of "The Gringo" mines the disavowals of the progressive narrative of America.[122] It portrays the cultural significance of an embodied white racial form to imperial expansionism and to the consolidation of the modern nation-state.

Set in the U.S.-Mexico borderlands, the story begins after its protagonist, Ygnacio, has been injured and his father and brothers killed when Anglo-Americans try to steal their family's cattle. Because he is "mistaken" as a white man, and thus an American, Ygnacio has been nursed back to health by a preacher's daughter, Prudence. Although eventually Ygnacio is discovered, because he does not speak much English, to be Mexican, the preacher agrees to care for him, at Prudence's urging. However, the preacher turns against Ygnacio when he suspects a romance developing between Ygnacio and Prudence, and Prudence consequently helps Ygnacio to flee. During his residency with the Anglo-Americans, Ygnacio obtains important information regarding the capacity of the U.S. army, but once he arrives in Matamoros, other Mexicans suspect him of being an American spy. Ygnacio's cousin Eutimio has gathered together highwaymen willing to join himself and Ygnacio as part of a larger guerrilla force, which Ygnacio knows is necessary to supplement the Mexican army if the latter is to defeat the U.S. forces. However, when challenged by Villegas, one of the other guerillas, to prove his allegiance, Ygnacio must ride out to a U.S. army patrol in order to draw it into the planned ambush. When he attempts to do so, his pronunciation of a few words in English—"Thees way, boyss!"—gives him away, an officer recognizing, "That's not a white man!"[123] Ygnacio manages to kill one of the soldiers, but misses the officer with his second pistol. The story ends with Ygnacio a victim of the officer's more advanced weaponry: "'¡Arma blanca!' [Ygnacio] cried, sliding his machete from its sheath. But the officer galloped forward without drawing his saber. Then he saw the revolving pistol, and the guns of Palo Alto went off inside his head."[124]

Paredes's story is compact in its telling, intertwining an exchange between Ygnacio and Eutimio about the advisability of recruiting townspeople and robbers as guerilla fighters with a flashback narration of the events that take place between Ygnacio, Prudence, and the preacher. In its concise exposition, Paredes explicitly ties the domestic racism of

American belonging to the nation's incursions into Mexico, a pivotal moment in its advancement into empire.[125] In a marked inversion of the cultural politics of assimilation, where whiteness eventually becomes "invisible," a (non-)marker of assimilation, Ygnacio's white skin is rendered highly visible in Matamoros.

Yet, while other Mexicans approach him with suspicion, the body provides Ygnacio little cover when he is betrayed by the primary *cultural* sign—his accent—that signals his otherness from the Americans. As such, Ygnacio's experience of double consciousness is itself doubled, without a home in either space. Instead, the intertwined narration of his family's death and displacement, Prudence's kindness and her father's angry repudiation of him, and the planned guerilla attack chaotically shuttle Ygnacio between these different spaces. At the same time, it becomes clear that the two experiences of double consciousness are not symmetrically structured. Ygnacio does not, indeed cannot, serve as a mediating bridge between the two sides, because his own experience is situated in the larger historical context of American expansionism. Ygnacio chooses the side he does in part because (as evidenced in the officer's words, "That's not a white man!") at this historical juncture, whiteness *comes to figure* in a tight constellation with other cultural attributes of language, religion, and class.[126] To this end, Ygnacio cannot but choose to sacrifice himself in order to prove his allegiances as a Mexican.

But Ygnacio chooses this side *only* in part for this reason; he also *chooses* to fight for Mexico, as an act of resistance against the violations his family and nation have endured at the hands of the gringos. In this respect, Ygnacio's death signifies the consequence of foolishly joining thieves, whose motives and therefore ultimately whose strategy for fighting the Americans differ significantly from his own. Ygnacio tells Villegas that "as long as we are seeking the same ends, and that we agree on the means," he is willing to submit to Villegas's command.[127] However, both their ends and means do indeed differ, as Villegas's men prefer to undertake a strategically risky ambush in order to more quickly sell the booty they recover from the attack. Again, the intertwined narration that precedes the confrontation between Ygnacio and Villegas proves crucial in representing Ygnacio's agency (doomed as it is), as even there Ygnacio wonders about the wisdom of including Villegas's men as part of the guerilla force.

"The Gringo" thus stages the tremendous costs exacted by the rigid polarities of separatist resistance and abstracted assimilation—of, that is, a minoritarian discourse of agency and domination divided into blackness and whiteness. It exposes the contradictions of imperialist expansion and domestic racism negated by a rhetoric of abstract equality. As David Theo Goldberg suggests, the racial order divides this particular subject "between the 'can' and 'ought,' between possibility and impossibility, requirement and liberty."[128] At the same time, against the enormous pressures of these historical conditions, the formal narrative also demands that its subject make an admittedly impossible choice and that it live—or die—according to the unpredictable consequences of that choice.

Ygnacio's death at the end of the story allegorizes the sedimentation of a symbolic economy that is still emergent at the end of the nineteenth century, where whiteness, assimilation, and citizenship become signs of one another and of national belonging. If it is absurd to think of Ygnacio as a "professional" Mexican(-American) in the way that Rodriguez and Liu describe, this is because the very concept presupposes an autonomous subject, free to choose or not choose racial affiliation. "The Gringo" in fact demonstrates that this very freedom of choice is an attribute awarded to the American citizen who comes into being (out of the white male body) only by banishing the threat that Ygnacio's cultural unintelligibility and racial indeterminacy augurs. Yet Ygnacio's racialization does throw into question his national allegiances, rendering him a potential spy and traitor in all the spaces he inhabits. Ygnacio therefore anticipates the arrival of the "professional" minoritarian subject, and the anxieties that this subject incites. In the following chapter, then, I consider narratives that actualize this threat: the "professional" minority who is the intelligence agent. Here, racialized spies do indeed become "traitors" of their "own people," a move that marks the historical transformation of the ties between race, class, ethnicity, and nation and the possibilities for their betrayal.

4 / Ethnic America Undercover: The Intellectual and Minority Discourse

> *Always ... the intellectual is beset and remorselessly challenged by the problem of loyalty. All of us without exception belong to some sort of national, religious or ethnic community: no one, no matter the volume of protestations, is above the organic ties that bind the individual to family, community, and of course nationality.*
> —EDWARD SAID, REPRESENTATIONS OF THE INTELLECTUAL

> *We live in an institution, and we live outside it. We work there, and we work with what we have at hand. The University is not going to save the world by making the world more true, nor is the world going to save the University by making the University more real. ... Change comes neither from within nor from without, but from the difficult space—neither inside nor outside—where one is.*
> —BILL READINGS, THE UNIVERSITY IN RUINS

As we saw in Chapter 3, Richard Rodriguez and Eric Liu assert that the cultural politics of minority discourse produces for its subjects a type of "professional" identity that these writers impugn. They both nevertheless participate in such a professionalization by "reporting" to their audiences on the intimate details of their family life, against the mandate by others to "not tell." For example, in *Hunger of Memory*, Rodriguez describes his mother's aversion to his autobiographical inclinations: "Just keep one thing in mind. Writing is one thing, the family is another. I don't want *tus hermanos* hurt by your writings. . . . Especially I don't want the *gringos* knowing about our private affairs. Why should they?"[1] The injunction to silence, one not uncommonly depicted in narratives by writers of color, bespeaks an anxiety that the minority insider might come to serve as a traitorous informant of his or her community.[2] In the previous chapter, I examined the way in which the minority neoconservative, and his rhetoric of assimilation, remain haunted by queer others who countenance the limits of the absorptive nation. In this chapter, I turn to the way in which the often unwanted attention of "outsiders," that is, the hegemonic discourses of the nation, haunts minority discourse.

This attention, I suggest, constitutes yet another set of grounds for possible duplicities and betrayals and requires us to go beyond the fact of minority discourse's cultural representations. That is, we must inquire about the conditions of production for all forms of minority discourse, oppositional and accommodationist, in order to understand how these representations might at once authorize and betray the subjects it means to represent.

By pointing to "conditions of production," I wish to emphasize further that the cultural work of minority discourse never occurs in a social and historical vacuum. The narratives, identities, and knowledge about raced subjects that minoritarian discourse struggles to create and legitimate are located within institutional, national, and global structures of power, as are the writers, readers, and critics who produce them. The hegemonic nation, privileged as it is within a *trans*national field of cultural and economic exchange, as well as professional and institutional pressures, overdetermine the politics of representation to which ethnic studies has obligated itself. Only by situating ourselves within these networks of power can we respond ethically to the prevalent charges that institutionalization and professionalization have superseded ethnic studies' prior and primary activist, practical, and "real" agenda. In this chapter, I argue that the fear of being "sold out" and given away by one's own is concretely realized in the troubled figure of the ethnic spy, who allegorizes the crisis of the "minority intellectual" as a self-representing agent and ethical subject within minority discourse. The two novels I discuss below, Américo Paredes's *George Washington Gómez* (1990) and Chang-rae Lee's *Native Speaker* (1995), not only illustrate the heterogeneities through which the knowledge worker betrays others, but also imagine alternative articulations for the intellectual responsibilities of minority discourse, especially within ethnic studies. The figure of the ethnic spy, like the minority intellectual, challenges conventional models of knowledge-power relationships by calling into question the extent to which the material processes and histories of race mediate the professional and political affiliations of intellectual and institutional power.

Conventional spy narratives have been predominantly concerned with the adventures of the white, usually male, patriotic spy. His agency is derived from the nation, whose geopolitical hegemony and state power he secures.[3] Paredes and Lee offer, instead, a markedly different type of agent. In their construction of the knowledge worker as intelligence agent, these novels explore Said's thesis that "the intellectual is beset and remorselessly challenged by the problem of loyalty" to national, religious, or ethnic communities. Knowledge production occurs within and against these bonds, at once constituting and compromising them. Minority discourse attempts to achieve representation on a multiracial terrain, engaging and negotiating the hegemonic nation in the interests of the minority subject. This double-speak gives voice to the minority subject, but also, I contend, cannot but compromise it. The novels thus probe two particular dimensions of Said's argument. First, Said suggests that the intellectual does not form an entirely separate "knowledge class," but, rather, is imbricated in and fractured by the social formations to which he or she is subject. Second, in positing the intellectual's loyalty to these communities, Said also implies that the intellectual might "fail" that community, a failure that amounts to betrayal.

What does it mean to "betray," and what is it that is betrayed, in this work? Paredes's and Lee's novels ponder how intellectual work is actually "intelligence work" but also imagine how ethical responsibility produces political agency that exceeds totalizing racial and national discourses. In the first part of this chapter, I consider critical debates as to the sociopolitical formation and political responsibilities of the intellectual and the impact of these debates upon the specific site of the university and of academic ethnic studies programs. The second and third sections then examine Paredes's and Lee's novels as allegorical interventions in these debates. They invent, through the trope of the spy-traitor, the "difficult space," as Bill Readings calls it, of the minority intellectual, in order to re-read the terms of knowledge-power and propose an ethics of betrayal in minority discourse.

The Intellectual in Minority Discourse

To define an intellectual is in itself a difficult task, and certainly there is no consensus among the many critics who have taken up the challenge.[4] Two issues frame much of this deliberation—the social function of the intellectual and the intellectual's position in terms of political economy. That is to say, discourse about the intellectual either asks about the moral or political responsibility of the intellectual and how one "proves" one's status as an intellectual, or it considers whether or not intellectuals constitute an autonomous class in capitalist societies. Formulating a definition from either one of these approaches almost invariably involves the other.[5] Moreover, intellectuals themselves, like other objects of discursive contention, have been shaped by these very debates. They are created and being re-created by what, in this case, is a self-reflexive debate about who can or must claim this name.[6]

Said suggests that the intellectual's capacity for "representing, embodying, articulating" messages "to, as well as for a public" comes with an imperative "to raise embarrassing questions, to confront orthodoxy and dogma (rather than to produce them), to be someone who cannot easily be co-opted by governments or corporations."[7] As such, the very raison d'être of the intellectual is "to represent all those people and issues that are routinely forgotten or swept under the rug."[8] In his description of how the intellectual produces and disseminates a kind of public knowledge, Said emphasizes the *critical* and *oppositional* consciousness that distinguishes the ideological position of this subject.[9] Nevertheless, the insistence on the intellectual's political role belies a less explicit anxiety, that the line between an "intelligentsia" (or the "experts") and "intellectuals" cannot be readily distinguished, and from certain perspectives does not exist at all. If the intellectual works both against and independently from the state and hegemonic discourses of nation, civil society, religion, and so forth, their "intelligence," and other forms of symbolic capital, continually threaten to render them a narrower subset of the technologically proficient or knowledge-rich intelligentsia. In other words, the demand for the intellectual's critical activity betrays the possibility that the intellectual might "slip" or be co-opted from his or her responsibility of oppositional politics into less noble, merely "academic" work.[10]

Fact management, knowledge production, and value critique are therefore tricky, overlapping practices. The material conditions and structural limits of subject formation delimit the *self*-consciousness demanded of the intellectual. Traditional intellectuals, as Andrew Ross surmises, "have had to forsake the high ground and recognize the professional conditions they share, for the most part, with millions of other knowledge workers."[11] The institutionalization of knowledge-power in the more general development of a rationalized, technocratic society organizes the emergence of such a professional-managerial intelligentsia.[12] Consequently, the concept of the "public intellectual," much romanticized and eulogized, has been replaced with a variety of "specialists," located in a range of institutions such as state agencies, corporations, NGOs, publishing houses, print and broadcast media, think tanks, advertising firms, and universities. It remains uncertain whether this bloc forms a "new class," insofar as there is little agreement as to whether this group recognizes and reproduces its own self-interests (or instead works in the interest of older capitalist classes) and whether the emergence of knowledge as a crucial productive force transforms conditions of class formation itself.[13]

What is clear though, as Pierre Bourdieu convincingly argues, is that this cadre of professionals are as beholden to the rules and stratagems of the semi-autonomous, professionalized fields in which they operate as they are to the "mandators" whom they claim to represent.[14] Nevertheless, Bourdieu maintains, representation is "always doubly determined," although the intellectual agent may very well be unconscious of this doubleness. The intellectual thus occupies a difficult and even contradictory position, making "a gift of his person to the group" as he abolishes himself in it, while also being determined *within* the institutional or professional field of representation.[15] Bourdieu describes a "sort of structural bad faith attached to the delegate," who must appropriate authority for himself by reducing himself "to the group," while then using that authority to establish himself in a field from which the group remains dispossessed.[16] This duality effects the political or cultural alienation of those whom the agent purportedly represents. In other words, Bourdieu suggests that the social formation and practices of the intellectual agent necessarily coalesce around a duality (or even multiplicity) of subjectivity. Yet, I would underscore, the "bad faith" and duality do not intrinsically amount an *individual* failing (although it is often culturally experienced and represented as such), because the *structural* conditions of representation overdetermine the diminished affiliation between the group and the agent.

The case of the minority intellectual that concerns this chapter, then, reverses the relationship between accident and obligation that we examined with regard to minority neoconservatism in the previous chapter. Here, although the intellectual *does* feel obligated and wishes to claim a fundamental, transparent, and immediate identification with other minority subjects, he or she fails precisely because the identifications between the intellectual, the represented collectivity, and the field are never complete and total. Rather, an excess of being escapes the reduction of the agent to the group, on one hand, and to the field, on the other. Moreover, as my analysis of the ethics of betrayal in *George Washington Gómez* and *Native Speaker* below will demonstrate, this excess emerges as an alterity that antagonizes *both*, the professionalized or institutional field *and* the formation of the represented group. Before turning to the allegories of the minority intellectual that the novels offer, however, let me first provide an account of the intellectual subject of minority discourse, in particular, the professionalized intellectual of ethnic studies.

In the formation of ethnic studies programs, we find a material site where knowledge-power constitutes racial and national identity, as well as facilitates betrayals of those affiliations.[17] Begun as grassroots and student-driven initiatives, cultural nationalist movements were considerably successful, especially on the West Coast, at establishing themselves within academic institutions, namely, in the form of ethnic studies programs.[18] This success, however, did not come without considerable ideological and political tension and compromise. While ethnic studies scholars produce a tremendous amount of knowledge about racial minorities, they have also been criticized for failing to provide for direct, relevant community programs.[19] Despite the growing number of racial minorities on university campuses (even in the face of affirmative action rollbacks), academic ethnic studies programs seem separated from and out of touch with the "communities" that constitute ethnic America. Its critics charge that ethnic studies is ineffective in initiating *real*, that is, practical, political and social change.[20]

I would like to argue, however, that this construction of racial and ethnic collectivity along the binary lines of the institution versus the community veils the way in which the university itself is a hegemonic site of political and cultural articulation, and that both ethnic studies and social movements are subject to local, national, and transnational politics. If the professionalization of the minority intellectual short-circuits his or her political efficacy, we might also marvel that ethnic studies programs (and the sometimes very radical critiques that they involve) have endured *at all* within the conservative institutional structure of the university. By perceiving the university as both a hegemonic *and* a contested site, we might provide an ethical account of the cultural politics possible within these institutions.

Institutional directives traverse various axes of identification and often mitigate the efficacy of oppositional politics. For example, the demand for academics in the field of ethnic studies results from the confluence of a liberal multiculturalism and the neoliberal market pressures to which the university responds as much as from an agenda of democratic access. Increasing rates of minority enrollment in colleges and universities produce individuals who perform eagerly according to the strictures of global capitalism, often instrumentalizing their own cultural insidership to facilitate transnational "development" and exchange. In this context, important questions face the cultural politics of resistance: What are the material and historical contexts of minority discourse? Who authorizes such discourse and by what process? What types of subjects are made legible and what differences exceed these categories, remaining unarticulated? What are the effects of this discourse? Racial and ethnic identities are constructed across multiple and wide-ranging sites, including churches, local "cultural associations," social service agencies, and cyberspace. For this reason, we must be cautious in positing a singular dichotomy, between the university and the community, and consequently naming an academic "we" who attempts to speak about—without really speaking as, with, for, or to—the objects of knowledge. Rather, we should conceive of the university, as one "difficult space" among many from which racial formations are made and unmade.

Toward this end, Bill Readings's *The University in Ruins* provides an impressive genealogy of the "idea of the University," from a statist project of Enlightenment rationalism to its present "ruin," the moment of transnational capital. Readings argues that the university proves a "ruined" institution insofar as it no longer serves the political economy of the nation by producing "national culture" and liberally educated citizens. Indeed, the nation-state itself no longer serves an essential purpose in a system of global capital. Without the unifying narrative of liberal, national culture, he further submits, the university becomes a corporation, managing information and knowledge in order to extract a surplus value in this administration.[21] While he might very well overstate the impotence of the nation-state and the university as ideological apparatuses—certainly changes in state policies regarding immigration and welfare continue to have immense impact—Readings's description of the "decentered" university convincingly situates the institution in a landscape of political and cultural deterritorialization.[22]

The situation of the academic then is perhaps best described as an uncomfortable and troubled one, where neither nostalgia for a lost tradition of culture or political radicalism nor capitulation to economic pressures of "accounting" suffices in the face of our ethical and pedagogical obligations to others. Readings specifies a notion of ethical work in the context of the university, suggesting that the pedagogical relationship foregoes rationalized "accounting" by attending to the question of account*ability* and justice—the obligation of the self to the Other. The position of the "amateur," or non-professional and non-authoritative, status of the student perhaps best articulates this ethical relationship for Readings. The ruins of the university make visible—as his analysis of the French student movements of 1968 demonstrates—the "excess of the subject": "[the students'] militancy challenges the representational claim of democracy, the claim that liberal democracy achieves exhaustive representation, reflects itself to itself."[23] If the university serves as an institutional face of the national culture, then the student embodies the limits of assimilation and unity in relation to it.

The implications of this argument are substantial for ethnic studies. To the extent that ethnic studies takes the "ethnic subject" and "ethnic culture" as its grounds of analysis, it continues to insist upon a discursive unity that draws up new disciplinary boundaries according to the legitimate(d) identities of "resistance." It thus invokes the "alibis" that, according to Readings, mystify academic work as a search for truth in the production of knowledge and representation. University-based knowledges do not simply provide second-order reflections of "real" identities and experiences that take place off campus. Instead, as Ross has written of the "new intellectuals," the intellectual subjects of minority discourse are "uneven participants on several fronts. They are likely to belong to different social groups and have loyalties to different social movements."[24] The minority intellectual personally participates in the politics of resistance *and* accommodation, loyalty and betrayal, in his or her knowledge production. Racial and national identities are performed—unevenly, temporarily, and contingently, but also historically, actively, and substantively—on campus as well as off. The minority intellectual, whom I am recasting, *pace* Readings, as the student of ethnic studies, both occupies the space of racial identity and exceeds it, both gives voice to the racial minority but also gives it away.

In one sense, by gaining access to the mechanisms of cultural and political representation, minority intellectuals no longer speak from a marginalized position. They have "gained position," and thus wield a symbolic power that alienates them from those whom they purport to represent. Yet, for the minority subject, working in the university also generates an anxiety that stems from a fear of loss and of integration into the structure of the field that Bourdieu describes.[25] I suggest that this anxiety registers an alienating separateness from both the institutional structure and from the community—a ghostly otherness disarticulated from both "here" and "there," never successfully incorporated into the institutional structure, but also no longer unselfconsciously identified with one's "original" home. For many, this anxiety manifests itself as a sort of anger, mostly directed at the university as a cultural center. But there also seems to be certain critical pleasures in the performance of the professional identity within the institutional context. This pleasure cannot guarantee the transformation of the institution itself, but the performance, in its parodic imitation and in its slippages, reveals the naturalized assumptions that generate the privileged citizen of national(ist) cultures within the institutional context. In the next section of this chapter, then, I examine both the representations of literal education and the allegorical portrayals of knowledge production in *George Washington Gómez* and *Native Speaker*. In the places where these two levels of the narratives intersect, the novels conceive this performance of professional identity as an ethico-political response to what has become an otherwise stalemated issue in ethnic studies: the academic/community divide in minority discourse.

The Knowledge Work of the Minority Spy

An investigation of the minority subject as a knowledge worker brings to bear the question of "excess" on Bourdieu's model of the fields of cultural production and political representation. As instances of what Bruce Robbins calls "the genre of the allegory of vocation," Paredes's and Lee's novels offer sophisticated accounts of the intersections, as well as divergences, between racial, economic, professional, and cultural status.[26] As the travails of the novels' protagonists, Guálinto/George and Henry, demonstrate, "gaining position" is hardly a simple game of self-interest, insofar as self-interest is itself heterogeneous and contradictory. On the one hand, the knowledge they produce is deemed authoritative because both the hegemonic nation and the ethnic community recognize them as racial insiders. On the other hand, their access to institutional and state power makes possible the betrayals that they enact, and the distance between them and the dominated group provides the very means and motives for the betrayal. As knowledge workers, they undertake the representational work of identifying and naming racial and ethnic others, but their knowledge about their objects proves to be only partial. Thus, the narratives imagine ways in which the agents' racial and ethnic situatedness antagonizes the discourses produced for the hegemonic nation by and about the minority subject.

While much has been written about Américo Paredes's exploration of identity and hybridity in the Texas borderlands that he depicts in the bildungsroman *George Washington Gómez*, critics have generally not commented on his protagonist's decision to become a spy at the novel's end. The novel opens in 1915, the year that sees the rise of an insurgency movement by Mexican Americans, *los sediciosos*, against the Texas Rangers, and ends with the onset of World War II. It traces the birth, youth, and education of George—whose Indian nickname Guálinto encapsulates Paredes's central thematic concern, George's conflicted subjectivity as he struggles between a romanticized American ethos of egalitarian progress and his sense of himself, rendered a "foreigner in his native land," as well as his pride in a Mexican heritage.²⁷ George comes of age under the care of his mother and Uncle Feliciano. Paredes's depiction of George centers largely on his education. It is one limited by the racial and economic hierarchies that make the classroom a "kind of hell," but one prompted by his parents' and uncle's overriding desire to see him become "a leader of his people."

Guálinto's struggles with the contradictory implications of schooling and formal education and with his own divided self are seemingly resolved at the end of Part IV of the novel, where, upon his graduation from high school, Guálinto finally commits to attending college, implicitly signaling his agreement to serve as a representative of his people. Guálinto decides to pursue higher education when he learns about his uncle Feliciano's *sedicioso* past, which Feliciano has also until then kept secret. Motivated by the death of Guálinto's father, Gumersindo, at the hands of the Texas Rangers, Feliciano perceived his own revolutionary activities to be in the interests of his people—in the need to defend their political rights and national interests—and Guálinto inherits this responsibility. Thus, Guálinto follows in his father figure's footsteps, a predetermined path about which he has been ambivalent in the past but to which he now sees himself obligated. The significance of Guálinto's decision to continue in school is further intensified in Paredes's illustration of the extant "representative" of the Mexican American community, the character of K. Hank Harvey, the graduation speaker who, despite his lack of fluency in Spanish, is considered "the foremost of authorities on the Mexicans of Texas."²⁸ In introducing what otherwise seems an extraneous figure to the narrative, Paredes parodies the authorized "expert" on this group: "K. Hank Harvey filled a very urgent need; men like him were badly in demand in Texas. They were needed to point out the local color, and in the process made the general public see that starving Mexicans were not an ugly, pitiful sight but something very picturesque and quaint, something tourists from the North would pay money to come and see."²⁹ Clearly, Harvey only furthers a hegemonic discourse that casts Mexican Americans as the premodern others of the modern, progressive nation. In contrast, then, Guálinto's personal education inherently incorporates the interests of his community and authorizes the self-representation of the minority subject.

Yet, in a complicating turn, the narrative moves from Guálinto's decision to attend college at the end of Part IV to a surprisingly different and seemingly discontinuous conclusion. Part V presents an adult George, who has served as a spy in Europe until the onset of World War II, returning to the Texas borderlands, where he works to maintain security along the U.S.-Mexico border. Now married to a white woman (a sociologist who, like Harvey, has studied Mexicans in the American Southwest, albeit with more tact and sympathy, but who, again like Harvey, does not speak Spanish), George disappoints his former classmates and friends when they urge him to join their political coalition. He admits to them that not only does his "company" prohibit him from becoming involved in politics, but that he would in any case be more likely to back the incumbent. As for "our people," he argues they will continue "clearing more brush" and "digging more ditches," "if that's all they can do."[30] When Feliciano surmises that his nephew's true job is as a government agent, George confides to him that "if any spying or sabotage takes place it will be by some of our own people."[31] In addition to explaining that he will not teach his children to speak Spanish, he bluntly expresses his scorn for the Mexican American activists: "Mexicans will always be Mexicans. A few of them, like some of those would-be politicos, could make something of themselves if they would just do like I did. Get out of this filthy Delta, as far away as they can, and get rid of their Mexican Greaser attitudes."[32] In all appearances, then, the Anglo-American George seems to have emerged triumphant, as in his former classmate, Eloida's, epithet, "*Vendido sanavabiche!*"[33] George seems to have clearly betrayed and "sold out" his people, exploiting his intimate knowledge of the community in order to manage and ultimately suppress their political interests.

Yet, while George affiliates himself primarily with the hegemonic nation and as an agent of the security state, this final section of the novel also opens with him daydreaming about living during the era of the U.S.-Mexico War. In his fantasy of the battle of Houston, he builds his own armed militia, populated by racial minorities, that valiantly defends itself against the United States:

> He would imagine he was living in his great-grandfather's time, when the Americans first began to encroach on the northern

provinces of the new Republic of Mexico. Reacting against the central government's inefficiency and corruption, he would organize *rancheros* into a fighting militia and train them by using them to exterminate the Comanches. Then, with the aid of generals like Urrea, he would extend his influence to the Mexican army. He would discover the revolver before Samuel Colt, as well as the hand grenade and a modern style of portable mortar. In his daydreams he built a modern arms factory at Laredo, doing it all in great detail, until he had an enormous, well-trained army that included Irishmen and escaped American Negro slaves. Finally, he would defeat not only the army of the United States but its navy as well. He would reconquer all the territory west of the Mississippi River and recover Florida as well.[34]

This fantasy—one through which Paredes strikingly redeems the sacrifice of self that Ygnacio performs in "The Gringo"—displaces George's American self by returning him to the rifted grounds of 1848 and holding out the possibility of another history and future for the subject. As María Josefina Saldaña-Portillo argues, George is "haunted in his dream life" by the Indian/Mexican Guálinto, whom he cannot fully negate.[35] The fantasy further evokes the history of insurgency with which the novel opens. It keeps alive *los sediciosos*' "Plan de San Diego," which called upon Mexicans, African Americans, Asian Americans, and American Indians to forge a new border republic in the Southwest, and countenances the history of incursion, conquest, and discrimination that "his people" have inherited.[36]

Therefore, as we saw with minority neoconservative subjects in Chapter 3, George keeps alive, if unconsciously, a revolutionary affiliation with "his people," whom, in his waking life, he must repudiate as clownish, childish, seditious, or savage.[37] The fantasy marks the limits of George's claim that, "I am doing what I do in the service of my country," by rendering uncertain what "my country" is.[38] As José David Saldívar contends, even as George attempts to constitute himself into an assimilated modern subject, racialized others haunt and rupture both his full incorporation into the nation and the state's attempts to close ranks against national outsiders.[39] The duality of George/Guálinto's subjectivity antagonizes the nationalist identifications he attempts to consolidate. In fact, the opportunity and decision to become an intelligence officer in itself betrays the extent to which the nation is highly vulnerable to invasion and subversion from both "within" and "without," as well as the state violation of the nation's own principles of democratic openness in the name of securing the nation.

The *specificity* of the contradiction that George embodies—and the ethics of betrayal that the novel poses—pertains to his situation as both an educated subject *and* the knowledge worker, an agent of intelligence. Bradley Levinson and Dorothy Holland suggest that while schools supplement the education of the home and one's immediate locality with "an educational mission of extra-local proportions," they are also the sites of "intense cultural politics" between the local (in this case, the minority) and the national.[40] Schools are a "contradictory resource" where students are taught to think of themselves as "somebody" within the systems of class, race, and gender that undergird national formations, while simultaneously effecting a sense of loss of self insofar as "encounters with formal education can result in a feeling of responsibility for one's lowly social standing."[41] While the educated person is produced through the cultural transmissions that education mediates, the student also employs his or her own interests in resisting or creatively incorporating that education. Likewise, while those in his family and community recognize that Guálinto/George must attain the symbolic and cultural capital that will legitimize him as a "leader of his people," the process by which he will secure these privileges, which are in turn meant to be reinvested into the community, also gives birth to the traitorous Anglo-American George. Paredes thus portrays the anxiety that haunts the minority subject as he or she seeks cultural and political representation, that the "insider," given the responsibility to represent, will use and betray the community rather than work in its collective interest.

Paredes's depiction of Harvey provides an image of the most familiar type of "expert" on racial and national objects. In his portrayal of the benevolent and affectionate racism that underpins Harvey's expertise, Paredes affirms earlier scholarly knowledge on these groups that worked mainly to reproduce the social, political, and economic hierarchies already in place. In contrast, the figure of George as the bearer of a more "authentic" expert knowledge is at once more prophetic and more troubling, as it predicts the multiplicitous character of the self-knowledge produced by minority "insiders." Yet, in its construction of George as a fragmented subject, Paredes advises that his protagonist's betrayal is itself complicated. Thus, on the last page of the novel, Feliciano challenges George's defense of his choice of profession as a matter of "service [to] my country" by asking, "Does 'your country' include the Mexicans living in it?"[42] It is a question that George would "rather not go into," because it exposes the impossible subjects who forestall the suturing of the hegemonic nation into a unified totality and it countenances the others to whom George owes loyalty.[43] George refuses to engage these others who evince the ethical obligation of the professional minority and the American self. The narrative, however, poses the need to account for this relationship.

Chronologically located between Guálinto's self-inscription as a leader of his people and George's emergence as the traitor of them is a period in the narrative left unspoken, his time at the university. As such, the literal and figurative dimensions of betrayal that I have outlined, that of the spy and of the intellectual, are structurally coupled and equated. The novel implies that while he is in college, the nation interpellates George as its assimilated subject and he emerges as the state's intelligence agent. Thus, his symbolic and literal separation and distance from other Chicana/os while at the university galvanizes his betrayal of them. This narrative, conceived during a moment in which minorities were by and large barred from the institutions of higher education, accordingly imagines the university as inculcating the minority subject into the hegemonic nation. The oppositional politics in which Guálinto engages during high school are therefore left behind and unvoiced here. It is, in many ways, a story that does not need telling—as the novel's silence intimates—because it so familiar: only by assimilating can one become an equal member and representative agent of the nation. As the conclusion of *George Washington Gómez* suggests, at this historical moment political and cultural equality is difficult to envision as anything but a salutary submission to the hegemonic nation.

Yet, the conflict set out in the closing of this novel also gestures toward the predicament of minority discourse that follows the civil rights and cultural nationalist movements' demands for political representation of cultural difference. As I have recounted in Chapter 3, these movements effected a paradigm shift on a national scale in which the nature of racial politics and the meaning of racial identity itself were altered. A burgeoning sense of collective identity based on race allowed for a minoritarian discourse of racial identity that critiqued the dominance of Eurocentric (i.e., white) and often biologistic conceptualizations of race. With this shift, self-representation became both possible and treacherous, as the minority subject entered a social terrain that remained highly uneven, despite claims by the nation of an already accomplished equality. Paredes's intimation that the subject of minority discourse remains conflicted by different sets of interests remarkably suggests the contesting claims that class and professional difference (or any of the host of other differences that cultural critics have since explored) effect upon racial identifications.[44] As Ramón Saldívar has argued, *George Washington Gómez* is a "curiously polytemporal text"; written between 1935 and 1940, set during the first half of the twentieth century, and published in 1990, it provides a "prefigurative instance of the state of Chicano literature and the Chicano subject at the end of the twentieth century."[45]

Paredes penned this novel after the mass deportations of Mexicans (and Mexican Americans) during the Great Depression and just before the onset of World War II, in which unprecedented (and disproportionate) numbers of Mexican Americans participated. After World War II, many Mexican Americans were consequently able to avail themselves of the provisions of the G.I. Bill. This new access to higher education provided Mexican Americans (especially in contrast to more recently arrived Mexican immigrants and *braceros*) an avenue into the middle class. But it also politically mobilized them around the civil rights movement, and later, in El Movimiento, the Chicana/o cultural nationalism that allied itself with the mobilization of other people of color in the United States and decolonization campaigns in the Third World. Gilbert G. González further argues that U.S. foreign policies that intended to prevent Mexican organizations from becoming "disruptive or divisive factors" and to promote "inter-American political solidarity" also provided for education reform in Mexican American communities, effectively ending segregation and introducing some curricular changes.[46] In the fragmentations and transformations that Guálinto/George undergoes, Paredes's novel traces these momentous changes, of which Chicana/os were both subjects and objects. Poised as it is just prior to the onset of World War II, the narrative considers what possibilities face a community that, prior, articulated its collective interest in the more singularly heroic and oppositional forms of the border ballad. The novel itself predates El Movimiento's collectivist articulations of race and the theorization of difference that postmodernist, poststructuralist, and feminist thought has more recently brought to minority discourse. Nonetheless, its seemingly "modern" (i.e., post–civil rights, post–cultural nationalist) perspective with respect to Chicana/o history denotes the extent to which racial formation has always been lived through multiple axes of difference.

It is this multiplicity that Chang-rae Lee attends to in his novel *Native Speaker*. Whereas Paredes's novel concludes with George's decision to become a spy of his own people, Lee posits this situation as a point of departure for his work. Published in 1995, *Native Speaker* focuses on a multiracial New York City nearly three decades after the race-based movements of civil rights and cultural nationalism began. My reading of *Native Speaker* in conjunction with *George Washington Gómez* asks the questions with which Paredes ends: What is the character of the betrayal that the ethnic intelligence worker enacts? Who is the subject and object of this betrayal, and how are we to understand interests, both self-interest and interest groups, as they play out in these treasonous acts? What replaces national interest, the "in the service of my country," when it no longer provides the ideological alibi of the minority spy? In this case, as Lee's novel illustrates, "self interest" is constituted through multiple axes of social difference, and representational politics becomes an even more difficult practice to control.

At the beginning of this novel, the wife of the narrative's Korean American protagonist, Henry, initiates a trial separation, leaving him with a partial, haphazard list of adjectives that describe him. Lelia's list (what Henry initially thinks to be a "love letter") portrays him as an "illegal alien" and an "emotional alien," as a "traitor" and a "neo-American." Because elsewhere in the novel, Lelia's figurative role as a cultural "standard bearer" and her "whiteness" are both stressed, her articulation of Henry's identity—especially as it reaffirms the alien status of the Asian American—are crucial to the development of Henry's self-image. Standing in as the hegemonic nation's arbiter of legitimacy and normativity, Lelia's catalogue names him as the duplicitous and illegitimate subject of American history.

Henry's sense of himself as a "fake" is further consolidated in his professional identity as a spy. The intelligence agency for which Henry works is not a state operation, but rather, Dennis Hoagland's independent agency, which specializes in "ethnic coverage," and whose clients vary, but include multinational corporations and foreign governments. Lee thus sets his narrative squarely in a post–Cold War moment, where nation-states no longer constitute the only or necessarily primary actors in political contests. In contrast to the task of the agent in many works of the spy genre, where intelligence work leads to state control over the object of scrutiny through the secret securing of knowledge about it, Hoagland already recognizes that all knowledge, and the power it garners, is partial, never totalized, and that no one can see the entire "game": "You know that no matter how smart you are, no one is smart enough to see the whole world. There's always a picture too big to see. No one is safe. . . . There's no real evil in the world. It's just the world. Full of people like us."[47]

Consequently, without the alibi of nationalist service, Lee refuses to romanticize Henry's profession, instead depicting him as rather self-conscious and self-deprecating: "We casually spoke of ourselves as business people. Domestic travelers. We went wherever there was a need. The urgency of that need, like much of everything else, was determined by some calculus of power and money. Political force, the fluid motion of capital. Influence on your fellow man. These basics drove our livelihood.... We pledged allegiance to no government. We weren't ourselves political creatures. We weren't patriots. Even less, heroes."[48] As spies, Hoagland's employees engage their subjects in casual relationships, and the reports they produce for their clients are meant to be objective, impersonal accounts of these details—"unauthorized biographies."[49] As Henry explains, the spies begin this process by creating "legends" of their own, "extraordinarily extensive 'stor[ies]' of who we were, an autobiography as such, often evolving to develop even the minutiae of life experience, countless facts and figures, though [they] also required a truthful ontological bearing, a certain presence of character."[50] These performances are stronger the more closely they ride the unstable line between fact and fiction, articulating but also reimagining the various subject positions of family, profession, ethnicity, and sexuality that the spy already inhabits.

Related in retrospect, after Henry becomes personally attached to one of his subjects, a Filipino psychoanalyst, Emile Luzan, these "stories" elicit Henry's feelings of guilt. For Luzan, he begins introducing into his legend the facts of his real life, but "no longer extrapolating: I was looping it through the core."[51] Thus, he finds himself trying to account for his own losses: his mother's death from cancer while he was still a boy, his struggles with his own masculinity against and alongside the model offered to him in the figure of his immigrant father, his sense of racial and cultural dispossession, his marriage to a white woman and the death of their son. When Henry attempts to warn Luzan about possible dangers the doctor might face, Hoagland pulls him off the case. Luzan thereafter dies in a boating wreck that is declared accidental, but which Henry suspects is the result of political machinations. Henry's likely betrayal of Luzan initiates his sense that his own encounters with traumatic loss are symptomatic of his part in the "selling-out" of those around him, his sense that he is responsible, because of something lacking in him, for the pain he finds in others.[52]

This guilty sense of responsibility strays from the emotional distance that the spy must maintain, as Hoagland and his colleagues repeatedly remind him. Henry's new assignment to John Kwang is meant as an easy and gradual reintroduction to the job and a test of his ability to carry it out. As the novel narrates his "infiltration" of the campaign and party structures of this rising New York City political star, Henry grows increasingly attached to and identifies with his subject. He finds that he is no longer able to represent Kwang, with whom he has begun to identify, in any "neutral" or non-self-interested manner, but wishes instead to know him more intimately, familiarly: "I believed I had a grasp of his identity, not only the many things he was to the public and to his family and to his staff and to me, but who he was to himself, the man he beheld in his most private mirror."[53] As Tina Chen surmises, "Henry becomes enmeshed in the complexities of his own performance; he is a performer who leaves behind the self-consciousness of impersonation to embrace the seamless transformation of imposture."[54]

Yet, by the end of the novel, a circuit of betrayed trusts and interests, manifested in two key revelations, expose this sense of (self-)certainty as a fiction. First, a firebombing of the campaign headquarters, which results in the death of one of Kwang's most trusted volunteers, Eduardo, ultimately leads to Henry's discovery that Eduardo was in fact working undercover for a rival candidate. The attack proves to be not the work of Hoagland and Henry's colleagues (a suspicion which has left Henry feeling utterly responsible), but of Kwang's own affiliates. Kwang tries to explain to Henry his reasons for having Eduardo taken out: "He was betraying us, Henry. Betraying everything we were doing.... I loved him, Henry, I grieve for him, but he was disloyal, the most terrible thing, a traitor."[55] Second, the exposure of the *ggeh* (a Korean "money-club") structure of Kwang's fundraising apparatus results in the arrests and deportation of numerous undocumented immigrants by the INS.

Henry comes to understand his role as an intelligence and social agent in both of these instances as only partial; he has only partial claim to, control over, and responsibility for the knowledge he has produced, the identity he has performed, and the consequences it has effected. But he *does* indeed retain this partial control and responsibility. In other words, *Native Speaker* does not exonerate Henry in the game of interests and intelligence. The novel's ultimate revelation that it is the INS who has commissioned Henry's collection of data on the *ggeh* members in order to deport the undocumented immigrants associated with Kwang's campaign offers a significant recognition of the complex interrelations between transnational and nationalist politics, demonstrating that the nation-state, although increasingly subject to and transgressed by transnational flows of peoples and capital, is hardly incapacitated. The swift roundup and deportation of the undocumented immigrants and Henry's sense of his having betrayed them points to his own formation as a subject of racial and national discourses: "Whether I wish it or not, I possess them, their spouses and children, their jobs and money and life. And the more I see and remember the more their story is the same. The story is mine. How I come by plane, come by boat. Come climbing over a fence. When I get here, I work. I work for the day I will finally work for myself. I work so hard that one day I end up forgetting the person I am."[56] Henry thus recognizes his betrayal of these immigrants as a self-betrayal, a negation of the diasporic past.

Set against the narrative of political intrigue, Henry also recounts the stories of his own life, including his fraught relationships with his parents and his attempt to reconcile with Lelia after the tragedy of their son's death and her discovery that he is a spy. As in *George Washington Gómez*, Lee's novel focuses closely on the cultural production of Henry as an object of education, especially, as the title suggests, through the question of language. Like Guálinto/George, school provides for Henry the locus of the intense cultural politics of language, and, again as with Guálinto/George, Henry finds the opportunity for his own assimilative survival and success embodied in the figure of the white teacher, in particular, the speech therapist.[57] Henry describes himself as having been "raised by language experts, saved from the wild":[58]

> [Miss Haven would] give each of us a small hand mirror so that we might examine our mouths as we spoke, and then she'd come around and practice with us. She would go from one student to the next, sit herself squarely before him or her, and say, *Now put your hand on my throat*. She wanted us to understand the vibration certain sounds required. If the kid wouldn't do it—most of us would automatically reach for her neck—she'd take the hand and move it up there herself and say something deep and thrilling like *vampire*, and you thought, this is a teacher, a person who can show, her mottled milky skin still damp with the sweat of other palms, her breath sweet.[59]

The teacher offers up her very body to the students as an instrument through which they might be domesticated and thus incorporated into the nation. Throughout the novel, as in this scene, Lee conceives of the execution of language as literally a bodily act. It is an act meant to be a seamless performance of the continuities of body, identity, and culture, but one that often instead exposes how education and other cultural negotiations construct such fluency.

Lelia, too, works as a speech therapist, a trait that Henry explains immediately drew him to her: "At first I took her as being exceedingly proper, but I soon realized that she was simply executing the language. She went word by word. Every letter had a border. I watched her wide full mouth sweep through her sentences like a figure touring a dark house, flipping on spots and banks of perfectly drawn light."[60] In this first meeting, Lelia discerns that Henry himself is not a "native speaker," despite his rather perfect approximation of standard English, suggesting that his body betrays the self-consciousness with which he performs the language. In contrast, English "fills" Lelia's voice and conversely her body inhabits the language with a natural(ized) continuity that makes her "an average white girl [who] has no mystery" and whose "job" is to serve as the "standard-bearer."[61] Henry's desire for Lelia is explicitly tied to the racial (her "whiteness") and cultural (her "perfect" English) privilege that she embodies. Instead, it is the tension between his "face" and his "voice," that is, the markers of his race and his education, that affords Henry his profession as a spy of his "own kind."[62] While his face registers him as the other of the national body that is the racial alien, his voice links him to a class that has "made it," has successfully assimilated to the dominant language of the hegemonic nation.

Henry's attraction to Kwang also rests largely on this trait. Among the "scores and scores of his versions" that Henry records, he is most drawn to the story, which I cite here at length, by which Kwang becomes an American, and further, an American representative of ethnic and immigrant minorities:

> Here is a man named John Kwang, born in Seoul before the last world war, a boy during the Korean one, his family not mercifully sundered or refugeed but obliterated, the coordinates of his home village twice removed from the maps.... He stole away to America as the houseboy of a retiring two-star general. Where he saved enough money to leave the general's house in Ohio and go to New York. Where he named himself John. Where he was beaten nearly to death and robbed of all his savings. Where he worked in a Chinatown noodle shop and slept outside next to the steam vent and awoke one morning to see that his feet had turned almost black with the cold. Where he knew hunger again, that unforgettable

taste of his other country. Where, desperate as he was, he took to stealing from others, one of them a young priest who saw something to salvage and took him to a Catholic orphanage. Where he first went to a real school and learned to read and write and speak his new home language. And where he began to think of America as a part of him, maybe even his, and this for me was the crucial leap of his character, deep flaw or not, the leap of his identity no one in our work would find valuable but me.[63]

Henry chronicles Kwang's biography as a series of movements plotted by the "where" that opens each sentence fragment, a narrative contingently driven by impersonal forces of violence and poverty. The break in this story, the "and where," indicates the supplementary force of a self-imaging that takes place, notably, when Kwang finally attends a "real school" and begins to "think of America as a part of him." Henry's closest affiliation to Kwang comprises this moment of the "crucial leap of character . . . the leap of his identity," in which education authorizes self-possession.

Henry attempts to separate emotionally the reports that he produces for Hoagland of Kwang from what he sees as the ethical impulse underlying the political work that Kwang's campaign espouses, the representation of the disempowered others whom Kwang embodies in his own history. Yet Kwang himself confirms for Henry the impossibility of such a separation between the personal narrative and the political: "When you are someone like me, you will be many people all at once. You are a father, a dictator, a servant, the most agile actor this land has ever known. And all throughout you must be the favorite chaste love of the people."[64] Kwang's status as the "favorite chaste love of the people" enables him to speak both for his constituency, the racial minority groups of Queens, *and* to a hegemonic nation. Thus, Kwang is pictured as a nodal point in a Rainbow Coalition–like alliance of minority interests that are translated into the language of "Americans" and political rights.[65] Lee hardly portrays this coalition as a harmonious coming together of racial minorities; Kwang labors to manage the difficult relations of his constituents, most notably tensions between African Americans and immigrant communities. Yet, the narrative imagines a remaking of American electoral politics, where campaigners offer constituents a remarkable message: "In ten different languages you say *Kwang is like you. You will be an American.*"[66]

The series of identifications produced by Henry's attraction to Kwang and his desire to see in Kwang a fatherly figure who articulates the dispersed interests of minorities is completed by his comparisons of Kwang to his own father. Henry's assessment of his own father tends to be rather harsh, a testament to both his disdain for his father's immigrant work ethic and apolitical presence in the American landscape and to the pain he harbors from his father's ability to convince him of his own fundamental inassimilability. The narrative ultimately, however, comes to a different resolution concerning Henry's father, aligning him explicitly with both Henry and Kwang through the language of betrayal. Lee characterizes the affinities between Kwang and Henry's father and between Henry's father and Henry himself through their differential relationships with others of their "own kind":

> If anything, I think my father would choose to see my deceptions in a rigidly practical light, as if they were similar to that daily survival he came to endure, the need to adapt, assume an advantageous shape. My ugly immigrant's truth, as was his, is that I have exploited my own, and those others who can be exploited. This forever is my burden to bear. But I and my kind possess another dimension. We will learn every lesson of accent and idiom, we will dismantle every last pretense and practice you hold, noble as well as ruinous. You can keep nothing safe from our eyes and ears. This is your own history. We are your most perilous and dutiful brethren, the song of our hearts at once furious and sad. For only you could grant me these lyrical modes. I call them back to you. Here is the sole talent I ever dared nurture. Here is all of my American education.[67]

For Henry, the truest "burden" that links him to his father and to Kwang is not their ability to forge an identity with others through sameness, but their shared histories of betraying their "own kind" through distance and difference. Paradoxically, however, if this is the "immigrant's truth," it is one engendered in their inhabiting the space between native citizen and foreign alien. In this passage, the difference marked by the "we," at first suggesting the spy, shifts with the introduction of a rather indeterminate "you," an interpellation of the audience as generic American readers, the disseminators of the "lyrical modes" and "American education" through which the betrayal is enacted. The spy's betrayal amounts to only one instance of the perfidious character of representation on a multiracial terrain.

Both Lee and Paredes foreground descriptions of the difficulties that the protagonists face in learning English, in interacting with white

Americans, and in their troublesome relationships as "insiders" of a particular minority community. This foregrounding suggests that it is their immediate experiences of the material processes and affective modes through which racial identities are constructed that make them expert spies.[68] These narrative accounts of racial difference authorize George and Henry as minority subjects. And like the minority intellectual, the minority intelligence worker's expertise lies in his or her ability to produce authoritative knowledge about this racialized experience and its cultural contexts. Rather than casting them as wholly disarticulated from racial formations, the novels depict how ethnic intellectuals antagonize both hegemonic and minority formations in the difficulties of their positioning. Michael Denning argues that the conventional spy novel mediates between the political conditions of modern social relations and individual experience by retaining a "fairly traditional plot" in which the spy provides a link between the individual's actions and "the world historical fate of nations and empires."[69] In the emphasis on individual agency, the spy novel displaces history "to secret conspiracies and secret agents, from politics to ethics. The secret *agent* returns human *agency* to a world which seems less and less the product of human action."[70] The narrative of the ethnic secret agent, however, like that of the minority intellectual, must grapple with *both*, the historical conditions that produce racial meanings as well as the ethical responsibilities of personal agency. Rather than the dichotomizing the terms of responsibility and determinism, *George Washington Gómez* and *Native Speaker* suggest, as Lee's Hoagland suspects, "it's just the world," brought into being by the negotiations, whether profound or absurd, between the personal and the historical-political. The parable that the novels provide for minority discourse, here of the minority subject as knowledge-worker/intellectual, thus casts the ethico-political project as the ongoing undoing of this binary of personal responsibility and impersonal history.

The Invention of the Minority Intellectual

George Washington Gómez and *Native Speaker* both truck with the generic conventions of the spy novel and the realist immigrant narrative or ethnic bildungsroman without wholly conforming to either. In establishing George and Henry as spies, Paredes and Lee respectively interrupt the seeming transparency of their accounts of minority ethnic boyhood and an American education by underscoring the vexed relationship between the subject as a professional agent and the subject as a member of a minority community. Yet, neither of these novels adopt the generic formula of the popular spy novel. As Chen contends, *Native Speaker* eschews the spy novel's hallmark (if fundamentally "non-mimetic") conventions of intrigue and adventure in its unglamorous (self-)representation of Henry. Likewise, *George Washington Gómez* only bandies with the genre in its positing of George as a spy, without offering any full-fledged plot to actuate this role. By absenting key features of both genres—forthcoming reliability in the realist ethnic novel and heroic adventure in the spy narrative—the novels challenge their readers' expectations for the production of generic subjects. But beyond noting that these novels, like much other minority literature, transgress generic boundaries, I would like to suggest that in the specific mode of their non-conformity, these works theorize themselves as allegories of intellectual production. By "inventing" their necessary reader as the intellectual who structurally identifies with the intelligence worker, these narratives imagine the intellectual as the ethical subject of minority discourse, whose responsibility to the Other continually unmakes and defers the self-certitude of intellectual authority.

The novels' formal concern with the extraction of knowledge about minority subjects begins with their reversal of the abstracting process of figurative language. Both novels literalize the metaphor, the "immigrant or ethnic minority is (like) a spy," by positing literal spying as a crucial element to narrative development. If metaphors rely precisely on the distance and difference between the vehicle and tenor of the trope, the novels' construction of the ethnic spy collapses the efficacy of this trope. It undermines the imaginative, that is, literary, aspect of the trope by which we understand that the minority subject is indeed *not* the spy, even while he or she shares some striking resemblances to being one. Nevertheless, precisely because the Asian American or Latina/o subject is always already assumed to be a treacherous threat—an alien and illegal presence encroaching upon the nation—the portrayal of the minority subject *as* the duplicitous agent itself cannot be said to be wholly unconventional and unexpected. Popular discourses widely manifest this image of the scheming, traitorous minority subject. What distinguishes Paredes's and Lee's novels, however, is that the object of surveillance and exploitation for the minority spy is not the nation but rather the community from which the spy hails. As such, the narratives do not simply "return" or abject the minority subject to a wholly alienated form of racial otherness in the nation by constructing them as spies; rather, Paredes and Lee situate the minority subject in a position of partial incorporation that is ambivalent, fraught, and generative.

Neither Henry nor George are able to comment directly upon the literalized metaphor of the ethnic spy that defines their subjectivity, even as the narratives closely link their professional and ethnic identities. They remain un-self-conscious of the figurative resonances that the trope implies. Indeed, as they perform their work they actually put the trope under erasure. That is, George and Henry are effective as spies only insofar as no one suspects them as such. Thus, they cannot admit that as minority subjects, they have always already been constructed as treacherous figures. Further, they cannot fully grasp the way in which their affiliative interest *in* their subjects compromises their surveillance of the minority community. For George, this is part of the question he would "rather not go into," and Henry only begins to recognize the performative effects of his attachments to Luzan and Kwang in the retrospective telling of his story. In George's performative dismissal of the political party and in Henry's utopian regard for Kwang's campaign, the agents intervene in the narratives of the subjects from whom they are supposed to remain detached, but with whom they simultaneously identify and have been identified. By suggesting that the political subject of minority discourse comes into existence through the (self) representations that the intelligence agent makes, the novels invert the relationships between knowledge and politics that George and Henry assume. Knowledge produces (them as) the political subjects of surveillance. The narratives then require *another* knowledge worker, one attuned to the novels' limits as both ethnic bildungsromans and as spy narratives. That is to say, the novels need a metareader of generic form. I am designating here this inversion of representation and subjectivity, and *our recognition* of the inversion, as the move to allegory that the novels perform. That is, the invention of the intellectual agent/reader corresponds to the subject's reading for allegory, a "secret" reading that reciprocally *rewrites* the novels *as* allegorical. In this way, the novels perform, as Henry writes of his perspective on Kwang, the "crucial leap of character . . . the leap of identity" between their reader and their minority subject.

If, as we saw in the Chapter 3, nationalist narratives of progressive assimilation strive to remove and abstract the minority subject from the material conditions and cultural images of social difference, *George Washington Gómez* and *Native Speaker* render the limits of this generic production of the minority subject in their depiction of what Lisa Lowe describes as "the material trace" of historical contradiction, that of racial formation.[71] In other words, if the New Journalism of minority neoconservatism aspires to produce a generic American self out of the particularized subject, the novels I have been examining in this chapter suggest that, at the historical juncture of the late twentieth century, the minority subject arrives in this process as a public or "professional" minority self, indelibly marked by the historical traces of race that forestall assimilation. Tellingly, neither novel insists that the politics of the professional minority need be a liberal or minoritarian one. Indeed, given their attachment to the promise of assimilation, George and Henry approximate the minority neoconservative Richard Rodriguez and Eric Liu more closely (although not exactly) than they do an oppositional or separatist politics of cultural nationalism. But, in their role as spies assigned to "ethnic coverage," the narratives do illuminate that the minority subject will have to continually "profess," even if it is in order disavow, his racial and ethnic identity to the hegemonic nation over and over again.

But, unlike Rodriguez and Liu, both Paredes and Lee imagine an alternative public form for the minority subject, the coalitionist multiracial politics—and their leaders—upon which George and Henry spy. In the political campaigns in which Eloida participates (and which George rejects) and that John Kwang spearheads, both authors propose a democratic politics that organizes the "alien citizens" whom the nation—and minority neoconservatism—persistently negate. Henry, who proves much more affected by this alternative politics than does George, writes that for him John Kwang indicates a "question of imagination": "Before I knew of him, I had never even conceived of someone like him. A Korean man, of his age, as part of the vernacular . . . a larger public figure who was willing to speak and act outside the tight sphere of his family."[72] In Kwang, Henry realizes the possibility of a "new plot" for the future, and consonantly describes him as "a trope, which is just a way to believe."[73] Thus, Henry declares, "my necessary invention was John Kwang."[74]

In both novels, the possibility that the minority subject might provide an organic representative of "the people," one fluent in the material histories and democratic aspirations of a multiracial constituency, conjures the "necessary invention" of just such a minority subject into being. In both novels, however, such a politics is also admitted as largely untenable or ineffective. As Daniel Y. Kim suggests with respect to *Native Speaker*, the minority discourse upon which such a vision depends remains largely absent from the nation's political vernacular, perceived, when at all, as "broken" English and alien otherness. However, as Kim further contends, *Native's Speaker*'s value rests not so much in the politics that a novel "could never give us anyway," but rather in "that politics that it might make us want."[75] Thus, he concludes, while the heterogeneous immigrant subjectivities and ethnic voices that the novel thematizes cannot be made into a "*political* vernacular," Lee does attend to them as the basis of a "*literary* vernacular" that inscribes a narrative of the nation's future.[76] Likewise, while George wonders with irritation about his revolutionary daydream, "Why do I keep doing this? Why do I keep on fighting battles that were won and lost a long time ago? Lost by me and won by me too? They have no meaning now," Paredes reprises the battle as a literary testament to the desire for a democracy that is yet to come.[77]

This literary vision of an alternative form of politics returns us to the debates regarding intellectual/academic knowledge production and political transformations as materialized in the relationship between ethnic studies and minority communities in the United States. It also couches my thesis that *George Washington Gómez* and *Native Speaker* allegorize the contradictory situation and ethical responsibilities of the minority intellectual. Both of these novels, I suggest, engage the problem of cultural practices as a form of politics by enacting the "necessary invention" of their reader as the minority intellectual, who, in turn, recognizes him- or herself as the invention of the ethical subject of minority discourse. This "necessary invention," I contend, hails the reader trained to read (for) political allegory, whose reading practices simultaneously establish the novels *as* allegories.[78]

Conventionally, allegories present, by concrete means, abstract ideas or events and significances external to the literal narrative. Traditional forms of allegory have comprised two sets of features germane to my argument here: (1) that allegories extend an expectation that the reader will recognize a second, figurative level of meaning that is usually much more significant than the literal content of the narrative; and (2) that this second level usually indicates a political/historical narrative of import or a meditation on abstract or philosophical themes. We might then say that the allegory is a duplicitous form, and, indeed, the OED defines the word as the "description of a subject under the guise of some other subject of aptly suggestive resemblance." Allegory depends upon its ideal reader who will recognize the themes and referents that the narrative does not enunciate. As a multivalenced form, allegory therefore also risks *not* being understood and instead being singularly identified with its literal level by the reader who does not read it "correctly." What might it mean, then, to think of the allegory as a form of literature that risks its own literariness in the interest of other themes and meanings?

If, as I explain in Chapter 1, narratives of betrayal provide parables for minority discourse, *George Washington Gómez* and *Native Speaker* caution us as to the practical limits of literary ethics. The literary forms that imagine justice to come and democracy to come always already depend upon the critical formation of their reading subject. The minority intellectual thus engages, however provisionally and imperfectly, the inventing of alternative political subjects through reading practices that make us, in Kim's word, "want" other possibilities and possibilities for others. The minority intellectuals that the novels ultimately invent are neither noble public intellectuals-cum-political leaders of liberal fantasy, nor conservative gatekeepers of a rarefied culture that academe houses. Rather, the novels proffer the flawed but responsible subject of the material and political histories and ethical obligations that constitute minority discourse. In short, then, by producing knowledge workers whose intellectual agency is always tethered to an ethico-politics of (self-)betrayal, the novels imagine and petition for an alternative project in American and U.S. ethnic literary and cultural studies to that of securing cultural capital, authoritative autonomy, and economic mobility for minority subjects. As political allegories, the narratives also then adduce an ethical pedagogy without which their political project of representing other others remains inoperable.

Emmanuel Levinas characterizes his sense of the pre-ontological, ethical reception of the Other "beyond the capacity of the I" as a "teaching."[79] *Readings* more fully elaborates this suggestive formulation of an ethical pedagogy in the specific context of the Western university in his analysis of the "scene of teaching." As Readings argues, in the wake of the demise of the Enlightenment project of nationalist pedagogy and "the idea of culture" upon which the institution founded its own professional, commercial, and political value in the past, an "antimodernist rephrasing of teaching and learning"—one that does not attribute to education the cultivation of autonomy and authority—offers an alternative future for intellectual practice.[80] Readings explains that such an ethical pedagogy envisions teaching as "answerable to the question of justice," and education as a site of obligation (rather than the transmission of knowledge or the emancipation of the subject as autonomous) through the ongoing, interminable work of thinking, or "Thought."[81] The scene of teaching, in which Thought remains at the forefront, does not engage this work in order to arrive at a truth or "final determination," but rather provides the site for thinking the impossibility of such an arrival: "what is drawn out is the aporetic nature of this differend as to what the name of Thought might mean: the necessity and impossibility that it should be discussed, despite the absence of a univocal or common language in which that discussion could occur."[82]

Native Speaker imagines such a "scene of teaching" in its closing pages. Henry, now "in between jobs," assists Lelia in her speech therapy practice, working with immigrant children. As they visit lower-income schools, Henry plays the role of the "Speech Monster": "I gobble up kids but I cower when anyone repeats the day's secret phrase."[83] In this case, where most of the students are foreign-language speakers, Henry describes Lelia's focus to be less on the actual words and utterances of the language itself and more on a welcoming to the language as a whole: "She wants them to know that there is nothing to fear, she wants to offer up a pale woman horsing with the language to show them it's fine to mess it all up."[84] This closing offers a moment of both astonishment and inclusion. The children wonder at the way in which Henry's voice, when unmasked, both succeeds and fails to "match his face": "They check again that my voice moves in time with my mouth, truly belongs to my face."[85] Then Lelia awards the students with badges, symbols of everyone having "been a good citizen": "Now, she calls out each one as best as she can, taking care of every last pitch and accent, and I hear her speaking a dozen lovely and native languages, calling all the difficult names of who we are."[86] Teaching here is, on the one hand, reduced to the management of subjects, facts, and bodies—Henry observes that the speech therapy class is, in fact, considered by many in the school as a "form of day care, ESL-style."[87] Lelia's calling the many "difficult names of who we are" does perform an interpellation of the students as citizens, through a common language that the students have only just begun to adopt. As in *George Washington Gómez*, where the classroom serves as the site for a utopian articulation of citizenship *as* the democratic project, it is circumscribed by the restrictions of class and race. It is only one moment in the institutional context of education, and one especially vulnerable to the lack of resources that stymie the development of these minority voices. As Henry explains, there are too many students for them to each receive individual attention, and Lelia's interaction with them is on a freelance basis, haphazard and infrequent.

Yet, this final scene of *Native Speaker* also troubles the privilege of authority and autonomy in a network of ethical obligations. As Readings explains, the scene of teaching "belongs to the sphere of justice rather than of truth," in which "the relation of student to teacher and teacher to student is one of asymmetrical obligation, which appears to both sides as problematic and requiring further study."[88] Henry's own vacillation between the students and Lelia foregrounds the discontinuities between the speaker, the listener, and that which is spoken, thus registering the *value* of teaching as the critical recognition of these asymmetries. Henry's performance and disrobing as the Speech Monster, and the children's surprise at the presence of a minority subject who inhabits the dominant language so "invisibly," exposes the heterogeneities that exceed the moment of incorporation. Henry's Speech Monster is a disruptive ghost in a narrative about intelligence and power, haunting and refusing a full identification with *either* the children or Lelia. Rather than portraying a one-directional transfer of knowledge and power—where either the teaching of language domesticates the children *or* they gain unassailable power in being able to represent themselves in the hegemonic language of the nation—the scene of teaching insists on a radical uncertainty over who it is that embodies privilege through knowledge and knowledge through privilege. If multiculturalism has been "a form of disciplinarity of difference in which the matter of alterity has been effectively displaced as a supplement," and if there is no giving of "voice" to marginalized groups in school that is not always already "the historical effects of multiple discourses through which power is effected," the haunted scene of teaching nevertheless maps the productive agency of desire—the excesses that cannot be integrated into liberal or consumerist models of personhood and citizenship.[89] Instead, desire circulates and produces new possibilities for articulating discursive identities, social relations, local and national imaginaries, and political agency. *George Washington Gómez* and *Native Speaker*, I thus argue, reconceive of minority intellectuals—academics, critics, and artists—as "students" of minority discourse in order to propose the ethical responsibility of the minority subject. Such a reconceptualization has several implications for ethnic studies. We must think of the student neither as the liberal citizen whose engagement with higher education is a process of "self-discovery," of learning—that is, of who he or she already essentially is—nor as a consumer interested only in the purchase of the commodified object of pedagogy, credentials. Instead, the ethnic studies "student" names at once, but always incompletely, the self and its others.

The meaning and consequences of the students' engagement in knowledge production in Paredes's and Lee's novel are certainly quite distinct from that in which undergraduate students, graduate students, and university faculty participate. To this extent, primary and secondary schools serve as one of the many alternative sites in and through which racial identity is constructed, and the formation of these identities can complement and contest those articulated elsewhere. Yet, the *self-critical mode* of this scene also provides a conceptual structure for the problematic of the minority intellectual as he or she engages in the production and dissemination of knowledge about his or her "own selves." If, as I have noted above, the minority intellectual's experience of the university is a ghostly one, this existence is in fact the product of extensive curriculum reforms on a global level that, as Thomas S. Popkewitz contends, "are concerned less with the specific content of school subjects and more with making the child feel 'at home' in a cosmopolitan identity that embodies a pragmatic flexibility and 'problem-solving' disposition."[90] As these reforms introduce local, decentered epistemologies, the different conceptions of "home" emerge as ambiguities—conflicts and tensions—such that competing social memories and "forgettings" are lived as institutional and personal anxiety.

However, as *Native Speaker* surmises, surprise and pleasure attend such anxiety as well; the ethical obligation of the subject to the Other opens out onto new, unimagined terrains for identification and articulation. To acknowledge alternative agencies, generated by the subject's location at the intersections of racial dispossession and symbolic privilege, is to understand ethnic studies not as a site where the work of self-discovery goes on, but rather as one place among many from which racial identifications are *made and unmade*, and as a site of an ethical pedagogy that insists on returning to the question of the possibility of justice in knowledge production and representation. Readings theorizes this critical pedagogy as the "drawing out of the otherness of thought that undoes the pretension to self-presence that always demands further study."[91] His insistence that justice "involves respect for an absolute Other, a respect that must precede any knowledge about the other," however, qualifies our restricted, pragmatic identification of that Other with/as the student by instead orienting respect not to the student as subject of educational reproduction, but as the bearer of a "shock" to the system.[92] If the institution assimilates the racial other through a multiculturalist pedagogy of reproduction, making him or her over into the "professional minority," *Native Speaker* suggests that the minority intellectual—the self-critical student of ethical pedagogy—remains obligated to *other others* who escape and exceed this process.

Native Speaker embodies these other others in the Asian female characters whose presence is integral to both the developmental narrative of ethnic boyhood and to Henry's assignment to Kwang, even as they remain at the margins of the present narratives themselves. As Henry reveals in his recounting of his final session with Luzan, his "single infidelity" during his marriage took place with a Chinese woman, the wife of one of his subjects, who, after the job and the end of the affair, "somehow crept back into my thoughts."[93] Henry recalls following the woman, whose husband abused her and who sports the "large fresh bruises about the side of her face and one eye," as she drove home from her family store: "She glanced over and saw me. . . . She didn't slow down or speed up and it was as if we were running on side-by-side tracks. She looked at me as if I were already dead, and then she turned her gaze back to the avenue and where she was going, the long way home to her husband."[94] Henry explains that until he had unburdened himself to Luzan about the affair—which initiates his own personal attachment to the therapist at the expense of his professional assignment—he remained for years "disordered by it, sickened."[95] The woman's silence here recalls the other figure of feminine silence in the novel, the unnamed Korean woman who moves in with Henry and his father after Henry's mother's death. Henry knows almost nothing about his father's housekeeper and lover, despite having lived with her for most of his life, and he refers to her simply as "Ahjuhma." An adolescent friend of Henry's deems her as a "total alien" and "completely bizarre," and Henry explains to a frustrated Lelia, who has been rebuked in her attempts to befriend Ahjuhma, that, "She's always been a mystery to me."[96] These figures, whom the narrative of ethnic assimilation and political intrigue cannot integrate, remain for Henry troubling figures of silent Otherness. Neither of these women can be made over into the subjects of domestic ethnic studies and minority discourse, but the novel does not successfully foreclose their claims on Henry either, instead memorializing them as troubling figures of obligation for him.

But Henry also recalls spying a scene between his father and Ahjuhma as they garden, in which they "were simply together and seemed to want it that way": "When they were finished my father stood up and stretched his back in his familiar way and then motioned to her to do the same. She got up from her knees and turned her torso after him in slow circles, her hands on her hips. Like that, I thought, she suddenly looked like someone else, like someone standing for real before her own life."[97] To "stand for real" before her own life, a life that Henry nonetheless cannot narrate as part of his own story of familial romance nor as part of the professional politics of Kwang's campaign, suggests the limits of racial and ethnic identification as a critical practice for the minority intellectual. This scene of transformation, in which Ahjuhma appears as "someone else," allegorizes the relationship of ethical responsibility to political agency by formally staging the arrival of disembodied Otherness into and as an embodied political-historical form. If these women occupy positions akin to that of Helen in *Mona in the Promised Land*, Henry's ethical responsibility to them takes on a specific political form in the disclosure that his work has led to the deportation of undocumented immigrants, in whom Henry sees what could have been his own political destiny. Henry explains that his own citizenship "is an accident of birth," as his mother delivered him when traveling from Seoul and never intended for him to "be an American."[98] As such, the deported immigrants pose the alien otherness by which Henry's American self is displaced.

The point here, then, is not that, by the novel's end, the "other women" have become *identified with* the deported aliens and with Henry, but rather that they stand at the gap between the citizen and the alien, the nation and diaspora, gesturing at the avenue, the "long way home," that the subject has otherwise missed. If, as we surmised in Chapter 2, desire offers an operative mode by which to trace the unmaking of the self that is fissured by ethical responsibility, I would like to suggest that these other women allegorize the "diasporic desire" of the minority subject. In countenancing the subject's desire for some time and place other than the here and now of citizenship and national belonging that is "to be an American," they proffer the politics by which the Other comes to "look like someone else" who stands "before her own life." In the following, final chapter, then, I will probe the ethical implications for minoritarian politics when we track the other as the emergent subject in narratives of diasporic desire and passionate betrayal.

5 / The Passion: The Betrayals of Elián González and Wen Ho Lee

> *The experience, the passion of language and writing (I'm speaking here just as much of body, desire, ordeal), can cut across discourses which are thematically "reactionary" or "conservative" and confer upon them a power of provocation, transgression or destabilization greater than that of so-called "revolutionary" texts (whether of the right or of the left) which advance peacefully in neo-academic or neoclassical forms.*
> —JACQUES DERRIDA, ACTS OF LITERATURE

> *To be a concrete agent in history is, after all, to be contaminated in turn by historically existing ideals and norms, no matter how contaminated these ideals and norms are.*
> —PHENG CHEAH, "POSIT(ION)ING HUMAN RIGHTS IN THE CURRENT GLOBAL CONJUNCTURE"

In April 2000, during the height of the media and political maelstrom surrounding the young Cuban boy rescued a little over four months earlier off the shores of Florida, the *Washington Post* ran a picture of Elián González hanging, arms akimbo, on a playground jungle gym, with a headline reading "The Passion of Elián." The story highlighted the local religious significance that had been attributed to the plight of this "miracle boy." The image, headline, and story elicited a symbolic order different from the otherwise tiresome framing of the case in mainstream media as a matter of national political interests versus private familial rights. In highlighting a terrain of religious meaning, this text implicitly asked: Could this child indeed (potentially) provide some kind of collective redemption in a world fissured by postmodern diversities? If so, whose redemption was it? Who were the Judas or Judases who betrayed this child-martyr? What sacrifice was needed from the child to make redemption possible?[1] With these questions in mind, this chapter compares the case of Elián González with a contemporaneous case that also became figured on a national screen in terms of martyrdom, scapegoating, and betrayal, that of the Chinese American Los Alamos physicist accused of spying on the United States, Wen Ho Lee.

The questions I initially ask about these two cases, as part of an ethical analysis of betrayal, are meant to evoke some political discomfort: What if Wen Ho Lee did in fact engage in espionage? What if we take seriously the traumas of Cuban exiles and their grievances against Castro's Revolutionary government? To pose these questions in the context of academic minority politics and discourse is to follow the injunction of critics like Gayatri Spivak and Rey Chow who urge us to accord to colonial and minority agents subjectivities as complex and contradictory as we are willing to grant to white, Western subjects. By forsaking the victim/oppressor binary, we might chart the multiplicities of domination, desire, and agency in minoritarian subjectivity. An ethical critique here rethinks the framework of rightist and leftist politics because, in Jacques Derrida's words, the "power of provocation" conferred by passionate language troubles these categories in minority discourse. And as I have already specifically argued in Chapter 2, such a critique must be willing to recognize that diaspora constitutes an other to the nation-state, an other whose desires the nation cannot resolve into its own narrative demands.[2] The radical alterity of this otherness can produce loyalties and desires that may, or even must, appear treasonous from inside the nation.

This then leaves us in a space that is fraught, where neither Right nor Left can claim a priori the higher moral ground, and betrayals loom in all directions. This is precisely the unstable terrain for emergent identifications and ethico-political agency that I have been describing throughout *An Ethics of Betrayal*. In this final chapter, I would like to draw out more sharply the ideological and material effects of hewing to the ethical dimensions of betrayal. This chapter continues the analysis of political rhetoric, and of the ethical grounds upon which such rhetoric depends, that I began in Chapter 3. However, following upon the radical pedagogy of intellectual self-critique that we saw allegorized in Chapter 4, this chapter focuses upon the responsibilities to the other that also antagonize the leftist and liberal subjects of minority discourse.

An idealized politics of resistance forecloses an ethico-political project; Rey Chow explains that idealism is a kind of "collective sentiment" that demands that critics disregard what they recognize to be "exploitative, coercive or manipulative" in "so-called 'oppositional' discourse."[3] Ethico-political action therefore involves "risk-taking" that "supplement[s] idealism doggedly with non-benevolent readings, in all the dangers that supplementarity entails."[4] Thus, this is admittedly dangerous ground, no matter how cautiously one treads, because it takes to task the most impassioned forms of minority discourse, ones grounded in civil rights.

"The Passion" invokes the suffering, sacrifice, and redemption of Christ, made possible, paradoxically, through Judas's betrayal of him. In the more concrete terms of these two cases, "the Passion" suggests to me the intensity of the intellectual and emotional commitment demanded by our political faiths. As I explain at length below, in the cases of Wen Ho Lee and Elián González, "passion" expresses a minoritarian discourse's commitment to leftist politics that can demand a closing off of avenues of interrogation—avenues that desire, namely diasporic desire, often insists on breaking out into the open, were we willing to de-idealize certain representations.

Imagining America in the New World Order

What was it about these two cases that drew such heightened political and media attention to them? After all, neither the separation of families through immigration nor the racial profiling of Asians was an especially new or unique occurrence. The significance of the Lee and González cases resides instead, I argue, in the narrative of the nationalist subject that they shore up. That is to say, each of these cases fashioned a narrative mode for the American subject by which to cope with the traumas of national deterritorialization and postmodern *dis*identification at the end of the twentieth century. As my discussion below will demonstrate, the popular narratives of each case attempted to reimagine America, to stabilize and smooth over the ruptures in national self-image wrought by the onset of transnationalism and global capitalism. For the United States, the nation-state most economically, politically, and militarily responsible for ushering in the "New World Order," the integrity of such a developmental narrative was central to its self-image. In other words, the dominant narratives, and their staging of crises and resolutions, assured the national subject that globalization was, in fact, an "Americanization," that could subsume or obliterate otherness, and the desires of the other, into the here and now of an idealized America.

As narratives, both cases vividly engaged the national imagination with elements of sentimentality, intrigue, bombast, hubris, and repentance. The protagonists were two very different people. Wen Ho Lee, a Taiwanese-born physicist, was fired on March 8, 1999 from his position at Los Alamos National Laboratories (LANL) for security breaches, after having been investigated for possibly having transmitted secrets on U.S. nuclear technology and capability to the People's Republic of China (PRC). The Cox Committee report, the result of a House Select

Committee investigation, found evidence of substantial advances in the PRC's nuclear sciences, which it linked to Chinese espionage and significant breaches of security during the previous four presidential administrations. At stake in Lee's case was the whereabouts of the "legacy files," the archival history of nuclear warhead development and testing that had been reportedly leaked to the PRC.

Lee was arrested on December 10, 1999, and charged in a fifty-nine-count indictment with compromising U.S. security, under the terms of the federal Espionage Act and the Atomic Energy Act. Although the investigation of Lee focused on him as a potential spy, he was not charged with passing nuclear secrets; the indictment indicated, however, that the security breaches had "secure[d] an advantage to a foreign nation." He was denied bail after the prosecution argued that, if released, Lee posed a formidable threat to national security because he could surreptitiously signal to another PRC agent the whereabouts of the missing tapes or other directives regarding them. After Lee spent eight months in solitary confinement, an expert witness for the defense argued in a second bail hearing that the prosecution had overstated the secrecy and significance of the missing files. Lee was subsequently released on bail, under the condition of house incarceration, at the beginning of September, 2000. Shortly thereafter, Lee and the prosecution reached a plea bargain agreement. Lee pled guilty to only one of the charges, was sentenced to time already served, made himself available for questioning, and agreed to drop any countercharges that he was being prosecuted because of his Chinese ethnicity.

Only two weeks prior to Lee's arrest, fishermen found Elián González clinging to an inner tube three miles off the coast of Fort Lauderdale, Florida, on Thanksgiving Day, November 25, 1999. The five-year-old child had left Cuba in a small aluminum boat that carried fourteen people, including his mother, Elizabeth Brotons, and her boyfriend, Lazaro Munero. Brotons had left Cuba for the United States with Munero and her son, unbeknownst to Juan Miguel González, Elián's father. Elián was one of only three passengers who survived after the boat began taking on water and broke apart. Both Brotons and Munero drowned, and their bodies were never recovered. The child was placed in the care of his great-uncle, Lazaro González, and his cousin, Marisleysis González, both relatives of the child's father living in the Little Havana section of Miami.

In January 2000 the INS ruled that Elián should be returned to Cuba, but the child's U.S. relatives sued the Justice Department to keep him in the United States and asked a Florida court to grant them custody. Cuban Americans living in South Florida took part in mass protests to support the Miami family during their custody struggle for Elián. In late March of that year, the Justice Department asked Lazaro González to sign a pledge to surrender the child if he lost the court battle; he refused the request. Federal agents seized Elián from Lazaro González's home on April 22 in a widely publicized armed raid and returned the child to his father, who had arrived from Cuba to reclaim his son. In May, a federal appeals court conceded the right of Elián's father to speak for the child and ultimately his right of custody over him. Elián returned with Juan González in June 2000 to Cuba, where he has since remained, for the most part, out of the media spotlight.

The release of Lee and the return of González to his Cuban father may have been the best, or, as some legal experts who saw both cases as "cut-and-dried" all along contended, the only solutions available under criminal law and immigration law, respectively. In fact, for many Americans, in both the Wen Ho Lee and Elián González cases, justice was eventually served, if unfortunately deferred for a spell. In placing these two narratives in conversation with one another, I am not necessarily arguing that they should have been resolved differently. Rather, in keeping with the critical responsibilities that an ethics of betrayal entails, I would like us instead to return to the scenes of crisis in order to defer these endings, so that we might consider alternative ways, as the *Washington Post* article did, of staging the crises themselves. The popular narration of these two cases reduced the complexities of desire to the polarized categories of innocence and guilt, national security and individual freedom, politics and family. In generating desires that move across the boundaries of these categories, the other of the nation-state undermined this construction of the national self. The narrative representations of these cases accordingly enacted an epistemic violence that marked the nation's inability to account for this other and its desires. To return to and restage the crises then affords the possibility for an ethics of betrayal that takes these desires seriously.

Lee and González functioned as symbols for social identification under the New World Order, but they also threatened to reveal the gaps and discontinuities in this social order. The national others in these narratives attracted most attention precisely when their suffering and redemption was most visible. Like the paradigmatic figure of Christ, whose Passion constituted a renunciation of all individual desires except for the singular mission of sacrifice for the collective good of humanity, the others of these narratives provided sacrificial examples of model Americanness under the New World Order. In contrast, the moments of Judas-like betrayal in each case, which I discuss at length below, represented failures in the functioning of the model minority construct and the idealized image of the nation it upholds. Public attention wavered at these points because they marked the failure of the totalizing nationalist fantasy, threateningly suggesting that globalization is indeed *not* synonymous with Americanization.[5]

In a world where the specter of Communism has been killed off, the fullness of the American promise—that one can somehow have both the traditional, hierarchical values secured by the family romance *and* the idealized equities of democratic modernism—is affirmed and managed by the private/public split.[6] The familial and the national served not only as analogies for one another, but comprised and disrupted one another, and when they did, they threatened profound failures of recognition between the self and its others. Indeed, they threatened a dissolution of the self. In other words, the triumph of the "traditional family" in the González case required that the conflicts of the domestic and global, of the national and the foreign, be completely elided. This was possible because, as the Lee case demonstrated, we (are to) believe that we now live in a globalized world *without borders and without history*. The narration of the Wen Ho Lee and Elián González cases functioned to cover over diasporic desire, that is, a desire that the American dream could not fulfill.

In so doing, the nation simultaneously constructed a progressive historical narrative about the relationship between the modernity of the nation-state and the postmodernity of transnational capitalism. By placing the United States at the center of this historical narrative, whereby the American ideal comes to encompass, through cultural and economic penetration, every corner of the globe, the narrative defused the threats that borderlessness, fragmentation, and fluidity, all hallmarks of postmodernity, posed to a unified national image. There is no space in this American imaginary for diasporic desire, rooted in lack and otherness; such desire, and its complex passions, cannot be countenanced and must be cleared away. Chinese Americans and Cuban Americans emerged not as unruly, productive agents of new terrains for imagining self and other, but as national objects, gratefully "liberated" or disciplined into model Americanness. The readings I forward below thus attempt to tease out the presence of diasporic desire in order to elucidate the temporal and spatial unevenness of social and cultural existence under the New World Order.

This thesis accounts for not only Lee's and González's visibility on the national screen. It also helps to explain the relative *invisibility* of the feminine, which so often conventionally figures otherness in the familial narrative of subject formation. Many questions have been raised, and for the most part left unanswered, about the roles of Lee's wife Sylvia and Elián's mother Elizabeth Brotons: Why did Brotons leave Cuba with Elián, and what was the nature of her relationship to her boyfriend, Lazaro Munero, and to Elián's father? To what extent did Sylvia Lee know about her husband's suspicious activities, did she engage in any of her own separately from him, and what was the state of their marriage?[7] There have certainly been attempts to map these women's own interests onto the binaries of the hegemonic narratives, but these accounts leave numerous gaps for contestation. Very little is known about Brotons; in the scores of pages written about Elián in the nation's papers, for example, only a handful even mention her by name. The mystery surrounding Brotons is almost matched by Sylvia Lee's near-silence in public on her husband's case.

In the midst of both cases, it was quite easy to lose track of Elizabeth Brotons and Sylvia Lee. This was especially true because more unambiguous figures of feminine loyalty captured public attention. Elián's cousin, Marisleysis Gonzalez, and Wen Ho Lee's daughter, Alberta Lee, were much more readily integrated into the narrative demands of the nation. In response to the question, "What did she want?" the figures of Sylvia Lee and Elizabeth Brotons offer little clear-cut evidence. These subjects resist symbolization. Their loyalties are questionable, their investments and sacrifices of self—were they selfish, were they selfless?—not easily discerned. As others, they remained resolutely inaccessible and they failed to shore up the totalized self-image that each narrative sought to capture. In contrast, Elián González and Wen Ho Lee offered to the nation an otherness that it could incorporate, or expel, from the body politic at will.

Model Minorities and Racial Profiles: Locating Cuban and Chinese Americans

Taken together, the national discord surrounding González and Lee revealed the anxieties over racial, ethnic, and diasporic differences that plague the nationalist subject. Both of these instances, especially when examined through the theme and tropes of betrayal and treason, offer insight into the meanings of belonging and exclusion, not only for minority subjects, but also for a more generic sense of the nation. The political strategies adopted by Asian (primarily Chinese) American and Cuban American activists in each of these cases, and the public responses they elicited, differed from one another in many ways. Yet, insofar as both cases presented the nation with revivals of the specter of Communism in a post–Cold War or New World Order, the two groups shared homologous positions in the complex terrain of racial formation at the beginning of the twenty-first century.

Thus, I begin this section with the fairly obvious claim that both Chinese American and Cuban American communities, separately, constitute model minorities. As we have seen in Chapter 3, the widely familiar construct of the model minority has usually been ascribed to those of Asian descent within the United States, but it is important to the meaning of Cuban American identity as well. The pages of an array of publications in the United States during the second half of the twentieth century attest that the Cuban exiles, who fled their island nation after Fidel Castro's defeat of the Batista government in 1959 and the installation of a socialist society there, have been welcomed into the United States as paragons of the economic, political, religious, and familial values that the nation attributes to itself.[8] As such, the stories of the remarkable economic and social rise of Cubans in the U. S. have long captivated politicians, journalists, and public commentators.[9] David Palumbo-Liu's description of the function of the Asian American model minority in the Cold War context, that "Asian Americans serve both to prove the rightness of American democracy as a *worldwide* model and to remind Americans of the traditional values it had cast aside in its rush to modernization," thus aptly describes the plight of Cuban Americans as well.[10] Both serve as fulfilling an idealized ethos of democratic capitalism and American exceptionalism.[11]

This construction of Cuban American model minoritarianism against the specter of Communism is not only a construct of right-wing politics. A particularly acerbic, if not uncharacteristic, attack on Miami's Cuban exiles contends:

> The monopoly on information concerning Cuba, which up until now has largely consisted of prime pickings from the ideological refuse heap of information conjured by the Miami exile community

and supported by the United Stated [sic] government—always eager to reinvest in the Cold War—is bent on the continual demonization of Fidel Castro and the hellification of that prickly anticapitalist state so close to our sovereign shore. The anti-Castro cultists seek their salvation in the capitalist market doctrine and their undiminished and militant faith in the frictionless character of its market laws. Such a position removes the inconvenience of having to undress such laws so as to reveal their inner workings and to evaluate the consequences of such laws in the lives of millions of poor and suffering children.[12]

Leftist support of Cuba's Revolutionary government thus also needs the *same* image of the Cuban American, as fanatically anti-Castro and a staunch supporter of U. S. capitalism, Christianity, and traditional family and social values, against which it can define itself.[13]

There are, however, also striking differences between Cuban American and Asian American model minoritarianisms that became especially prominent in the Elián González case. Perhaps the most important is that because of their size, concentration, and location in the key electoral state of Florida, Cuban Americans have managed, unlike Asian Americans, to amass considerable, and some argue, disproportionate strength in national politics. The visibility and clout of Cuban Americans on the political scene contrasts dramatically with that of Asian Americans. For the latter, an important aspect of their model minority status has been precisely their economic success combined with a political *invisibility*, and this is perhaps nowhere better illustrated than in the case of the Lee family itself. Lee's daughter Alberta, who became an outspoken advocate for her father's release, described Lee as "clueless" about American law and government, despite being involved in some of its most highly classified matters of national security. Alberta Lee herself had, prior to her father's arrest, distanced herself from Asian American studies and political activities as an undergraduate at UCLA, because, she has stated, "I thought it was whining."[14]

In the early months of the year 2000, during the midst of both cases, few observers compared the two communities' politics of representation. Among those who did, like legal and political commentators Phil Nash and Albert Yee, there was a decided sense that the Cuban American community had been much more successful at garnering support for its cause than Asian Americans had. While Lee wasted away in solitary confinement, Elián had become a diminutive star. From the position of retrospect, then, each case was poised for a dramatic "reversal of fortune." At the beginning of the year, it seemed quite likely that Cuban Americans would succeed in their protests to keep Elián in the United States and that the Justice Department would successfully try and convict Wen Ho Lee. Of course, as it turned out, neither of these conclusions was foregone. Thus, the raid on Elián's Miami family's home, the forcible removal of the child from the care of his great-uncle and cousin, and the child's return to his father, stand in stark contrast to the dismissal of the majority of charges, and all of the most serious ones, against Lee, an unprecedented apology from the judge in the case, and his release from prison.

In part, the representation of race and ethnicity was responsible for these dramatic shifts, especially in public perception. In the case of Wen Ho Lee, as articulated first by Asian American activists but eventually, if slowly and at some times reluctantly, by the news and popular media, the question of martyrdom and betrayal came to be seen as rather straightforward. Lee became figured as a scapegoat, a citizen profoundly betrayed by the state, through a violation of one of the most sacred principles of the nation, abstract equality before the law and the right to fair trial. The federal government—in particular, the FBI, the Department of Energy, and the Justice Department—seemed clearly to have violated Lee's rights. Even if mainstream media were slow to adopt this point of view, they did so ultimately, most famously in the *New York Times*'s mea culpa of sorts after the Justice Department and Lee struck a plea bargain agreement in September of 2000.[15] This particular argument, that Lee was a scapegoat, eventually prevailed because civil rights discourse had successfully re-read racial injustice in the past. What has broadly come to be known as "racial profiling" is a narrative that can unify experiences as disparate as "driving while black," Japanese American internment during World War II, and, in Lee's termination, "downloading while Asian."[16]

The charges of racial profiling against the federal government gained credence when the former head of counterintelligence at LANL publicly announced that there was no evidence that Lee had passed along atomic secrets to the PRC and that Lee had been singled out because of his ethnicity.[17] Subsequent testimony during the trial by expert witnesses suggested that the importance and level of secrecy of the files that Lee had been accused of mishandling had been overstated. This further weakened the claims of the FBI and Energy Department, enough that Judge James Parker ordered the government to produce evidence of ethnic profiling, including a classified report of computer security violations at LANL. A survey by the Committee of 100 and the Anti-Defamation League concluded that a substantial number, one out of every four, Americans held strong anti-Chinese attitudes, further affirming for many Asian Americans that Lee had been a victim of pervasive racist sentiment in the United States.[18] Thus, "racial profiling" provided a narrative mode for cross-racial alliances between Asian Americans and other people of color, especially African Americans, in the Lee case.

When cross-racial comparisons were made over the course of the Elián case, it was also primarily to black Americans. But these comparisons drew upon the racial and ethnic *tensions* between African Americans and Cuban Americans in Miami, as well as the differing impact of U.S. immigration policy on Cubans and Haitians (the other primary group of asylum seekers in Florida). That is to say, whereas the activists involved in the Lee case allied themselves with other communities of color by embracing the dominant terms of minority discourse, the discursive history of racial hierarchy and model minoritarianism in Miami made such alliances virtually impossible.[19] Both the Lee and González cases were staged against the black/white poles of America's racial terrain. Both were haunted by the specter of Communism and its construction of the model American minority subject. Yet the strategies of maneuver in each instance articulated racial, ethnic, and national belonging to strikingly different effects. These differences turn on an ambivalence that characterizes betrayal, and rest here on the contradictions of national, racial, and ethnic belonging. In the following two sections, then, I examine the circuits of identification, betrayal, and desire at work in the narrative modes of each case.

"The Passion of Elián": Staging Cuban Diasporic Desire

Much consternation was directed at the use of Elián as a "political football." Commentators expressed concern that both the Cuban American exile community and elected officials had delivered the child into a symbolic realm at the expense of the "real" considerations of his developmental needs and familial attachments. In contrast, I am arguing that the narrative production of Elián González, on the part of both liberals and conservatives, took place in the realm of the national imaginary, so deeply naturalized as to feel obvious in its moral implications for the flesh-and-blood child. Although each side argued for different outcomes, both vied for a narrative that fully subsumed and assimilated the other, without any stain of excess or desire left over. "Having Elián" protected and masked the *dis*-order of personal and national existence under a globalized and multiculturalist New World Order. Ultimately, it anchored a developmental narrative of global relations that swept away remnants of the Cold War, and with it, the necessary objects of Cuban exile passion.

For Cuban Americans, the narrative of Elián was a tragedy, a grave betrayal of democratic rights. A desire for the "arrival" of (and return to) an imagined Cuba organizes Cuban diasporic nationalism, an arrival that Castro's rule seems to render perpetually impossible. This desire took Elián as a savior or redeemer of the Cuban people.[20] American media have widely reported on this aspect of the Cuban American response to domestic and international politics. Cuban Americans' hard-line leadership has long labeled as sellouts those (Cubans and non-Cubans alike) who advocate (or appear to advocate) engagement or appeasement of Castro. This particular rhetorical trajectory stretches back to the first arrivals of political exiles from the island, key political leaders in Batista's regime and economic elites who fled the Revolution and the government's subsequent nationalization of private property. It has been promoted especially by organizations such as the Cuban American National Foundation, established in the early 1980s as part of the Reagan administration's Cold War strategies. As Jesús Arboleya explains:

> The Cuban American National Foundation was never representative of the entire community, even though it tries to present itself as such. What it does reflect is the degree of domination the ultraright sector of Cuban American businessmen has managed to impose on the rest of the community. That control is based on the predominantly conservative ideology of Cuban émigrés and on the marginal benefits that the new counterrevolutionary upsurge has brought to a part of the community. That control has also been exercised through the application of all kinds of coercive measures against those who have dared to defy it.[21]

In addition to the Cuban American National Foundation, the politics and exploits of Jorge Mas Canosa, the long-time leader of exile activists, and of paramilitary groups who were held responsible for bombings and other acts of intimidation (including a role in the scandal of the Watergate burglary during Richard Nixon's reelection campaign), have all been explained as protests against "Castro-appeasers."[22]

Thus, while Cuban Americans served a key function in U.S. Cold War politics, anchored in good part by the community's embodiment of an idealized American self-image, the community's position within the United States was simultaneously shot through with ambivalence. As Agustin Tamargo wrote in 1989, during the Reagan-Bush administration, in defense of the Cuban "sufferers in exile" who refuse assimilation: "Some [Cuban Americans] can exchange what is their own for something borrowed, others cannot. Some can frivolously enjoy the freedom and prosperity they did not produce themselves. Others believe this enjoyment, as it is not a product of the Cuban people, is a subtle form of betrayal."[23] Many protestors in the Elián González case worried that Cuban "spies" had infiltrated their ranks, and they branded as Castro's agents anyone advocating Elián's return, declaring that "'Elián's street' is sacred ground," where such viewpoints were unwelcome.[24] Mainstream journalists in return suggested that these protestors exhibited a "one-sided" notion of free speech.[25] While many observers believed that a younger generation of U.S.-born Cuban Americans had become distanced from exile politics, the Elián case saw an upsurge of political and personal interest that crossed generational, gender, racial, and class lines among Cuban Americans.[26] Figured as the child-savior—in some versions he was compared to Jesus, in others to Moses—González embodied the hope and desire of Cuban exiles for a restoration to and with an imagined Cuba.[27]

Since Elián himself had lost his mother—a loss that they easily attributed to Castro's repressive regime as well—the child's own lack, recent and visibly raw, materialized the passionate desires of Cuban emigrants. The symbolic representation of Elián-as-savior, rather than as "real" child, was further overdetermined by the exile activists' arguments that Castro's regime had effectively vitiated familial rights to any child, such that Juan González's paternal claims to Elián were farcical.[28] Consequently, the demand to retain Elián in the United States was a matter of stopping up losses in two directions. For the Cuban exile subject, Elián-as-savior held out the promise of spatial and temporal restoration of an imagined Cuba, and this restoration would also reciprocally save Elián from his own loss, recuperating him to wholeness by supplying him with a "mother Cuba." As one commentator wrote of the child: "Elián represents the salvation of a people, the slandered and unseen exile, the homeland in chains, and in the purest sense, our condition as human beings who find ourselves in another's land."[29]

In its betrayal of Elián, the symbolic body of Cuban diasporic desire, America betrayed the entire Cuban community. The United States, as harbinger of democracy, failed to make good on its promise of rights and freedom. The Cuban American community perceived America as having collaborated with the Castro government and subsequently of having extended the reach of Castro's authority. Thus, when Cuban exiles later compared the loss of Elián to the terrorist attacks of September 11, 2001, as some did, the language of catastrophe was dramatic but not insincere.[30] The betrayal for the Cuban exile community amounted to a symbolic castration. It revealed the impossibility of its imagined self; its phallicity as the "true Cuba" had been uncloaked as a fiction.

What remains underarticulated in the narrative logic of this version of the Elián case, is that Elián himself had turned traitor. In other words, Elián's transformation from savior to a desiring other has remained, for the most part, undiscussed by both Cuban American leadership and mainstream American observers. The child's father, Juan González, was consistently portrayed as a handmaiden to Castro.[31] For this reason, the child, who in his reunion was smiling and affectionate with his father, became a "deserter" of Cuban Americans. The child's happy return to his "home" thus played an important ideological function for politically committed leftist scholars and activists who have long been unable to tolerate much criticism of the Revolutionary government. For leftists long enamored with the "New Man" ideal of the Revolution, identified with Castro and, perhaps to an even greater extent, with the late Ernesto "Che" Guevara, the desire for a socialist democracy requires an impassioned fervor that mirrors the intensity and structure of Cuban diasporic nationalism.[32] As Irving Horowitz writes:

> To this day, Castro esteems the purity of self-sacrifice, almost (but not quite) to the point of the Christian notion of sainthood. The party cadre may not always be sanctified, since sometimes they are called upon to engage in violent acts. But in their devotion to party, state, and nation, the Communist Party member is the apotheosis of what the Cuban society as a whole was to become under socialism. Cuba was to be the showpiece for the hemisphere and ultimately for all of the developing world. Indeed, many claims to leadership in the Third World came to rest on this quite special concept of moral man.[33]

Elián's return marked a triumph for both Communist Cuba and sympathetic leftists. In the David and Goliath story of Revolutionary Cuba and its tenacity against international hostilities, spearheaded by U.S. foreign policy, the restoration of Elián to the island provided a key victory for the Castro government.[34] Thirty years of mass emigrations, including the

Freedom Flights of 1965–73, the Mariel Boatlift of 1980, and the *balseros* crisis in the summer of 1994 (when a record number of Cuban "rafters" sought to flee the economic fallout in Cuba after the collapse of the Soviet Union), had proved an embarrassment to the Revolutionary government. The jubilant return of Elián, as well as Juan González's complete lack of interest in defecting to the United States, signaled the continuing vitality of the dream of a socialist democracy. But, this particular leftist fantasy entails an idealization of Cuban state forms and of Castro as a political leader. Framed by the bilateralism of Cold War discourse, this idealist fantasy of Cuba permits no critique of abusive state practices.

Both the "vestigial Hegelianism in Cuban-in-exile ideology, and the spectralized Marxism persisting on the island," as Ricardo L. Ortíz has described the ongoing political conflict between the Castro government and Cuban Americans, enacted idealized fantasies of Cuba that made tolerable the historical juncture of Cold War modernity.[35] However, the case of Elián González was meaningful not only for Cuban nationalisms—whether anti- or pro-Castro—and their identification with an idealized Cuba. I believe that possibly the most long-term, resonant, and subtle significance of the case might very well have been for the self-image of America and the ideological ruptures it threatened to that self-image. The Elián case represented the Cuban nationalist's attempt to restore an imagined Cuba "here" rather than "there." Thus, at the same time, it obviated the American fantasy, which, ironically, is at once the Cuban dream, the dream of capitalist "freedom." The "betrayal of Elián" threatened to uncover the fiction of unified national formation, for *both* American and Cuban nationalisms, through the *antagonistic* relationship of the two nationalisms. It consequently laid bare a certain *intolerability* between these competing claims. The security of the American self-image, the ideal of the American dream, necessitated the disciplining of Cuban nationalism. For this reason, the state could justify its own dealings with its avowed Cold War foe at the expense of Cuban American interests, even though those latter interests seemed to accord more fully with the policy and political positions repeatedly adopted by the United States during the Cold War.

The alignment of sympathies in the Elián González case was organized by the Cuban American model minority status, which rests on the double, and what, in the end we can see as the contradictory, qualities that Palumbo-Liu describes: the domestic versus the international *and* the traditional versus the modernist. Cubans were model minorities because of the fact that they were exiles, because they held Castro's

Cuba in contempt and found salvation in America, *and* because of an ethic of hard work, God, and the family. As a model minority, the Cuban exile reflected back to the generic American subject its own idealized construction, its own impossible desire that it resolves through the model minority. The model minority offered a fetish by which America convinced itself that the Cuban was fully American, and that neither suffered any kind of lack. On the other hand and at the same time, the model minority was a diasporic group of exiles always looking to a return, for whom American democratic capitalism was (only) a proxy for Cuban democratic capitalism.[36] In other words, as Palumbo-Liu makes clear, model minority status is not only founded on these contradictions, but also evokes a strong ambivalence on the part of the nation in response to them.

If the Cuban exiles and their Republican supporters saw Elián's residency in the United States as a triumph of modern democracy—best demonstrated in Senator Connie Mack's introduction of a bill to grant Elián citizenship—they ran up against the other premise of model Americanness, that the private sphere of the family is off-limits to the state, except to protect its integrity and sanctity.[37] There was no way to predict beforehand that in this showdown the traditional would trump the modernist, the rights of the family would subsume those of the individual. But central to this reversal of fortune was the national desire on the part of Americans for Cubans to "give up the ghost," as it were— to kill off the specter of Communism, of Cuba, and thus ultimately, of diasporic desire. The Cold War narrative of national formation needed the Cuban to function as a model minority, to play the part of the displaced exile raging against the ills of Communist authoritarianism. However, in the New World Order, the Cuban American model minority not only became unnecessary, but the exile proved disruptive to the reimagining of the national self under globalization.

Many outsiders accordingly trivialized the Cuban community's preoccupation with Castro and Communist Cuba as an outdated preoccupation on the part of an exile community, what one writer described as the "Cold Spat" between "Cuba and Cuba," two "palmy, balmy banana republics" who trafficked in "active discontent."[38] From this perspective, the Cuban community was finally called to account, forced to forego its "banana republic" political modes and live within the laws of the nation. As a result, Anglo-Americans and black Americans both found Cubans insufficiently loyal to the United States, as was demonstrated in the opinions of black and white non-Latinos who strongly favored

González's return to Cuba, a consensus widely divergent from the wishes of the majority of Cuban Americans.[39] In fact, as polls demonstrated, as a group, black Americans favored even more strongly than whites the child's return to Cuba, and objected more strongly to the rhetoric used by Miami-Dade County mayor Alex Penelas suggesting that he would refuse to uphold the law if the federal government attempted to forcibly remove Elián.[40] There would be little forging of cross-racial alliances in this case, because the diasporic desire it unleashed overdetermined the local economic and political hierarchies already in place in South Florida. Americans, black and white, found this situation intolerable. As an editor at the *Miami Herald* observed, "Every single argument about why Elián should stay begins and ends with Fidel Castro. . . . There is no sympathy and not much empathy for that position."[41]

It seems telling, then, that in the aftermath of the decision to return Elián, the impact of the case on the Cuban American community was described in terms of the group's tarnished *image*: "The Elián Gonzalez custody struggle united and invigorated anti-Castro Cuban exiles in Miami, but their campaign to keep the boy in this country hurt their image and may have helped those who favor easing the U.S. economic embargo on Cuba."[42] In particular, the "anti-patriotic actions" of Cuban protestors were objects of negative attention. José Cárdenas, then the head of the Cuban American National Foundation, put it even more bluntly when he explained, "I think that the American people sort of began to resent it being forced into their living rooms every night. . . . They just wanted all those shouting people out of their living room."[43] The impassioned demands of Cuban American protestors that Cárdenas describes, I suggest, reflected not just a defective image *of* Cuban Americans *to* non-Latinos in the United States. Rather, because of the fetishistic role performed by the Cuban American model minority, what the American subject wanted banished most of all was this noisy confrontation with alienation, loss, and otherness, a seemingly uncontainable diasporic desire that betrayed the American dream.

The Betrayal of Wen Ho Lee: Disavowing Diasporic Desire

Critics derided Cuban American inability to build alliances with other minority racial and ethnic groups in their protests over Elián's plight. In Lee's case, such alliances proved crucial, but they depended, as I argue here, upon a domestically contained discourse of civil rights against charges of diasporic and national difference. Similar alliances probably could never have been forged in the Cuban situation, precisely because passionate Cuban American protest threatened to break out of the national frame of minority discourse. In both cases, the Republican Party seemed to come out the loser, as its support of Cuban exile politics and Asian-baiting eventually fell flat before a larger American public. But an ethical critique of the Wen Ho Lee case—and the mode by which model Americanness was secured there—reconsiders the political implications of these conclusions.

The protest on the part of Lee's advocates, it seems to me, *forecloses* the *possibility* of diaspora: that one might act on an enduring desire for *some time* and *somewhere other* than the self-presence, the here and now, that the nation demands. Because Cuban Americans not only stoked and kept alive the disruptive desire of diasporic longing for national return, but paraded it on the streets and broadcast it to the entire country, the state had to discipline it, even at the risk of betraying the nation's claim to democratic exceptionalism. The nation could not countenance this diasporic desire rooted in the trauma of exile. In contrast, Lee's advocates seemed to assert that one *only* rouses oneself to political passion in order to *dispel* any hint of diasporic desire and to prove one's loyalty to the nation. The *content* of desire, then, ultimately matters much less to understanding either case than does the *structure* of a belonging that does not reflect the nation's image back to itself but is instead aimed at some other time and place.

As numerous observers were quick to point out, it made little sense that Lee, a Taiwanese-born Chinese immigrant, would spy for the PRC, especially out of any ideological commitment. In response, federal agents took recourse in the neo-Confucianism that they attributed to "Operation Kindred Spirit," as the investigation into Lee's "Chinese connection" was named. The government argued that, rather than depending on any loyalty to the Communist state, the PRC regularly played upon a more deeply rooted sense of "Chineseness" to recruit overseas Chinese as intelligence agents, an appeal that, according to federal agents, might have found its mark in Lee. The FBI saw the PRC's hospitable treatment of Lee and his wife on their visits to China as "standard PRC intelligence tradecraft," to "encourage Chinese living abroad to visit ancestral villages and family members as a way of trying to dilute loyalty and encouraging solidarity with the authorities in Beijing."[44] How does this cultural politics structure diasporic desire? In asking this, I am not positing an inherent form of true Chineseness. Rather, I take it as a performative content for a diasporic existence that cannot be reconciled to the demands of loyalty by the United States. The narrative production of Wen Ho Lee, I suggest, covered over the possibility of alternative structures of belonging, thus bolstering a narrow conception of social formation with a totalizing vision of Americanization.

Alberta Lee's role in the protests emblematized the model minoritarian—and, I should add, quite successful—mode of political action. Her presence figured the moral sentimentality necessarily attributed to Lee's victimhood: "She became the human figure in the story, the alter ego of her dad, who was silent behind bars. The news media needed her to bring life to their stories, and she was willing."[45] As her father's "human" face, Alberta secured a sense of his innocence by projecting her own political innocence. She had no *desire* to assume the role of the outspoken, disagreeable minoritarian subject. In fact, she claimed an ignorance of the legal and cultural histories of racial exclusion in the United States, an ignorance that had been ruptured not by any willfulness on her or her father's part, but in the failure of the state. As the national other, the Lees' *only desire* was to fulfill the desire that American subjects have for them.

As he has been popularly imagined, Wen Ho Lee fulfilled this role as redeemer rather successfully. His betrayal was followed by redemption not only of himself, but of the entire minority collective that saw itself embodied in his plight—and, because of the broad appeal of the discourse of racial profiling, this extended well beyond Asian Americans to people of color from other racial and ethnic groups. If Elián atomized Cubans from other Americans, Lee's case symbolically articulated the concerns of a broad range of minority subjects. Yet, if we take seriously the other interpretive possibility, grounded in a haunting "what if," Lee also threatened a much broader range of peoples "duped" into good-faith advocacy by an agent whose desires were not their own. I am not arguing that Lee was actually a spy, but rather, calling attention to the structural possibility of such a critical truth. Certain questions plagued the narrative of scapegoated victim. As a former counterintelligence officer, whom I quote here at length, argued:

> Lee's guilty plea to a single count of mishandling national security information means that there will be no dramatic day in court to judge what really happened. However, under the terms of his deal with the government, he must explain his conduct to FBI debriefers, and those explanations will be put to the test of the polygraph. Some of the questions that most certainly will be posed are:

Why did you transfer 410,000 pages of sensitive information from the classified directory of your computer to the unclassified directory? This deliberate effort required you to defeat multiple security mechanisms in the Los Alamos system.

Why did you copy this information to tapes, and later make copies of these tapes? What did you do with these tapes?

What legitimate work purpose did you fulfill by making these tapes? The data on these tapes represented the most sensitive information in the Los Alamos computer system. Your colleagues and superiors affirm that your particular job did not require you to aggregate and use such files.

After you were barred in late December 1998 from entering the "X Division" secure offices, why did you make 18 attempts to enter this area, including one attempt at 3:30 a.m. on Christmas Eve?

Why, between Jan. 20 and Feb. 10, 2000, when the FBI was interviewing and polygraphing you, did you bypass security mechanisms to electronically access your secure computer in the "X Division" and delete hundreds of classified files that you had previously declassified and moved into the computer's unclassified directory?

During an FBI-administered polygraph examination, why did the results indicate deception when you were asked (1) "Have you ever given codes to unauthorized persons?" and (2) "Have you ever given W-88 (warhead) information to unauthorized persons?"

Have you ever provided classified nuclear weapons information to an unauthorized party?

If, as you have contended, your file transfers, downloading and other risky security practices were common to many of your co-workers, why is it that FBI investigators failed to locate a single other employee in your work area who had engaged in such actions? Who are these co-workers?

Please explain why the search of your office and home resulted in the recovery of classified documents that you had "declassified" by either cutting off the classification markings or by masking the classification markings before making copies of them.[46]

Some of Lee's advocates hedged on the question of Lee's innocence, especially prior to the plea bargain agreement, arguing that they were primarily calling for due process and a fair trial. Of course, this was not the case for his daughter, nor for Cecilia Chang, a long-time friend of Lee's who started up the Wen Ho Lee Defense Fund, for whom the personal ties of friendship and family meant that loyalty could only be made manifest by insisting on Lee's innocence.

And, insofar as they argued against the racial stereotype of the treacherous Asian alien, Asian American activists precluded the possibility of Lee's guilt as well. Lee's culpability would have been devastating to the Asian American community, even for those who were less closely associated with Lee than Alberta Lee or Cecilia Chang but who had invested so much significance in Lee's status as *scapegoated American*, a good citizen whose *only* crime was his Asian birth.[47] In this vein, Lee's advocates delimited his acts to ones of carelessness, not espionage or treason. If Lee had in fact provided the PRC with the computer codes, the scapegoat defense would have been rendered moot.[48]

The fact that Lee's defense team, after his release from jail, managed to have certain documents remain sealed, in spite of demands by Asian American activists who wanted all evidence of racial profiling in Energy Department investigations to be made public, is telling. Moreover, those documents that were unsealed revealed that Lee had actually made many more copies of the tapes than had been previously known. According to the documents, both Lee's attorneys and prosecution lawyers learned of the existence of these tapes after negotiations were drawing near a close, and the revelation almost entirely undermined the plea bargain agreement itself.[49] Relatively little consideration was given to these incidents by both the media and Asian American activists. In calling attention to these matters, and in more generally hypothesizing that Lee was a spy (and I stress, I am *only hypothesizing*), I am not suggesting that there is necessarily some evidence damning to Lee in those documents.[50] Indeed, Lee has addressed many of the questions concerning his violation of security measures and downloading of sensitive materials at LANL, although there remains disagreement as to how satisfactory his explanations are.[51] Rather, I am explicating how, as a symbolic body, Lee secured an idealized fantasy that Asian Americans, and minority Americans more generally, needed to uphold their image of themselves as fully deserving of citizenship rights and trust. This imaginative production of Lee left no space for other desires, for desires that did not reflect back to the minority subject (and the American public at large) an idealized image of itself.

The banality of *professional* desire, the explanation that Lee downloaded the files as part of a job search to make himself a more attractive candidate, "a kind of immigrant striver with an international portfolio—a job seeker rather than a spy," in the end rationalized his actions and put to rest most of the troubling questions of his case.[52] It also defused the possibility of the more insidious or explosive Cold War narrative of diasporic desire, largely because it did not necessarily run into irreconcilable contradictions with the nationalist narrative. As many commentators at the time observed, the stories surrounding Lee's arrest and also the politics of the Republican-backed Cox Report itself, which precipitated the investigation of Lee in the first place, depicted a cloak-and-dagger world of espionage and intrigue, worthy of, as one diplomat suggested, the spy novels of John Le Carré.[53] Prosecutors argued that Lee should be denied bail because he had information "so valuable that a hostile nation could conceivably plan a Ninja-style commando raid and airlift him out of the country," and that the data and codes were sensitive enough to "upset the 'global strategic balance.'" This narrative played uneasily alongside transnationalist trends that sought to curry favor with the PRC. But rather than settling the issue, I contend, this tension raises even more questions regarding the ethics of political and legal action in the Lee case.

The question of professional desire received attention, for the most part, indirectly, with respect to the impact of the case on the position of Asian Americans in the nuclear labs, and in the sciences more broadly. Yet, the Lee case potentially revealed as much about professional allegiances and conventions of belonging and exclusion as it did about race and nation. It exposed the extent to which the daily life of nuclear weapons labs involved antagonisms between state demands for secrecy and those for open inquiry and exchange by the scientific community. In fact, Wen Ho Lee's defense team was able to procure the key expert witness, John Richter, to testify that the data Lee was accused of stealing was not as sensitive as the prosecution had portrayed, precisely because of these tensions. Richter saw his participation as an attempt to rein in the actions of federal agents, who he felt had long acted like "thugs" toward scientists.[54]

Thus, putting questions of espionage aside altogether, Lee's betrayal could be said to have definitively occurred at this other level, the level of the "priesthood" of nuclear scientists, centered in the close-knit world of Los Alamos. That is, he broke the "fundamental trust" that underlies the world of nuclear weapons research by revealing the laxity of security arrangements at LANL and eroding the nation's confidence in its security. The kinds of security measures—for example, polygraphs of the lab scientists—that had been unnecessary under the "sacred trust" of the profession, were now justified. Lee's "downpartitioning" of the classified codes from classified to unclassified directories was therefore a "mortal sin," regardless of his motives, against the normative assumptions of the vocation.[55] In testifying for the defense, Richter aligned himself with Lee, but Lee's own actions threw the sense of professional trust *between* scientists into disarray. Many of Lee's colleagues and friends from the scientific community thus found both Lee's actions *and* the government's tactics in the bail hearing to be highly troubling.[56]

Lee's case also revealed a tightly spun web between the professional production of knowledge and the legal and military conventions of national formation. The indictment of Lee relied heavily on the Atomic Energy Act of 1946, under which an entire body of knowledge was classified, named at its very origin as secret and its security as in the supreme national interest. Under the terms of this law, not only the disclosure but even the "mishandling" of nuclear secrets constituted crimes with serious penalties, including life imprisonment.[57] As Virginia Carmichael explains:

> Crucial to the development of the cold war ... were the ways in which the cluster of ideas around that of atomic warfare was manipulated and imaginatively displaced, through mobilization of fears and anxieties, into ideas of ownership, secrecy, and defensive aggression.... The idea of national security was certainly not new, but with the development and use of electronic technology and atomic weapons it had become a qualitatively different idea. Even more than other ideas, that of national security was actively driven by its opposites: breach, espionage, betrayal, treason, aggression, take-over, overthrow, revolution.[58]

The scientist-spy embodied the dual meaning of "intelligence" in a Cold War world. The CIA often recruited foreign students in the sciences as spies, waiting for them to return home and move through their professional ranks until they had access to sensitive information to remit as intelligence.[59] Moreover, in 1987, the Department of Energy created its own counterintelligence organizations, which promoted exchanges between foreign and American scientists, favoring collection of intelligence in this manner (often to the chagrin of other federal agencies like the FBI).[60] The use of this type of open "scientific intelligence" had become such a routine matter that it was known as ASKINT; "ask intelligence" derived information from open visits, conversations, and observations between

U. S. and foreign scientists. In the case of China, much of this information was made available by PRC officials themselves in order to deliver a political message to the United States about Chinese capabilities.[61]

Thus, despite any claims by the profession that scientific knowledge is politically or ethically neutral, from the very beginnings of the national security state and the military-industrial complex at the end of World War II, through its full-scale operation beginning in the late 1950s after the decline of McCarthyist anti-Communism, and until the fall of the Eastern Bloc in the early 1990s, scientific knowledge not only played a key role in the production of Cold War bilateralism, but was the very discursive and material universe that constituted it.[62] It was repeatedly lamented that U. S. national security had long depended upon attracting "the best brains the world has to offer us," and that a waning in the number of Asian American scientists applying for appointments at nuclear labs would have a long-term impact on U. S. military dominance. Anxiety over the state of the security and the future of nuclear research further increased when the Association for Asian American Studies and Asian Pacific Americans in Higher Education endorsed a call by Ling-Chi Wang, the chair of the ethnic studies department at the University of California–Berkeley, for Asian Americans to boycott federal labs.

This discourse, especially when adopted by Asian Americans themselves, was firmly rooted in the model minority image and the fantasy of the American dream it secured. For example, Xiao-huang Yin, chair of the American Studies program at Occidental College, wrote in the *Los Angeles Times*:

> To many aspiring Asian Americans, particularly immigrants, a career as a research scientist means guaranteed freedom and employment security, awe-inspiring enough to symbolize the realization of their American Dreams. It is no accident, then, that Asian American contributions to science have been singular. There have been six Chinese American Nobel Laureates, five in physics and one in chemistry. As they earn distinction in science, Asian Americans are lauded by the mass media as the latest success story of the American Dream. In fact, it is mainly their accomplishments in science and academe that have made Asians the "model minority" in U. S. society.[63]

In explaining his own role as a member of the "nuclear brotherhood," Lee invokes the political neutrality that science affords him, stating, "I had never had much interest in politics.... I stuck to science and math, which are much more fascinating to me and have a clear benefit to humanity. They are also far less volatile than politics."[64] But he also portrays himself as a good citizen: "My research on the numerical modeling of nuclear reactors and reactions has been used in many countries, and I was proud that my work contributed to America's safety and to global nuclear security. I ... took [my research] very seriously—if I didn't do my job well, the consequences could be dire."[65] The decrease in applications by persons of Asian descent to national defense laboratories after Lee's termination and indictment only further highlighted the fact that Asian Americans have long been key participants in the construction of national security.

The good faith of Asian American activists' efforts notwithstanding, the fight to clear Wen Ho Lee's name comprised a struggle to clear the road for a person of color to participate in the development of weapons of mass destruction and the ongoing military and economic hegemony of the United States on the global stage.[66] This is a critical truth that might be so obvious that it would not need arguing, if it were not so readily elided by the entrenched domestic boundaries of civil rights discourse, through which legal and political critics examined the Wen Ho Lee case. I am not dismissing the veracity of racial profiling as one of the most potent technologies for the surveillance and disenfranchisement of people of color, nor faulting those who have insisted upon juridical and legal redress in this arena. However, I am arguing that we must also begin accounting for the *other* stakes, which include the *others of the nation-state*, in our political modes of minority representation, without which we will fail to understand the heavy ethical weight of the cultural politics we engage.

The "betrayals" of Wen Ho Lee and Elián González foreclosed the possibility of the desiring other in order to secure a developmental narrative about global relations under the American New World Order. But if the symbolization of Lee and González reduced them to the demands of Americanization, this does not mean that their narratives offer no openings or avenues for an ethics of betrayal. If in these narratives the diasporic desires of the other had to be barred in favor of the nationalist subject, the readings I have been forwarding here direct us to a different subject who cannot be reduced to the demands of the American imaginary. As I detail in my next and final section, when we read the cases of Elián González and Wen Ho Lee as screening a developmental narrative about the United States under the New World Order, there emerges at its margins the shadowy figure of the subject of human rights who haunts this nationalist narrative of citizenship and civil rights.

Hearing the Subject of Human Rights

One of the strongest arguments made by liberals seeking to end the trade embargo on Cuba has been that the United States long ago opened up lines of political and economic exchange with Communist China, and had more recently granted the PRC "most-favored-nation" (or nondiscriminatory trade) status, suggesting anti-Communist tactics are an anachronistic holdover from the Cold War and irrelevant to the New World Order. This position gained even more popular support, as I have explained above, after the Elián González case, as Cuban exiles risked their position of idealized model Americanness. The political and economic incentives for this rhetoric are certainly apparent. U.S. corporations and U.S.-based multinationals see in Cuba a fertile ground for market enterprise and profit development, and neoliberals believe that democratic reforms will follow the penetration of global capital.

At the same time, Wen Ho Lee's supporters were quick to denounce the state's actions by employing a particular analogy that depended upon a rigid distinction between the First and Third World. As one member of the Committee of 100, an Asian American advocacy group, stated, "The behavior of the U.S. government's in conduct [sic] in the [Wen Ho Lee] case is no better, I repeat no better, than the behavior of third world dictatorships that the U.S. is wont to criticize."[67] This comparison was meant to tease out the unintended irony of Lee's case in order to chastise the state for seemingly discriminatory behavior. However, its very familiar premise, the mutual exclusivity of First World democratic liberalism and Third World repressive authoritarianism, short-circuits a more radical critique of the mutually invested and mutually contaminated formation of the First and Third Worlds under global capitalism.

What does the ethico-political analysis of the Wen Ho Lee and Elián González cases intimate about such liberal discourse, which maintains rigid distinctions between the First World and Third World, civil and human rights? Wendy Brown proposes that "the political potency of rights lies not in their concreteness . . . but in their idealism, in their ideal configuration of an egalitarian social, an ideal that is contradicted by substantive social inequalities."[68] As such, "the democratic *value* of political emancipation lies partly in its revelation of the *limits* of political emancipation."[69] In this respect, I wish to consider in this section how the civil (or "first-generation") rights so crucial to the American imaginary are extracted from the subject of human (including "second-generation" and "third-generation") rights more broadly conceived on a globalized terrain.

This kind of reading elucidates, as Pheng Cheah describes it, the mutual contamination of the many "worlds" of global capitalism, rather than construing this globalized terrain as an uncontaminated universe free of the "historicity of history."[70] In an idealist universe, the ethical subject finds itself trapped in a zero-sum game that cannot countenance competing claims to rights *as equally valid*. In other words, in such a universe, the legitimacy of the claims of one side necessarily dissolves those of the other; one has rights by "being right," and not because of the particular contingencies that constitute material history.[71] However, in an ethical framework of rights, as Cheah adopts from Jacques Derrida's model of deconstructive justice, there is no horizon of justice smoothly and evenly crossed over all at once and once and for all. Rather, justice is an "avenue" and an "arrival" that keeps its own time and that is produced *in* the very texture of historical contingency, rather than abstracted out and away from it. Cheah further elaborates on Derrida's conception of justice in order to provide an alternate model of human rights discourse from the ones conventionally available to us. Rather than imagining human rights as a transcendent, natural property, Cheah contends, we must understand them as "violent gifts" at once bestowed and compromised by the material-historical structure of global capitalism. As Cheah observes, Hegel describes international relations as "a maelstrom of external contingency and the inner particularity of passions, private interests and selfish ends, abilities and virtues, vices, force, and wrong" that threaten to "expose" the ethical whole and its claim to universality.[72] Likewise, most contemporary discussions of universal human rights focus on what Susan Koshy calls the "mythical opposition" between cultural relativism, especially as it has been espoused or attributed to the former colonial nations of Asia and Africa, and the universalism associated with Western liberal democracies.[73]

For Cheah, however, the historicity of human rights ideals provides them with their disruptive, normative force. The "normative force" of human rights provides a way out of the theoretical bind between the "realist cynicism" attributed to relativism and the rational universality demanded of a conception of "human dignity" free from the incursions of economic or political interests.[74] Rights will never be able to transcend their own contamination by global capital, "for the very constitution of a subject entitled to rights involves the violent capture of the disfranchised by an institutional discourse that inseverably weaves them into the textile of global capitalism."[75] The resulting universality that global capital produces is real and unequal, one that "caricatures" the ideal universality of first-generation/First World human rights discourse. As Cheah concludes: "Rights are thus not, in the original instance, entitlements of intersubjectively constituted rational social agents but violent gifts, the necessary nexi within immanent global force relations that produce the identities of its claimants. Yet rights are the only way for the disfranchised to mobilize."[76] Extraction from this contamination, an extraction that attempts to get to the "pure" subject of rights and dignity in order to articulate "an exhaustively universal vision of human rights," is constitutively impossible.

Nevertheless, this impossibility does not dismantle the project of human rights: "My point is that an irreducible-because-systemic contamination occurs in the very court of claims in which the voice of the oppressed can be heard, although it is in this court alone that justice can be done and we cannot *not* want this justice-in-violation."[77] Thus, rather than reducing the contingency of human rights to the straightjacket of historical determinism, Cheah names it as the possibility of radical alterity that is "original to and constitutive of historical actuality." We do not choose human rights as rational agents, nor does capitalism not choose rights. Instead, the historical relations of global capitalism produce us as "finite historical actors" who can envision change through the normative force and effectivity that human rights present. While the different voices of human rights discourse all prove complicit in various forms of violation, "the line of force that joins them together in the service of the global capitalist economy can also mutate to separate their interests and pit them against each other and against capitalism."[78] An ethico-political agency that envisions change therefore must harness the unpredictable ambulation of rights discourse on a global terrain.

What does this mean for a political critique of communist, communitarian, and capitalist states under the New World Order? The discursive structure of liberal rhetoric that frames U.S. foreign policy on Cuba and China dehistoricizes human rights, particularly by limiting their accountability to the question of civil rights under global capitalism, in order to secure the national imaginary of the American citizen. In contrast, the ethical subject of betrayal cannot claim its own "right to be" in a space ideologically uncontaminated by the political and economic imperatives of global capitalism, nor can it idealize Cuba and the PRC as "outsiders" to global capital. From this perspective, then, Cuba and the PRC stand as ghostly remainders of the Second World of the Eastern Bloc, whose undoing marked the founding of the New World Order. At the same time, however, both Cuba and the PRC share the material conditions and colonial histories that characterize the Third World as well. Straddling the (now disintegrated) Second World and the Third World, China and Cuba figure, not as anachronisms, but instead as singular examples. They instantiate the modernities and postmodernities of global capital in stark contrast to the idealized ethos of liberal democracy under the New World Order. In the global arena of human rights discourse, especially since the demise of the Soviet Union, human rights have become increasingly identified with civil and political rights, described as "first-generation rights," associated with the liberal democracies of the French and American revolutions. This narrowing of the definition of human rights functions to the exclusion of the "second-generation rights"—of social and economic entitlements—rooted in socialist revolutions, and "third-generation" or solidarity rights, such as a right to development, that originate in anticolonial movements. The "belated" entrance of China and Cuba, as remnants of the Second World into the New World Order, ruptures the American imaginary in which human rights mean first-generation rights and which assumes their security as a fait accompli in the West.[79]

The subjects of civil rights abuses in Cuba and the PRC—those severed from due process, freedom of speech, free press, freedom of assembly, and subject to cruel and unusual punishment, torture, and political repression in each of these nations—do not inhabit a space outside of liberal democracy and global capitalism. Rather, they bear witness to the violent historicity of "existing ideals and norms," a witness that betrays the universal promise of liberal democracy. The subject of civil rights abuses in Cuba makes her claims within the historical texture of the ongoing Cuban Revolution and *its* claims for the Cuban people to social and economic rights and the right to development *against* imperialist intervention. This contradiction throws into relief the aggressively expansionist grounds of "American freedom."[80] In other words, the claims of Cuba for self-determination and collective rights are not idle alibis to be easily dismissed; the neoliberal discourse of human rights makes all too clear that the "freedom" of Cuban people touted in the United States is at once the rendering of the nation into a comprador state. Likewise, as Chow writes of the image of China projected onto the world screen after the 1989 Tiananmen massacre:

> As the champion of the unprivileged classes and nations of the world, Communist China has shown itself to be a failure, a failure that is now hanging on by empty official rhetoric while its people choose to live in ways that have obviously departed from the Communist ideal.... The apparent absence of the [foreign] "enemy" as such does not make the Chinese case any less third world in terms of the exploitation suffered by the people, whose most important colonizer remains their own government.[81]

China thus also offers an example of the grounds contaminated by the histories of colonialism and neo-imperialism, on and through which a discourse of rights comes into being. The figurative "departure from the Communist ideal" that Chow describes with reference to the Chinese also finds a material body in Cuban emigrants, whose experience provides the context for the González case.[82]

Thus, to take China and Cuba as objects of critique is not so much a question of denouncing Communism, in either of these sites or elsewhere, but rather to account for the political, economic, and cultural revolutions there as "necessary events of a positive present of which we, living in the other half of the globe in 'capitalistic freedom,' are still a functioning part."[83] As ghostly remainders in the New World Order, China and Cuba make visible the West's continued sense of a "coming threat" that Marxism has posed and continues to pose. In surveying the post–Cold War, neoliberal triumphalism that declares Communism to be dead and gone, Derrida discerns that the *possibility* of a return, which must continually be denied and conjured away, haunts the West. The specter, of which Marx wrote in 1848 in "The Communist Manifesto," was one of a "coming threat." At the end of the twentieth century, it "would represent a threat that some would like to believe is past and whose return it would be necessary again, once again in the future to conjure away."[84] The coming and going of the specters, Derrida surmises, are passages that cannot be made to heel to a linear narrative of historical progression. After all, if capitalist societies must not only declare Communism dead and buried, but must also deny its having taken place at all by insisting that it "was only a ghost," they fail to perceive that "a ghost never dies, it remains always to come and to come-back."[85] China and Cuba, as specters of Communism, evince this "hauntology" by offering the embodied presence of those others who lived the "hot wars" of the twentieth century, fought in Asia, Latin America, the Caribbean, Eastern Europe, and Africa. Only through the tremendous violence done unto the others of the hot wars, was the Cold War administered in the interests of *its* subjects in the United States and the USSR. If global capitalism "is not a totality but a textual network," as Cheah argues, these sites embody what Aiwha Ong describes as an "alternative modernity" that exists in simultaneity with the modernity of the Western nation-state and (post)modernity of transnationalism.[86]

The narrative production of Elián González and Wen Ho Lee attempted to cover over the uneven and shifting modalities of historical agency so as to secure the integration of national and transnational imaginaries centered in the United States. But the diasporic desires that were feared and foreclosed in these national others can shift our attention to the material and historical terrains inhabited by the subject of human rights, a subject who otherwise cannot be made self-present in the American imaginary. The individual freedoms granted to American citizens in the late twentieth century were extracted from the violent discipline of those caught in the "textile of global capitalism," a worldwide order that the United States arrogates through military and economic aggression. For this reason, the ethics of betrayal compels us to risk shifting our attention to the imagined spaces toward which the others of the nation-state lead us, spaces where the discourse of civil or first-generation rights will not suffice in meeting the demands articulated there.

Epilogue: The Traitors in Our Midst

The brevity of the appellation (September 11, 9/11) stems not only from an economic or rhetorical necessity. The telegram of this metonymy—a name, a number—points out the unqualifiable by recognizing that we do not recognize or even cognize, that we do not yet know how to qualify, that we do not know what we are talking about.
—JACQUES DERRIDA, "AUTOIMMUNITY"

I am a patriotic, loyal American. I am not a terrorist, nor am I spy.
—JAMES YEE, FOR GOD AND COUNTRY

After the attacks on the World Trade Center and the Pentagon on September 11, 2001, the question of betrayal seemed to take on an immediacy and urgency that would have been difficult to imagine when I first began writing *An Ethics of Betrayal*. And yet, it remains difficult to know *what* exactly happened on September 11. For every narrative that marks 9/11 as a singular event irreducible to anything in the nation's—or the world's—past, there are reminders that the state of emergency it supposedly inaugurated is "more of the same" for both people of color in the United States and for colonial and postcolonial subjects elsewhere. For every suggestion that American citizens would now have to face up to the complex ecologies of international politics, there was boasting assurance (trumpeted first and foremost by the Bush-Cheney administration) that Americans would not have to give up their "way of life." And for every suggestion that there was no justification for the massive loss of life that took place on September 11, there were the historical recountings, albeit muted in mainstream discourse, that cast the attacks (not to mention the political conditions in Afghanistan and Iraq) as chickens coming home to roost or, perhaps more poetically, the specters of U.S. Cold War and neo-imperialist machinations around the world returning with a fury.

But, even if we remain unable to read the "telegram," as Jacques Derrida calls it, of September 11, in the intervening months and years, the nation has of course gone on. It has survived, and even, we might daresay, reconciled itself to September 11, by churning out its discourse of retribution and war. Precisely because the war on terror that September 11 inaugurated marshaled the lexicon of loyalty, betrayal, responsibility, and faith in potent and spectacular forms, the ethical inquiry that I have described in the preceding chapters remains crucial in the political projects of minority discourse. This, even as the ethical subject of that discourse can never apprehend the conditions of September 11 in their totality. The minority subject's own "taking-place" has been implicated in the occurrence of the event, and induces us to stop being, in Rosalind Morris's words, "shocked," and leads us instead to be "disillusioned" with the idealized forms of innocent sovereignty that citizenship promises.[1] Through an ethics of betrayal, we might recast the possibilities for responsibility and freedom or agency in ways that seek to do justice to all the "victims" of September 11: those who died in New York, Virginia, and Pennsylvania; those victims of hate crimes in the U.S. after the attacks; those detainees suspected of terrorist activities in the U.S.; those Afghani and Iraqi citizens killed in U.S. wars of retribution and "liberation"; those U.S. troops from minority and working-class or impoverished backgrounds who find themselves in the military because it offered a promise of economic and professional security and mobility unavailable to them in other sectors of the U.S. workforce; those "enemy combatants," held in places like Guantánamo Bay and Abu Ghraib, subject to illegitimate standards of detention; and those countless others whose very presence cannot be registered within the American imaginary.

An ethics of betrayal will necessarily fail these victims of September 11, even as it tries to account for the singularity of each loss. It will fail because the claims of each of these others are absolute and irrefutable. And it will fail because the claim of each other will contradict the claims of every other other. But an ethics of betrayal will also justify neither the political and military rhetoric of U.S. international policy nor that of Islamic fundamentalism. It cannot be satisfied with adequate representation as a model of justice, so neither of these discourses will suffice to understand what is at stake in the world after September 11. In this conclusion to *An Ethics of Betrayal*, then, I will briefly describe the reimagination of belonging and exclusion, according to the terms of victimhood and betrayal, which the emergence of a supranational discursive formation of "America" attempts to ensure. Articulating nation, diaspora, religion, and race in order to secure anew the nationalist subject's innocent and ideal sovereignty, this discursive formation rebounds upon the nation and its others in ways that are at once old and new. The ethical subject enters onto this emergent discursive terrain to imagine and encounter those "traitors in our midst" who supplement, antagonize, and threaten to undo an expansive, assimilative America.

Since September 11, the nation has become subject to the proliferation of terms that describe an "America" that is global in its reach and constitution—and that recognizes itself as such. The language of an "axis of evil" (which recalls but is not identical to the "evil empire" of the Cold War), of a "new Europe" and an "old Europe," and, more generally ubiquitous, of the "terrorist," all promulgate the discursive constitution of the New World Order. Certainly already emergent during the first Gulf War, the consolidation of this discourse has violently accelerated after September 11 and the implementation of the current war machine. The terrorist attacks of September 11 spectacularly put the nation on notice as to the fragmentation and flexibility of postmodernity, now readily embodied in the decentered, highly mobile transnational networks of people, capital, and technologies through which Al-Qaeda functions. The ongoing assumption of the narrative of the New World Order, that globalization is a unified process of Americanization, strives to ameliorate the trauma of that notice. An emergent supranational discourse therefore ironically posits itself as a principled defense of national sovereignty.[2] The violence that the United States enacts in the name of an "international community," the New World Order, or "America" (referring to something along the lines of what Tony Blair alluded to when he observed that "We are all Americans now") founds this global order and law.[3] The declared state of emergency announced by and through the war against terror suspends one international order so as to found a new one, violating specific articles of both constitutional and international law in order to protect them "as a whole" from "an alien system of legality."[4] As John Milbank surmises, because the perceived threat is to "sovereignty as such," "law in a state no longer applies."[5] The state of emergency that the war on terror announces therefore enacts what Derrida refers to as the "mystical foundation of authority," wherein law can claim no legitimacy beyond its own force.[6]

The supranational discourse of the state of emergency marks both a culmination and a transformation in the world-historical projects of Western empire and democracy.[7] The narrative of the New World Order—whose emergence began with the collapse of the Soviet Union and the fall of the Berlin Wall and continued through the first Gulf War into the war on terrorism and the invasion of Iraq—imagines a final "home" for history by liberating the world once and for all. The language of the Bush administration, of being "with us or against us," where to be against is to be part of the "old" (whether "old" is characterized as Islamic totalitarianism or as an "old Europe") relies upon the residual divisions of the Old and New Worlds of national sovereignty. At the same time, however, the New World Order witnesses the haunting of its "modernity" by its spectral others, by the alternative modernities it has enabled. The westward march, that is simultaneously the march of the West into the East (and the South), creates its own "hauntology" in the multitudes of others from the Americas, Africa, and Asia sacrificed in order to uphold the nation's idealized image of itself. September 11 marks the necessary return of these others displaced from democratic rights and governance.

The rhetoric of domestic or homeland security, in conjunction with a *global* war against terrorism, tries to have it all ways at once. The state attempts to uphold U.S. sovereignty while propelling the limitless expansion of American ideals—and global capital—as a transnational force and universal principle. However, we find fault lines in this strenuous effort to unify citizenship, national sovereignty, and colonial and diasporic formation in singular terms under the New World Order—for example, in the case of Maher Arar. Arar, a Canadian citizen of Syrian birth was detained at the John F. Kennedy International Airport in New York City by federal agents on September 26, 2002, because officials believed he might be connected to Al-Qaeda. Arar was "returned" by U.S. officials to his "homeland" Syria, where, he alleges, he was tortured for ten months. Released by the Syrian government without explanation on October 5, 2003, Arar seems to have been an object of "extraordinary rendition," the CIA's covert practice of turning over suspected terrorists to foreign agents in order to extract information through torture. At the time I write this, Arar's lawsuit against the United States has been dismissed by a federal court because, as the judge explained, the court was unable to review the decision by U.S. officials to send Arar to Syria, due to security and foreign relations concerns. Arar's case highlights the contradictions that homeland security, a global discourse of human rights and democracy, (post)colonial and diasporic histories, and religious and ethnic affiliation pose to one another. Arar, it would seem, embodies the subject of human rights whose claims literally cannot be heard in the American imaginary. But to say that such a subject exists outside the American imaginary does not mean that he or she does not live *within* the United States. Indeed, the accelerated consolidation of the New World Order promises to rebound upon Americans, both "generic" and minority, at "home" and abroad. In this vein, José Padilla, the Latino U.S. citizen and former gang member detained as an "enemy combatant," stands as a domestic counterpart to Arar. Padilla, suspected of having links to Al-Qaeda and plotting to manufacture a "dirty bomb," symbolizes the domestic counterpart to Arar *and* the intermediary between the racialized citizen and the terrorist alien, whose claims remain almost equally difficult to "hear."

If pre–civil rights nationalist discourse overtly equated racial otherness, foreignness, and criminality, based on naturalized assumptions consolidated through legal, scientific, and political knowledges, post-9/11 nationalist discourse sutures another version of this symbolic economy, but with a crucial difference. Because hegemonic liberal discourse promotes the transnational exporting of U.S. domestic civil rights, overt or explicit images and references to racial difference prove legitimately impossible. The terms of national belonging and exclusion constellate instead around formations of religious fundamentalism, cultural practice, terrorist politics, and embodied resistance to disciplinary regulation and surveillance. The invasive practices authorized by the USA PATRIOT Act to facilitate the surveillance of U.S. citizens have been accompanied by such military and intelligence "innovations" as extended detention without legal representation of those deemed "enemy combatants," the ready and publicized return of torture as a legitimate intelligence-gathering strategy, and secret military tribunals authorized by the Bush administration in November of 2001, in which any non–U.S. citizen can be tried and disciplined, including being subject to a death sentence penalty.

The state cannot simply return to the practices of racial profiling and moral panics that reigned throughout World War II and the Cold War, because the liberal discourses of civil rights pose a formidable object to such a straightforward recourse. Instead, with the institution of the USA PATRIOT Act at "home," and through the transnational penetration of American media, capital, and goods and a global war machine generating a rhetoric of global, democratic freedom, the state constitutes a new vocabulary for belonging and exclusion to speak to the psychic and social anxieties of the nation. Through the various social, legal, and military/police measures they employ, the nation and the state create the subjects and objects—the loyal citizens and the treasonous terrorists—of the New World Order, of an American imaginary stretched to its limits. And this discursive production of the national imaginary refracts upon those within the United States in ways that are also simultaneously familiar and innovative. America creates the (suspected) terrorist through a capacious rearticulation of crime and war, and the criminal and the foreign enemy, by drawing upon but also reworking conventional racial and national imagery. The popular and official discourses and the practices of the state in/of emergency reconstitute domestic juridical practice, law enforcement procedures, international military strategy, and immigration policy, producing the "suspected terrorist" as a subject of global geopolitics *and* as subject to domestic American surveillance and discipline.

It remains to be seen what the (im)possibilities for democracy and justice will be in the intersections, and contradictions, of this regenerated American imaginary. However, in offering a brief reading of one final work, I would like to suggest the urgent necessity of an ethics of betrayal in the political project of seeking justice for others after September 11. I turn here to James Yee's political memoir *For God and Country: Faith and Patriotism under Fire* (2005) as a parable of the emergent subjects of the war on terror—articulated in the supranational discourses of racial, national, and religious difference—and of the others to whom these subjects are held responsible. In *For God and Country*, Yee—a Chinese American convert to Islam who served as a Muslim chaplain at the Guantánamo Bay prison facility, Camp Delta—chronicles his tenure at "Gitmo," including the suspicion under which he labored there perceived to be "Chinese Taliban," and his arrest and detention in 2003 for mutiny and sedition, aiding the enemy, and espionage, charges which were subsequently dismissed.

A third-generation Chinese American, Yee describes himself as having grown up, in his mother's words, "terribly American." Besides a childhood almost entirely devoid of Chinese cultural practices, Yee describes his military education at the West Point Academy as "continuing a tradition of military service" that had begun with his father, who enlisted in the army soon after the end of World War II.[8] He portrays his decision to convert to Islam when a young adult as in keeping with his own belief in the nation's liberal promise to "all people, regardless of their circumstances" that they might "lead an extraordinary life"—indeed, often depicting Islam to be a simpler monotheism and more reasonable and tolerant faith than Christianity, with which Islam shares fundamental theological tenets.[9] When deployed to Saudi Arabia after Operation Desert Storm in 1991, Yee, who adopts as his Arabic name Yusuf, makes his first pilgrimage to Mecca, where he "was overwhelmed by the diversity of those traveling to the holy mosque": "My parents had instilled in me the importance of diversity, and I'd never seen anything as truly diverse as this."[10]

Later, after having returned to civilian life, Yee decides to study Islam and Arabic intensively in Damascus, and it is in Syria that he meets his wife, Huda. In Huda, Yee offers another figure of reconciliation between liberal modernism and Islamic faith, portraying her as a devout Muslim who at once "chooses" him: "Most people from the West assume that a woman in the Middle East is married off by her family, but that wasn't my experience. Though her family introduced us, it was just the beginning. Huda decided for herself who she wanted to marry, and she chose me."[11] Yee's depiction of his own decision to become an army chaplain then follows from this construction of an ideological rapprochement between Islam and liberal democracy. Yee negotiates the antipathy toward Islam that he encounters in the military by maintaining an exemplary professional demeanor through which he can insist on the compatibility of his patriotism and his religious faith. Indeed, after the September 11 attacks, he becomes "the U. S. military's poster child of a good Muslim—a devout chaplain who comfortably served both God and country."[12] He further emphasizes that two days before his arrest, he received the best officer evaluation report (a type of military job review) of his army career.[13] Throughout his memoir, then, Yee portrays himself as, in Mahmood Mamdani's terms, the "good Muslim" who adopts the U.S.'s self-image of fully achieved freedom and democracy.[14]

However, the narrative troubles this assimilative portrait of Yee by enumerating his increasing dismay at the conditions of life for detainees—the harsh physical environment, the violations of the Geneva Conventions of 1949 in the disciplinary and interrogation practices at Camp Delta, and the routine violation of detainee religious rights—that he encounters upon his relocation in 2002 to Guantánamo Bay. Yee comes to suspect that his position is a token one, not one established out of a "genuine desire to respect the prisoners' right to practice their faith," and that he occupied a contradictory role: "I was being asked to provide religious support to prisoners, but because they were 'enemy combatants' rather than criminal prisoners or even prisoners of war, their right to religious support didn't really exist."[15] Moreover, Yee details the disorganized state of the operating procedures at Camp Delta, as well as the interagency surveillance and mistrust that pervaded the soldiers' everyday life. Given that the unofficial slogan "Never pass up an opportunity to keep your mouth shut" indicated the military command's policy toward media inquiries regarding operations at Camp Delta, Yee's detailed catalogue of the abuses and disarray at Guantánamo both establishes him as a patriotic insider who has had access to privileged information and as a traitor of the codes and military culture by which this insidership was secured. Thus, Yee continually risks slipping from "good Muslim" to "bad Muslim," by revealing the shortcomings of the avowed American self-image.

Yee's complaints to his commanding officers about the abuses that detainees suffer—in particular regarding the use of Islam as a "weapon" (e.g., in the mishandling of the prisoners' Qur'ans) by soldiers—compound growing concern about his loyalty, which is already under suspicion because he is Muslim.[16] The narrative both begins and culminates with his arrest as he returns to the United States for a visit to his family. *For God and Country* grapples with the contradictions between the liberal national imaginary and the neoconservative politics of the security state in a remarkably daring and sophisticated manner. In telling his own story, Yee mounts a defense of detainee rights that betrays the violations of international accords on human rights and the treatment of prisoners by the United States. This exposure leaves Yee vulnerable to charges that he is undermining the war effort and is a traitor to the nation, even as Yee unwaveringly professes his own loyalty to the nation's highest principles and ideals. Yee recognizes that his arrest and imprisonment positions him as *loyal to and identified with* the Gitmo detainees, even though his own detention occurs at naval brigs in Jacksonville, Florida, and Charleston, South Carolina. As Yee writes of the scene when he is escorted by the Naval Criminal Investigative Service to a military hospital: "The chains around my ankles dragged behind me, and I recognized the look on the faces of those watching me: I was a detainee."[17] The experience of double consciousness recurs in his transfer from Jacksonville to Charleston, when he is subject to the sensory deprivation techniques that a Guantánamo detainee had described to him and he begins to believe that the guards escorting him will kill him—that he has "effectively vanished from the world."[18]

Although Yee is soon cleared of espionage, sedition, and aiding the enemy, he continues to face charges of mishandling classified information and of conduct unbecoming an officer, namely, that he has carried on an adulterous affair and had downloaded pornography onto a government computer. Besides providing the government a cover for Yee's arrest and imprisonment, the charges function to dispute Yee's claims to loyalty on a second front. Not only has his loyalty as a patriot been questioned, but so too his fidelity to his family and Islamic standards of moral conduct. Notably, *For God and Country* refuses to respond to the latter charges. Although he does relate his assurances to Huda that the stories about adultery are fabricated and that a computer forensics report countered the accusations that pornographic images had been downloaded or stored on his laptop computer, he never directly responds to the charges in his narrative. Instead, Yee repeatedly emphasizes that these charges amount to a public diversion from the "real questions" of the violations of his own civil liberties and the conditions at Guantanamo.[19] For example, he writes about his preliminary hearing:

> I couldn't believe it. Since my arrest, I had endured accusations that I was a traitor to my country, was referred to in the media as "part of one of the most dangerous spy rings discovered in the United States since the Cold War," and was considered such a threat to national security that I had been held in solitary confinement for seventy-six days. But apparently the government wasn't interested in any of that. Instead it was a greater priority and matter of national importance to prove that I was an adulterer.[20]

Ultimately, all charges of mishandling classified information were dropped, and the allegations of adultery and pornography were dismissed upon appeal. Nevertheless, the working conditions Yee encounters (e.g., he is prohibited from having contact with anyone who had been stationed at Guantánamo Bay, and he discovers that his case has become part of at least one briefing on counterintelligence, such that the army continues to portray him as a spy and terrorist) prove so hostile that he resigns from the service after being granted an honorable discharge in January 2005.

Yee's strategic negotiation of the fractured subjectivity that the state has imposed upon him ingeniously addresses the question of his own reliability as a narrator, which after all is the most crucial generic feature that a political memoir like this one must establish. If the state has tagged Yee as duplicitous and untrustworthy, the narrative refuses to dignify the personal charges with a response. In constructing a sphere of privacy around Yee, the narrative performatively establishes him as a private citizen whose marital relationship and personal faith can be protected from public exposure. By insisting that his behavior at Guantánamo, even during the most provoking of incidents, was "always measured and professional," he implicitly defends this right to privacy.[21] In hewing to the liberal division between public accountability and individualized privacy, Yee establishes himself as both a good citizen and true patriot who can be trusted, despite his admission in the epilogue that, "I am sure that many will discount me. . . . I may be a former captain and a chaplain, but I'm also an accused terrorist and spy."[22] It is this tone of measured reasonableness that then prevails in his acknowledgment to his supporters, including congressional representatives who meet with him after his ordeal: "My experience in Washington gave me a renewed sense of appreciation for how our government operates. When it works properly, it's a thing of wonder."[23] By affirming himself to be "a patriotic, loyal American," Yee necessarily distances himself from the enemy combatants while retaining a humanitarian concern for them: "The military's inability to apply justice fairly to its own citizens certainly suggests an inability to apply it fairly to foreign nationals held in Guantanamo."[24]

And yet Yee's silence simultaneously recalls an earlier account he provides of Shaker, one of the Guantánamo detainees, who "goes mute" as a way of coping with the isolation of Camp Delta. As Shaker explains to Yee, he has taken a pledge of silence on the Muslim holy days of Friday as a way of maintaining hope: "It's going to be a day for me to enjoy my own type of privacy."[25] If, by the memoir's end, Yee wants to reestablish himself as a private citizen, Shaker's "enjoyment" of his own "type of privacy" illumines the others from whom the right to privacy and other civil rights have been materially extracted.[26] In light of Yee's extensive exposition of the interrogation techniques employed at Camp Delta, the "right to remain silent" that Shaker claims for himself fundamentally contests the terms of national sovereignty—and its security—upon which this purportedly and expansively "universal" liberal right depends. Insofar as Yee has been identified with—and has provisionally recognized himself as—a detainee, *For God and Country* invokes an alternative imaginary for the subject of the war on terror, what I have described at the end of Chapter 5 as the emergent subject of human rights whose claims can hardly register in and cannot be reconciled to an American imaginary. The war on terror poses the possibility and necessity for such an alternative imaginary in starkly contradictory terms, as "a fundamental choice . . . between [American citizens'] safety and the rights of citizens of other nations to their liberties."[27] Yee pointedly remarks with regard to his discovery of the charges being leveled at him, "In fact I stopped believing in many things," hinting at a divided consciousness whose "appreciation" for the state cannot be "renewed."[28] While he continually avows the liberal ideals of religious tolerance—a tolerance Yee implies ironically that Islam embodies more fully than does American nationalism—his tenure as a detainee shifts the locus of this belief to an international framework of rights.

In its representation of Yee's subjectivity, fractured between being "one of 'them'—a Muslim" and the desire to be "a soldier, a citizen, and a patriot," the memoir locates an emergent collective subject with which minority discourse will have to reckon.[29] While Yee himself notes the similarities between his own case and that of Wen Ho Lee (e.g., the fallacious charges of sedition and treason that ultimately betray the government's grave mishandling and violations of civil rights), the relationship that Yee's narrative configures between himself and the detainees also suggests the historical transformations in racial discourses underway. The charges leveled against Yee, and the discourses of rights and religion to which he turns as he defends and identifies with the Guantánamo detainees, cannot be neatly reconciled to traditional critiques of racial profiling. Rather, the histories of civil rights politics *and* September 11 produce Yee, like Arar and Padilla, as a "suspected terrorist," a subject of global geopolitics *and* subject to domestic American surveillance and discipline. In its rendering of the conditions and politics of detention the memoir offers a discerning account of the emergent subject in the war on terror.

Finally, however, we should note that even as Yee refuses to directly answer the defamatory allegations about his own moral conduct, he nevertheless stakes his political grievances against the state as most immediately centered on the personal and psychic damage that the subject of surveillance and detention endures. Yee accomplishes this dual task, of protecting his right to privacy while simultaneously exhibiting personal, individualized damage, by narrating Huda's harrowing experiences of his apparent disappearance after his arrest and the search of their home by FBI agents, as well as her suicide attempt and ongoing anguish at the scrutiny that their family has endured. Although Yee depicts Huda as a particularly appealing figure of Syrian Islamic womanhood for liberals—a woman who makes choices regarding her faith and her personal life—in order to dispel dominant images of the Muslim woman-as-victim, the narrative returns to gendered victimization in order to hold the state morally accountable.[30] As we attend to Huda's role in Yee's narrative construction of the emergent subject of human rights and the powerful political critique it levels against the state, we must remember too the other others to whom this emergent subject will be responsible. Huda embodies the Other who shoulders the burden of the subject's taking place, to whom Yee and the reader retain a responsibility. An ethics of betrayal, as I have described throughout this book, recognizes acts of betrayal as the arrival of otherness that disrupts and defers self-presence. As such, to speak of an "ethics of betrayal" after September 11 is to speak less about a programmatic agenda than about the structure of otherness itself. Our attention to the subject of human rights thus does not exhaust our ethico-political responsibilities, but rather memorializes the heavy cost that "traitorous" others in our midst bear in the name of the trust, rights, and privileges granted to any subject of rights.

Notes

Chapter 1

1. Chang-rae Lee, *Native Speaker*, 314.
2. Rorty, "Justice as a Larger Loyalty," 56.
3. Here and throughout *An Ethics of Betrayal*, I use the terms "subject" and "subjectivity," on the one hand, and "self" and "selfhood," on the other hand, in counterdistinction to one another. I do so to distinguish the modalities of minority and liberal discourses from those of contemporary cultural criticism and critical theory. While liberal and critical discourses never exist separately from one another, the notion of a minority subject aspiring to or authorized with selfhood suggests the specific political investments of each. In very general terms, liberalism posits the self as an *a priori* condition of social formation, a discrete and bounded agent that acts upon the world and effects changes through its will. Cultural criticism and critical theory take the subject as the more unstable "subject of enunciation," which is both enabled through the structural and discursive operations of power, and which also acts, although with limited agency, upon the structural and discursive formations in which it finds itself. The subject supplements and is excessive to the self, an excess that will be crucial to understanding the ethical possibilities of betrayal. In a similar vein, I distinguish between "the Other" and "others" to indicate the relationship between the existential conditions of ethics and the sociopolitical grounds of critical theory. "The Other" stands as a figure of the impersonal "Otherness" of existence that cannot (as I explain in this chapter) be thought or known. My reference to "others" and "other others" addresses those bodies, groups, and subjects to whom Otherness has been attributed.
4. Levinas, "Ethics as First Philosophy," 84.
5. Ibid.
6. Levinas, *Existence and Existents*, 60.
7. Ibid., 63. Levinas utilizes in particular Husserl's formulation of a "non-

theoretical intentionality" in consciousness and Merleau-Ponty's emphasis on the primacy of perceptual experience as a situated and embodied one in his own conception of a non-reflective passivity that grounds first philosophy. Merleau-Ponty insists that consciousness itself is situated in the material body, is incarnate, such that reflection is always outpaced by unreflected life or existence. Thus, in Levinas's words, self-consciousness is always situated as an "intimate carnation" that "no longer purely and simply displays the exteriority of an object" ("Ethics as First Philosophy," 79). If this self-consciousness is a reduced one, in that the limits of what it might grasp become more readily visible in the body's materiality, it also affirms a "self-consciousness and absolute being" through a surplus of the non-intentional consciousness, the "consciousness of consciousness" and unknowing knowledge that is indirect, implicit, and aimless.

8. Levinas, "Ethics as First Philosophy," 78.
9. Levinas, *Time and the Other*, 70, 77.
10. Ibid., 74, 71.
11. Ibid., 81.
12. Judith Butler, "Ethical Ambivalence," 25.
13. Levinas, "Ethics as First Philosophy," 82.
14. Ibid.
15. Ibid., 85.
16. Ibid.
17. Derrida's description of ethics as "hospitality" provides a significant thread for conjoining the ethical to the juridico-political, a theme that will be troped in a number of the works that I examine in this book. For Derrida, if the subject experiences its own being as, in the Heideggerian sense, being "thrown" into existence, the ethical project amounts to an attempt to make oneself at home, a project of "hospitality": "Insofar as it has to do with the *ethos*, that is, the residence, one's home, the familiar place of dwelling, inasmuch as it is a manner of being there, the manner in which we relate to ourselves and to others, to others as our own or as foreigner, *ethics is hospitality*" (*On Cosmopolitanism and Forgiveness*, 16–17). Hospitality thus signifies a reckoning with the dislocation of being, one that, as a first philosophy, is "ethicity itself" (*Adieu to Emmanuel Levinas* 50). In *Adieu to Emmanuel Levinas,* Derrida also addresses Levinas's deployment of sexual difference and "feminine alterity" to figure the ethical hospitality of the Other (36– 45). However, as I will discuss below, the political implications of this figuration are not unproblematic, nor even as salutary as Derrida suggests, given how this homogenized and abstracted generalization of difference always conceals the racial and gender privilege that is put under erasure in a reading of politics as "*the* political."
18. Derrida, *Adieu to Emmanuel Levinas*, 29.
19. Ibid., 29–30.
20. Ibid., 33.
21. Ibid.
22. Ibid.
23. Ibid., 59, 61. For extended discussions of the theoretical relationship between deconstructive ethics and politics, see Critchley, *The Ethics of Deconstruction*; and Critchley, *Ethics—Politics—Subjectivity*.
24. Critchley, *The Ethics of Deconstruction*, 220.

25. Derrida, *Specters of Marx*, 22.
26. Ibid. Derrida distinguishes eschatology from teleology when writing of this justice to come. The *eskhaton*, he explains, refers to an "ultimate event" that "can exceed, at each moment, the final term of a *phusis*, such as work, the production, and the *telos* of any history" (*Specters of Marx*, 37).
27. Derrida, "Force of Law," 27.
28. Ibid., 28.
29. Ibid.
30. Derrida, *Specters of Marx*, 25.
31. Ibid., 29.
32. Derrida, *Rogues*, 11. Derrida's reflections on democracy to come in *Rogues* proves especially pertinent to U.S. ethnic studies and American studies, because he takes as a point of departure Tocqueville's description of democracy in America as the actualization of democracy itself, such that: "The people reign over the American political world as God rules over the universe. It is the cause and the end of all things; everything rises out of it and is absorbed back into it" (quoted in *Rogues*, 14).
33. Ibid., 14–15.
34. Ibid., 33.
35. Ibid., 38.
36. Ibid., 40.
37. Ibid., 29. Likewise with respect to justice, Derrida argues that justice "doesn't wait"; although justice is never self-present—that is, one can never essentially say a decision (or an individual making the decision) is just—a decision is nonetheless called for ("Force of Law," 26). The demand for a decision is always an urgent one; its immediacy sets limits. One can never make a decision after gathering "infinite information" and "unlimited knowledge of conditions, rules or hypothetical imperatives that would justify it" (ibid., 26). Even if this infinitude were available to the judge, Derrida argues, "the moment of decision, as such, always remains a finite moment of urgency and precipitation" (ibid., 26). A decision always interrupts, with a type of finality, the processes of deliberation that precede it.
38. Derrida, *Rogues*, 39.
39. Ibid., 40–41, 47.
40. Ibid., 18.
41. Ibid., 75.
42. For a further discussion by Derrida of what takes place in the world as "strategic politics," always in the "name of democracy," see *Politics of Friendship*.
43. Derrida, *Rogues*, 84.
44. Ibid., 86.
45. Bow, *Betrayal and Other Acts of Subversion*, 3.
46. Ibid., 8.
47. Ibid., 11.
48. Ibid., 25.
49. In her perceptive theorizing of Asian American subjects as "impersonators" who enact "double agency," Tina Chen distinguishes between performative acts of impersonation and denigrated forms of imposture in order to expose how Asian American performance is too often misread as acts of betrayal rather than as performances of divided or multiple allegiance (*Double Agency*, xvii). My goal in *An Ethics*

of Betrayal is not to reinscribe all such acts of performance and impersonation as betrayal, but rather to understand why betrayal provides such a particularly abjected form of agency against which other possibilities are imagined.

50. In *Scenes of Subjection*, Saidiya Hartman offers an especially powerful warning in this respect. She describes how "emancipation" constructed former slaves according to a new disciplinary regime whereby the individual was defined as free primarily through notions of "responsibility," which amounted to his or her "blameworthiness" before the law.

51. Nevertheless, as I suggest above, *sexual* difference takes on a significant representational dimension for theorizing the Other—one that, as feminists have suggested, cannot escape the social implications through which it becomes intelligible. My discussion in this section further elaborates the political assumptions and ramifications that an "alterity without context" entails.

52. Ahmed, *Strange Encounters*, 142.

53. Ahmed, *Differences that Matter*, 159.

54. Ibid.

55. For example, Ahmed notes that in his work, Levinas contradicts his own insistence on the Other's unrepresentability with references to the Other as an "alien being," which implies that the Other is *a* "being," albeit one that is unlike the self.

56. As Ahmed argues, if we insist that the representation of the Other in figures of unbelonging or dispossession does not accord those particular bodies the status of the Other *per se*, we risk eliding "the relation between particular others who are dispossessed, and the Other as radically other who cannot belong within these figures" (*Differences that Matter*, 61). At the same time, although it might seem even further contradictory, the insistence that existential otherness is prefigural because it is preontological, can also clear the way for what Ahmed describes as "stranger fetishism," the production of a "universe of strangers" that disregards the political and historical processes "whereby some others are designated as *stranger than other others*" (*Strange Encounters*, 6). The figure of the "stranger neighbour" proves an "effect of the processes that imagine [that the other] can either be taken in, welcomed or expelled," an attempt to recognize unintelligible alterity, to assimilate the unassimilable (ibid., 141). These processes, in their attempt to represent the unrepresentable, take otherness as the essence of the alien. In naming the alien resident or the stranger neighbor as the figure of Other, certain bodies are inscribed as fetish objects that domesticate Otherness. These bodies accordingly are "assumed to contain otherness within the singularity of [their] form ('entire being')" (ibid., 143).

57. Ahmed, *Differences that Matter*, 66.

58. Li, *Imagining the Nation*, 2.

59. Behdad, *A Forgetful Nation*, 107, and Sean McCann, "Connecting Links," 77. We should note that the advocates of cultural pluralism during this era ranged in terms of their stance toward national formation and politics. At their most radical, social thinkers such as Randolph Bourne anticipated a "trans-national America" that seemed to contest the very sovereignty of the nation by advocating that new Americans be permitted dual citizenship and multiple geopolitical affiliations. Nevertheless, in *Our America* Walter Benn Michaels has shown that by the 1920s modernist literary and social discourses reified cultural pluralism *as* racial difference by linking culture to "inheritance."

60. McCann, "Connecting Links," 76.
61. Oboler, *Ethnic Labels, Latino Lives*, 31.
62. Ngai, *Impossible Subjects*, 4.
63. Singh and Schmidt, *Postcolonial Theory and the United States*, 12.
64. The traditionalists in these cases felt that the Constitution "must follow the flag" (else the nation would descend into tyranny), and they were accordingly anti-imperialist because they feared that *ex propio vigore* would mean the incorporation of racially undesirable others into the nation. For modernists, however, Teutonic constitutionalism, a belief that Anglo Americans had a particular "racial genius" for the law, provided a basis for ethno-juridical jurisprudence that imagined itself as thoroughly modern insofar as it grounded empire not in tyranny but, rather, in "science" (Weiner, "Teutonic Constitutionalism," 58). See also Amy Kaplan's discussion of how the threat perceived as inherent to "alien races" ultimately overran concerns that the republic might replicate European absolutism in "annexation without incorporation" (*Anarchy of Empire in the Making of U.S. Culture*, 6–7).
65. Kaplan, *Anarchy of Empire in the Making of U.S. Culture*, 3–11. See also Mae Ngai's discussion of the contradictions in the status of Filipino migrants in the United States, who as U.S. "nationals" were afforded neither the status of citizens nor that of aliens, but did retain the right to move freely within the territorial United States until the passage of the Tydings-McDuffie Act. As Ngai observes, "Filipino migrants were the corporeality of contradictions that existed in American colonial policy and practice" (*Impossible Subjects*, 97).
66. Kaplan, "The Birth of an Empire," 1075. Kaplan also describes in detail the way in which the relationships between blacks and whites in the United States were intertwined with the question of empire well before 1898. As she writes, U.S. conquest of Indian and Mexican lands in the antebellum period was fundamentally linked to the expansion of slavery and emancipation (*Anarchy of Empire in the Making of U.S. Culture*, 18). The re-entrenchment of the color line proved necessary to quell anxiety about "race mingling" on the battlefield during the Spanish-American War (ibid., 121–45). The work of Lisa Brock and David J. Hellwig also discusses the questions of race and empire facing African Americans at the end of the nineteenth century. While the African American press in the United States often expressed concern about "the extension of racism via imperialism," the presence of black soldiers as part of U.S. forces during the Spanish-American War (for the first time since slavery) meant that the black press generally approved of their involvement and offered support for troops fighting in Cuba in 1898; tensions over this contradiction proved stronger in the case of the Philippines (see Brock, "Introduction: Between Race and Empire," 13–14; Hellwig, "The African-American Press and the United States Involvement in Cuba," 71–72). See also Carol J. Batker (*Reforming Fictions*) for a discussion of African American Progressivism and its claims to national belonging, which depended upon the demarcation of foreignness in others.
67. Oboler, *Ethnic Labels, Latino Lives*, 38. Moreover, despite the distinctions that Latin Americans may have wished to draw amongst themselves according to national, class, or racial specificity, U.S. nationalist discourse homogenized or elided such differences by characterizing all Latin Americans by the specious name of "Mexican." Further, María Josefina Saldaña-Portillo describes in detail the construction of the "Mexican" in contradistinction to the indigenous "Indian," which stems from a racial

logic set in motion by the Treaty of Guadalupe Hidalgo. As she explains, the terms by which Mexicans were incorporated as U. S. citizens (and Mexican lands as part of the nation) differentiated them from the "savage tribes" of Mexico's northern territories, who threatened this "incorporation" ("Wavering on the Horizon of Social Being," 142). As Saldaña-Portillo demonstrates, the provisions in the treaty that "protected" Mexicans from these "savages" codified the legacy of Spanish imperialism, which constructed the humanity and citizenship of all its *criollo*, *mestizo*, black, and Indian subjects against those Native Americans who refused to recognize the governmentality of the Spanish crown and, subsequently, the Mexican republic (ibid., 145).

68. Despite the treaty's promise to protect the property and civil rights of Hispanos, the state and federal systems for determining land titles and claims in the territories acquired in 1848 functioned to the disadvantage of most Mexican American landowners (Meier and Ribera, *Mexican Americans / American Mexicans*, 69–102). The courts tended to demand authorized documentation of land ownership, to not recognize communal private property, and to require continuous occupation of land grants (ibid.). For example, in the cases of New Mexico, Colorado, and Arizona, fewer than a third of the petitions by *hispanos* were confirmed. And even in those cases where such claims were upheld, many petitioners had to sell off most of their land to cover legal expenses (ibid., 95). Backed by the courts and rationalized through the auspices of capitalist restructuring, corporate agribusiness acquired previously family-owned lands. As Ramón Saldívar has explained, this process not only displaced *hispanos* onto increasingly smaller plots of land, and ultimately into a sharecropping relationship with Anglo landowners, but eventually led to the hiring out of Mexican Americans as wage laborers, rather than as tenant farmers. Mexican Americans and Mexican immigrants came to constitute a migrant workforce for Anglo American farmers, their labor controlled by an extensive network of economic and legal mechanisms: "By the late nineteenth and early twentieth centuries these efforts had produced a new sociospatial, cultural, and geopolitical reality in the former Mexican territories, resulting in communities experiencing the development of new forms of social modernity" ("Border Subjects and Transnational Sites," 376). Furthermore, while the treaty extended citizenship rights to Mexicans, the state precluded from this category those Mexicans whom it determined to be of "black" and "Indian" heritage (Saldaña-Portillo, "Wavering on the Horizon of Social Being," 147).

69. This process culminated in such initiatives as the mass deportations of the 1930s during the Great Depression and the 1950s "Operation Wetback," both of which "repatriated" hundreds of thousands of Chicana/os, including an untold number of U. S.-born citizens, to Mexico (see López, *White by Law*, 142–45; Gómez-Quiñones and Maciel, "What Goes Around, Comes Around, 38; and Flores, "Citizens vs. Citizenry," 272–73).

70. López, *White by Law*, 38.

71. Lowe, "The International within the National," 31.

72. In its response to the legal challenges brought on by Japanese Americans to the government's military orders, the Supreme Court confirmed, especially in *Korematsu v. United States* (1944), that U. S.-born Asian Americans continued to be perceived as aliens whose civil rights were contestable. In *Korematsu*, the Court ruled that despite the need for care such that racial hostility was not translated into a violation of the rights of citizens, "public necessity must sometimes justify the existence of

such restrictions." As Angelo Ancheta surmises, "Discounting the centrality of race, the majority opinion concluded that Korematsu was not excluded because of racial hostility but because the United States was at war with Japan" (*Race, Rights, and the Asian American Experience*, 32). Consequently, the Court imposed a supplementary national identity, one meant to displace and obscure racial difference, in upholding the removal of Japanese Americans. On the effective formation of the Japanese as an Asian transnation in the policies and legal decisions surrounding the internment, see Chuh, "Transnationalism and Its Pasts."

73. See Lauren Berlant (*The Queen of America Goes to Washington City*) and Ali Behdad (*A Forgetful Nation*) for discussions of the constitutive ambivalence of the nation that structures the racial antagonisms and cyclical movement between nativism and openness to immigrants in the U.S. As Behdad argues, the nation's ambivalence to immigration, an ongoing coexistence between "hospitality and hostility" to immigrants, has been productive of a core national identity that gets to have it both ways, sustaining a myth of an immigrant America which, despite deep social differences, somehow also coheres as a singular civic identity (*A Forgetful Nation*, 32). Nativism therefore does not so much contradict liberal discourses of hospitality as constitute a repressed component of the latter, which, when it does inevitably erupt in national discourse, demarcates the alien from the native (ibid., 129). Nativism owes the longevity that it has enjoyed in its demands for a singular imagined community (which Behdad locates as occurring as early as the debates between Thomas Jefferson and Alexander Hamilton) to its inventiveness during moments of historical transformation, so that the outsider has been variously imagined as political alien, as medical danger, as communist, and, most recently, as terrorist.

74. Ngai, *Impossible Subjects*, 2, 8. See Kandice Chuh ("Hierarchies of Color") and Suzanne Oboler (*Ethnic Labels, Latino Lives*) for further discussion of, in Oboler's terms, the complex fusion of "xenophobic nationalism and a domestic racism" that plagued the racialized alienation of Asians and Latina/os in the U.S. and the partial enfranchisement of African Americans (32). Moreover, while certainly the histories of Asian Americans and Latina/os are quite distinct from one another, both the cultural exclusion *and* the immigration of Asian Americans and Latina/os in the United States have also been *mutually imbricated* within this larger context of empire-building and domestic racism. The U.S. colonization of the Southwest territories and its broader imperial designs on the western hemisphere, justified within the ideological imperatives of Manifest Destiny, were in large part mobilized as attempts to trade with Asia (Palumbo-Liu, *Asian/American*, 339–40). The importation of *bracero* labor during the twentieth century resulted in part from labor shortages created by the various Asian exclusion acts, providing a pool of cheap labor to appease employers who otherwise lobbied against immigration restrictions. That Latina/os and Asian Americans were similarly situated in the United States as symbolic outsiders to the nation is provocatively evidenced in the words of a congressman in the debates over the Foraker Bill in 1900: "I am opposed to increasing the opportunities for the millions of negroes in Puerto Rico and the 10,000,000 Asiatics in the Philippines of becoming American citizens and swarming into this country and coming in competition with our farmers and mechanics and laborers. We are trying to keep out the Chinese with one hand, and now you are proposing to make Territories of the United States out of Puerto Rico and the Philippine Islands, and thereby open wide the door by which these negroes

and Asiatics can pour like the locusts of Egypt into this country" (quoted in Oboler, *Ethnic Labels, Latino Lives*, 37). In fact, the established legitimacy of Asian exclusion here provides the rhetorical potency to Filipino, Puerto Rican, and, more generally, Latin American exclusion as well. With the Chinese Exclusion Act already instated and Japanese immigration soon to be restricted with the 1907 Gentleman's Agreement, the precedence for excluding groups from access to the United States according to the precepts of racial hierarchy was well established. The Foraker Bill in 1900 denied territorial status, constitutional protection, and citizenship to *puertoriqueños* in order to protect the national body from racial outsiders.

75. David Theo Goldberg, in *The Racial State*, offers a more general discussion of the process by which the state secures homogeneity within the nation through such a dual racialization—the displacement of heterogeneity onto both a racialized interior (the urban ghetto) and exterior (the colonized territory).

76. Kaplan, "The Birth of an Empire," 222.

77. Ibid.

78. Ibid., 226. See Charles Bright and Michael Geyer ("Where in the World Is America?") for a consideration of how the modernization of the United States, while fundamentally transnational in scope and form, nevertheless broke with forms of European colonialism in its globally projected national image of democratic sovereignty and self-governance through universal principles.

79. Kaplan, "Romancing the Empire," 236–37. As Vijay Prashad points out, the history of countries throughout the western hemisphere mirrors that of the United States, challenging its claim to exceptionalism, "since they too comprised European colonies whose new residents massacred most of the earlier populations, fought wars of national independence against Europe (José San Martín and Simon Bolívar stand in for George Washington), and have since created various means to manage their cultural and political differences" (*The Karma of Brown Folk*, 59).

80. As Kaplan explains: "In the immediate reaffiliations during and following the war, this analogy was rapidly dismantled in America, where it became more pressing to emphasize difference, that 'they,' unlike 'us,' were incapable of self-government to which revolution aspires. After the war, only anti-imperialists compared Aguinaldo of the Philippines to George Washington, a trope tantamount to treason in its betrayal of the American past" ("Romancing the Empire," 237). David Noble further explains that historians of the nineteenth century equated the indigenous civilizations of the Americas (in particular, the Aztecs and the Incas) with those of the "Orient," and identified both (as well as the rule of the Catholic Spanish, albeit to a lesser degree) with despotism ("The Anglo-Protestant Monopolization of 'America,'" 259). As such, "all the other American nations were not [considered] real nations because their peoples existed outside progressive history.... The end of history as the perfect liberty of fraternal citizens existed, for them, only in the United States" (ibid., 265).

81. As Ngai explains, the decolonization of the Philippines and the repatriation and exclusion of Filipino migrants in the 1930s and 1940s further confirmed this abstracted character, restoring benevolent assimilation "to the status of myth, disembodied and abstracted from its putative beneficiaries." Consequently, the experience of imperialism and of Filipino migration during the early twentieth century was "willfully forgotten by a public determined to erase the colonial past from the American imagination" (*Impossible Subjects*, 126).

82. Palumbo-Liu, *Asian/American*, 321.
83. Ibid.
84. Ibid.
85. My argument here thus slightly revises Lauren Berlant's description of the "hypocrisy" of democratic nationality in the U.S. Berlant writes: "From the beginning, entire populations of persons were excluded from the national promise which, because it was a promise, was held out paradoxically: falsely as a democratic reality, and legitimately, as a promise, the promise that the democratic citizenship form makes to people caught in history. The populations who were and are managed by the discipline of the promise—women, African Americans, Native Americans, immigrants, homosexual—have long experienced simultaneously the wish to be full citizens and the violence of their partial citizenship. . . . Over the long term some of us have been American enough to provide labor but not American enough to be sustained by the fullest resources of democratic national privilege" (*The Queen of America Goes to Washington City*, 18–19). The analysis I forward here suggests that even the "partial citizenship" of some, troublesome in and of itself, has been anchored by the imagined alienation of *other* others in the nation.
86. Lisa Lowe, in *Immigrant Acts*, and Palumbo-Liu, in *Asian/American*, have each offered extensive analyses of the way in which Asian immigrants in particular have mediated the contradictions of capitalist modernity, racial hierarchy, and democratic egalitarianism. Palumbo-Liu argues that Asians necessarily played the part of the quintessential "marginal man" in the modern drama of alienation precisely because African Americans could not: "The 'exotic' east lends itself to certain mystifications, whereas the history of slavery in America, while certainly secured in part by ideological imaginings, has nonetheless embedded blacks more concretely and determinedly in the material" (*Asian/American*, 87). Furthermore, Palumbo-Liu contrasts the characterization of the "marginal man" with W. E. B. DuBois's concept of double consciousness. In particular, DuBois's description highlights the central role of institutional racism in creating the psychic conflict of the minority subject, a political inflection that was erased in most representations of the Asian in America (ibid., 299–300). Also, see Colleen Lye's *America's Asia* for a meticulous history of the consolidation of the "Asiatic racial form" in literature, policy debates, and public conversation in response to industrialization and neocolonial expansion. Lye offers, among other things, an original account of Japanese American internment as the "end of exclusion" and as liberalism's New Deal project for incorporating Asians into the welfare state. All of these critics complicate the notion that the history of Asian exclusion has been determined solely by the images of the "yellow peril," and suggest the close affiliation of this stereotype of the Asian threat with that of the model minority. In contrast, Ngai explains that the "wetback" stereotype, generated from the specificities of *bracero* labor and what she describes as the "national boundaries of class," correlates images of embodied material labor with those of illegal status/alien citizenship for the Mexican American. The particularized racial formation of the Mexican as foreign and illegal, but nominally "free" (i.e., free to quit, free to move), helps to account for why, as I discuss in chapter 3, Asian American neoconservatism produces a collectivized stereotype of the model minority distinct from the Uncle Toms and *pochos* of black and Latina/o minority discourse, respectively (*Impossible Subjects*, 131–33). Ngai further explains how the construction of the Mexican wetback stereotype—and its association with racialized

poverty (e.g., "Asiatic poverty")—became the primary image from which a middle-class Mexican American critique attempted to disentangle itself in the mid-twentieth century (ibid., 159–60).

87. The discussion here synthesizes substantial and thoughtful critiques of pan-ethnicity, of "culture" as a disciplinary formation, and of pluralist/ethnic canon and archival formation offered by Claire F. Fox ("Comparative Literary Studies of the Americas"), Kirsten Silva Gruesz ("Utopía Latina"), Jane Juffer ("The Limits of Culture" and "In Search of the Latino Public Sphere"), Susan Koshy ("The Fiction of Asian American Literature"), and Viet Thanh Nguyen (*Race and Resistance*).

88. Gruesz, "Utopía Latina," 54.

89. Juffer, "In Search of the Latino Public Sphere," 264.

90. Nguyen, *Race and Resistance*, 4.

91. Koshy, "The Fiction of Asian American Literature," 342.

92. Miller, *On Literature*, 18. This is of course not to suggest that only fabulous or speculative accounts are literary, since one of the accomplishments of literature is to "de-form," or rewrite, even the seemingly most banal subjects (e.g., in the genre of realist fiction) into something heterogeneous to its "literal" referents.

93. Attridge, "Introduction: Derrida and the Questioning of Literature," 23.

94. Ibid.

95. Derrida, *Acts of Literature*, 48; Attridge, "Innovation, Literature, Ethics," 23. My use of the terms "discourse" and "social [racial, national, etc.] formations" throughout *An Ethics of Betrayal* draws from Ernesto Laclau and Chantal Mouffe's important theoretical work in *Hegemony and Socialist Strategy*. Elaborating upon Michel Foucault's notion of discourse as the strategic organization of tactical elements within fields of force relations, Laclau and Mouffe emphasize the *articulation* of these elements within a discursive field (the terrain of the social) that in turn constitutes social relations. The articulation of discourses is performative, in that there is no unified subject that effects articulation. Rather, partially fixed "subject-effects" constitute themselves in the process of articulation. Articulation is also radically contingent, in that there are no teleological guarantees nor predetermined necessity or unity to the conditions of the articulation. And it is symbolic and overdetermined in nature: "There is no possibility of fixing an ultimate literal sense for which the symbolic would be a second and derived plane of signification. Society and social agents lack any essence, and their regularities merely consist of the relative and precarious forms of fixation that accompany the establishment of a certain order" (*Hegemony and Socialist Strategy*, 98). Discursive articulation itself establishes the relation among elements, "such that their identity is modified as a result of the articulatory practice," and these elements are partially fixed, as "moments" of the discursive formation, by way of "regularity in dispersion" within the structured totality of the discourse (ibid., 105). These discursive formations can never be completely sutured and closed off. If social discourse determines a meaning for the elements within itself by equating or relating them to one another, those elements also always exceed the fixed meaning of the discursive moment. Because "no social identity [is] fully protected from a discursive exterior that deforms it and prevents it becoming fully sutured," discursive formations are always open to this multiplicity, excess, and rupture (ibid., 110–11). The figure of the traitor, I contend, in a very precise manner indexes this openness; the act of betrayal is a discursive articulation that "deforms" social identity. Furthermore, acts

of literature fundamentally antagonize social discourses; they are a crucial site from where and method by which the openness of the social can be imagined.

96. Miller, *On Literature*, 68.
97. Attridge, "Introduction: Derrida and the Questioning of Literature," 21.
98. Ibid., 15.
99. Ibid., 5.
100. Derrida, *Acts of Literature*, 74.

Chapter 2

1. For a synthesis of the extensive scholarship and criticism in postcolonial and area studies of diaspora, as both a conceptual framework and as referencing specific historical experiences, see Kalra, Kaur, and Hutnyk, *Diaspora & Hybridity*.

2. Critical engagements with this issue include, to name only some select works: (a) in Asian American studies, Kim and Lowe, "New Formations, New Questions"; Eng, "Out Here and Over There"; Palumbo-Liu, *Asian/American*; Chuh and Shimakawa, *Orientations*; Grewal, *Transnational America*; and Lim et al., *Transnational Asian American Literature*; (b) in Chicana/o and Latina/o studies, Bonilla et al., *Borderless Borders*; Romero, Hondagneu-Sotelo, and Ortiz, *Challenging Fronteras*; José David Saldívar, *Border Matters* and *The Dialectics of Our America*; Poblete, *Critical Latin American and Latino Studies*; and Fregoso, *meXicana Encounters*; (c) in American studies, Lowe and Lloyd, *The Politics of Culture in the Shadow of Capital*; Kaplan and Pease, *Cultures of United States Imperialism*; Singh and Schmidt, *Postcolonial Theory and the United States*; and Rowe, *Post-Nationalist American Studies*.

3. For example, see Sau-ling C. Wong, "Denationalization Reconsidered."

4. For example, David Leiwei Li writes that, although diaspora can generate helpful "multivalenced formation," the movement away from the "compelled solidarity" of Asian America "not only disregards 'race' as a central category of address and analysis, but also virtually dismisses 'nation' as a viable ground for critical alliance" (*Imagining the Nation*, 202). Likewise, Sau-ling Wong worries about the risks involved with abandoning the nationalist project of "claiming America," whereby "certain segments of the Asian American population may be left without a viable discursive space" ("Denationalization Reconsidered,"137).

5. According to models of internal colonialism, both U.S. minorities and colonized natives elsewhere provided the racial otherness against whom white nationalist/imperialist domination proceeds.

6. "Globalization" here indicates the increasing penetration and expansion of capital that has resulted in the deterritorialization of peoples, information, technologies, finances, and ideas (Appadurai, "Disjuncture and Difference in the Global Cultural Economy," 6–10). Inderpal Grewal further clarifies these processes, practices, and networks by describing "transnational connectivities" that characterize not only deterritorialization and flow, but also exclusions, incompleteness, and unevenness in the globalization of neoliberal political economies (*Transnational America*, 22–24).

7. Appadurai, "Disjuncture and Difference in the Global Cultural Economy," 12.
8. Appadurai, "Heart of Whiteness," 413.
9. See, for example, Chuh, "Transnationalism and Its Pasts."
10. Ong, *Flexible Citizenship*, 11.
11. The 1965 reforms formally ended a national-origins "quota" system of

immigration that had effectively inhibited the influx of certain groups of immigrants and that allowed for liberal immigration from northern European countries. Whereas national limits regulated flows of immigrants into the United States, the 1965 reforms replaced this criteria with standards aimed at bolstering employment and investment as well as family reunification.

12. See U. S. Dept. of Commerce, Bureau of the Census, *Profiles of General Demographic Characteristics 2000*. Since 1965, immigrants from Asia, Latin America, and the Caribbean have come to make up 75 percent of all arrivals in the United States (Camarota, "Immigrants in the United States—2002," 8). The number of Asian Americans increased from one million in 1965 to over 12.5 million in 2000 (U. S. Dept. of Commerce, Bureau of the Census, *Profiles of General Demographic Characteristics 2000*, 1:1). Similarly, the Mexican-origin population, which makes up more than 50 percent of all U. S. Latina/os, grew to a total of 20.6 million in 2000 (ibid.). About half of this increase has been attributed to international migration, and the Latina/o population as a whole numbered 35 million (ibid.; also, Camarota, "Immigrants in the United States—2002," 8). Latina/os now constitute 12.5 percent of the population in the United States, approximately equal to the African American population (U. S. Dept. of Commerce, Bureau of the Census, *Profiles of General Demographic Characteristics 2000*, 1:1). Despite more recent policy reforms, most notably the 1986 Immigration Reform and Control Act (IRCA), that seek to limit Mexican-origin immigration, many of the legal and economic dimensions of immigration ensure a continued influx of Mexican migrants (Baker, "Demographic Trends in the Chicana/o Population, 6–7).

13. Ramirez, "It's Not Just Black and White Anymore," 478.

14. Visweswaran, "Diaspora by Design," 11–12.

15. For example, rather than the product of hard-fought battles of civil rights movements for political representation, their socioeconomic mobility proceeds from the reorganization of capital on a global terrain, where generalized strategies of unpaid labor and the exploitation of co-ethnics, to name only two instances, are deployed across ethnic communities (Visweswaran, "Diaspora by Design," 14).

16. That is to say, the emergence of a transnational elite has as its counterpart a transnational underclass that provides much of the flexible labor from which global capital draws. A critical perspective on globalization thus articulates the positions of laborers, many of whom are women of color, working in *maquiladoras*, sweatshops, service economies, and other establishments of the "free market" as sharing globalized conditions of economic inequity, even as they appear in specific and localized forms.

17. Eng, "Out Here and Over There," 32. Eng's suggestion that we employ diaspora, as well as queerness, as "theoretical vantages" in our analysis of minority cultural production indicates the grounding of various nationalisms in systems of patriarchal hierarchy and, moreover, compulsory heterosexuality. As Eng explains, both the diasporic subject (in his argument, the Asian immigrant) and queerness have been marked as "exterior or eccentric" to the configuration of "home" in the politics of the nation-state and of normative heterosexuality. The oppositional stance that minority discourse has taken responds to these constructions of home by claiming space in the public sphere for the minority subject. But such a claim to citizenship proper comes at a high cost, "purchased through the emphatic possession of a popularly devalued private realm, constituted as both the feminine and the homosexual" (ibid., 35).

18. See also Avtar Brah's formulation of "diaspora space," which names the "intersectionality of diaspora, border, and dis/location as a point of confluence of economic, political, cultural, and psychic processes" (*Cartographies of Diaspora*, 181). As Brah contends, the idea of diaspora carries within itself the concept of borders as well as that of the indigenous or native.

19. Kalra, Kaur, and Hutnyk, *Diaspora & Hybridity*, 29. My discussion here and throughout *An Ethics of Betrayal* takes "minority discourse" as, in Homi Bhabha's description, a supplement to the hegemonic, liberal, and neoconservative discourses of the nation, whereby the cultural difference of minority subjects exceeds the self-identity of the nation (*The Location of Culture*, 154, 162). If the nation seeks to assimilate the heterogeneity of its constituents to a singular authoritative discourse, its subjects are always in the process of undoing this consolidation. Through their "performance" of the nation, subjects attempt to represent the nation according to their own multiple interests and thereby "continually evoke and erase" the totality of the nation (ibid., 150). Abdul JanMohammed and David Lloyd's further elaboration of minority discourse in the U.S. context, that it refers to a "theoretical articulation of the political and cultural structures that connect different minority cultures in their subjugation and opposition to the dominant culture," provides a useful entrance for critical race theory by describing linkages *between* heterogeneous minority cultures (*The Nature and Context of Minority Discourse*, ix). However, in this chapter, I argue that while minority discourse bars the nation from its "eternal self-generation," it is also itself continually interrupted and deferred from achieving the social formation to which it aspires (see Bhabha, *The Location of Culture*, 148).

20. Lim et al., *Transnational Asian American Literature*, 22.

21. In focusing on the diasporic other as the unincorporable and unassimilable difference that installs the subject of nationalist or minority discourse, my argument also means to resist the tendency for discussions of diaspora and migration to slip into an abstract and romanticized metaphor for generalized humanity. For further discussion of this tendency, see Ahmed, "Home and Away." As the setting of betrayal, diaspora registers the limits of affiliation and identification and provides the ground for critical "estrangement" that recognizes the other as Other.

22. Kim, "The Strange Love of Frank Chin," 286–94.

23. The play has been described as an "extended metaphysical conceit" about Chinese American "ontological alienation" as well as a self-conscious search for a language that will mediate the Asian American subject's relation with others (Li, "The Production of Chinese American Tradition," 323; McDonald, Introduction to *The Chickencoop Chinaman*, xvii).

24. Chin, *The Chickencoop Chinaman*, 37. When Tam and Kenji protest, the Lone Ranger insists, "I'm the law, China Boys, it's a curse I'm a givin ya to thank me for, not a blessing. In your old age, as it were in your legendary childhood . . . kiss my ass, know thou that it be white, and go thou happy in honorary whiteness forever and ever, preservin your culture. AMEN" (ibid., 37). Thus wielding the phallic authority of the law, the Ranger names Asians as "white," because they are known to be "legendary obeyers of the law, legendary humble, legendary passive" (ibid., 37). The Ranger leads the Asian in America back into an identity formulated by way of a benign orientalism. Multicultural ethnicity, "preservin your culture," functions "rehabilitatively," as Ruth Hsu terms it in "Will the Model Minority Please Identify Itself?" Sanctioned by

national discourse as a harmlessly quaint, "China Boy culture" preserves the distance between whites and Asians without threatening the power of whiteness.

25. Li, "The Production of Chinese American Tradition," 323.

26. Ibid., 323–24.

27. Chin, *The Chickencoop Chinaman*, 40.

28. Ibid., 41–42.

29. Ibid., 42.

30. Ibid., 8.

31. Derrida contends that at the core of history "there is something of an abyss" that refuses totalization, such that, "History can be neither a decidable object nor a totality capable of being mastered" (*The Gift of Death*, 4–5). Instead, historicity is fundamentally tied to a responsibility that intercedes in the subject's grasping of the self-present (ibid., 5).

32. Ling, *Narrating Nationalisms*, 25.

33. A similar type of reading is possible regarding the presence and silencing of the biracial character of Lee, through whom the possibility of a miscegenated selfhood is both proposed and foreclosed. Kenji's pronouncement about Lee's pregnancy seems to hope to recuperate Lee—an otherwise vocal, antagonistic, and possibly promiscuous figure of unintelligible racial desire—to the cultural politics of panethnic racial formation.

34. As such, the ethnic narrative generically aligns less with realism than with the "legend," a "dramatization of its metaphoricity, its textuality and seriality, and its 'reality' as a kind of continual storytelling" (Chow, *Ethics after Idealism*, 111). If, as Chow contends, "behind each mother is thus always another mother," Leslie Bow describes this "other mother" as the structurally necessary "prefeminist" Asian woman who "exists as excess" and cannot be disciplined to a normative ethnic narrative (*Betrayal and Other Acts of Subversion*, 84). This line of Asian American feminism thus approaches the Asian (American) woman as, in Laura Hyun Yi Kang's terms, a "compositional subject" who is "composed, composite, and positional" in and through representation (*Compositional Subjects*, 27).

35. Bow, *Betrayal and Other Acts of Subversion*, 84.

36. In *Imagining the Nation*, David Leiwei Li has demonstrated that these images amount to two sides of the same coin with respect to the status of Asian Americans in U.S. racial and national discourses. *The Chickencoop Chinaman* depicts this duality in the collaborative reactions of Charley Popcorn and the Lone Ranger to Tam and Kenji.

37. Of course, as many observers have pointed out, the loss of innocence is a rather recurrent theme in American history, leading one to wonder just how often Americans can lose and regain their innocence. After all, the Civil War, the bombing of Pearl Harbor, and, most recently, the September 11, 2001, attacks have all been characterized in the terms of innocence lost. As for its racial and ethnic inflections, the question of American innocence lost and found forms a broad and significant undercurrent for *An Ethics of Betrayal*.

38. Jen, *Mona in the Promised Land*, 3–4.

39. Ibid., 6.

40. Friedman, *Mappings*, 168.

41. Jen, *Mona in the Promised Land*, 49.
42. Ibid., 14–15.
43. Ibid., 49.
44. Ibid., 14.
45. Ibid.
46. Ibid., 15.
47. Ibid., 52.
48. Ibid.
49. Ibid., 53.
50. Ibid., 119.
51. Ibid., 40. This aspect of the novel links the Asian Americans' status as the model minority and their socioeconomic function as a "middleman minority"—that is to say, as entrepreneurs of small businesses who play a mediating role between the dominant racial group and other minorities. Indeed, as numerous social historians and scientists have pointed out, this was a role that Asian Americans largely inherited, beginning in the 1960s, from Jewish Americans. In addition, Jen incorporates into her portrait of restaurant life, elements of an ethnic enclave economy—a concentrated network of enterprises that have been built, financed, and staffed by a single ethnic group. While these businesses shelter co-ethnics with fewer marketable skills from an open competitive market, they also pay low wages to these workers, enforce reciprocal obligations from these workers in financial ventures, and structure workplace relations along the lines of the patriarchal hierarchy of the family. The Pancake House thus maps the dual exploitations through which the model minority emerges: the exploitation of other racial minorities and that of co-ethnics. Certainly, the Pancake House manifests neither the middleman minority nor the ethnic enclave economy in its entirety. Instead, Jen's portrait is both partially emblematic of each, and forward-looking, gesturing to the expansion of Asian American enterprise from urban locales to suburban areas by the end of the twentieth century.
52. Ibid., 57.
53. Ibid., 277.
54. Ibid., 109.
55. Ibid., 21.
56. Ibid., 294–95.
57. Even those minor characters who appear throughout the novel—for example, Seth's well-meaning but naively liberal stepmother Bea, who gives Mona the bus fare to (as I discuss below) run away, and another, more distant friend (and an object of Barbara's affection) Andy Kaplan who, as Seth informs Mona, actually initiated the charade of Sherman before passing the role on to Seth—play integral parts toward the narrative outcome. These many points of relationality overdetermine the final crisis for Mona.
58. Bow, *Betrayal and Other Acts of Subversion*, 9.
59. As Inderpal Grewal observes, in U.S. minority literature, "choice" is the crucial element of narrative movement from "tradition" to "modernity," for both the subject of modern nation and of liberal feminism. The centrality of choice proves the hallmark of the liberal democratic agenda, and its imbrication in neoliberal consumer culture, which purports to offer to the subject options not available in "traditional" cultures

and societies (*Transnational America*, 65). Consequently, although Asian American women's narratives might not be promoted as feminist per se, they link minority discourse closely to a liberal feminist project.

60. Derrida, *The Gift of Death*, 21.

61. Jen, *Mona and the Promised Land*, 300, 302.

62. Butler, *The Psychic Life of Power*, 23. Melancholia, a topic that has recently generated much critical interest in cultural and ethnic studies, proves a subset or corollary question for an ethics of betrayal. Indeed, we might conclude that the traitor is marked by the affective character of melancholia, but an ethics of betrayal, I contend, furthers this line of critical inquiry, insofar as it probes the political questions of agency and responsibility even more forcefully.

63. Jen, *Mona and the Promised Land*, 303.

64. Friedman, *Mappings*, 168. For further discussion of the novel's portrait of identity as performative and relational, see Lin, "Mona on the Phone"; and Furman, "Immigrant Dreams and Civic Promises."

65. Jen, *Mona and the Promised Land*, 303.

66. I should make clear, in regard to my argument with Friedman's reading of *Mona in the Promised Land*, that I am not suggesting that the cultural forms represented in the novel and the epilogue are not indeed portraits of hybridity. Nor do I wish to suggest that hybridity is not a viable and even preferable alternative to other models of cultural politics, namely, assimilation or glib, separatist multiculturalism. However, I do maintain that the cultural work performed by the narrative *exceeds* hybridity as an *end* in the ethical negotiation of difference and identity. As such, *Mona* presses against the limits of national incorporation and subject-formation with its concern for the diapsoric other, suggesting that hybridity cannot entirely shoulder the weighty responsibilities the minority subject encounters. For a succinct discussion of the dangers involved when hybridity becomes a "positive eventuality" or a "constructed anchoring device" for thinking diaspora, migration, and globalization, see Kalra, Kaur, and Hutnyk, *Diaspora & Hybridity*, 87–104. For an extended treatment of the conditions, limits, and possibilities of hybridity as "critical transculturalism," see Kraidy, *Hybridity, or the Cultural Logic of Globalization*.

67. Jen, *Mona and the Promised Land*, 298.

68. Read as an ethical betrayal, Mona's desire here for the *figure* of desire, for the "other woman," suggests something like a rapprochement between deconstructive ethics and Lacanian psychoanalysis. Mona's desire for the other woman recalls Lacan's answer to the question of "what does the woman want?" with the enigmatic observation that "she simply *wants*" (*Feminine Sexuality*, 132). The answer, Lacan points out, has no content. Rather, its significance inheres in the very structure of the question, the position of femininity in relation to desire. Mona's desire in the epilogue refers to the impossible demand to do away with the social and symbolic separation from her mother that has made (Asian) American selfhood possible. The demand is an impossible one insofar as Mona would cease to exist as a socially intelligible subject (in minority discourse) if the demand were somehow met; she would "fade" away (we might recall Charley Popcorn's confounding inability to make sense of Tam in *The Chickencoop Chinaman* as exemplary of such a fading away). Mona's desire thus stands in for this impossible condition of objective indifference. Her desire stands in a relation of excess to the self; it remains barred and inaccessible to the conscious subject who

speaks. It emerges, therefore, displaced and inverted, in Mona's uncanny sense that there is an "other woman" who would satisfy her and whom she might satisfy. If this other's desire could be satisfied, we might imagine, then perhaps Mona too would find some satisfaction for herself. The narrative, however, ethically refuses to allow us to make this mistake, keeping the "question mark" of subjectivity open by retaining the "what does she want" as the ongoing "she wants" of Mona's desire (*Feminine Sexuality*, 132). For detailed treatment of the possible connections between Levinasian ethics and Lacanian psychoanalysis, see Harasym, *Levinas and Lacan*.

69. Schroeder, "The (Non)Logic of Desire and War," 52.
70. Bergo, "Inscribing the 'Sites' of Desire in Levinas," 68.
71. Butler, *The Psychic Life of Power*, 29.
72. Bergo, "Inscribing the 'Sites' of Desire in Levinas," 71.
73. Jen, *Mona and the Promised Land*, 60.
74. Ibid., 61.
75. Ibid., 152.
76. Ibid., 194.
77. Ibid., 197.
78. Ibid., 207.
79. Ibid., 215.
80. Ibid., 219.
81. Ibid., 231.
82. Ibid., 281–82.
83. Ibid., 251.
84. Ibid., 255.
85. Ibid.
86. Margolis, "Huckleberry Finn; or, Consequences," 334.
87. Ibid., 331.
88. Ibid., 338.
89. Ibid., 337.
90. Ibid., 340.
91. Jen, *Mona and the Promised Land*, 141.
92. Ibid., 140–41.
93. Margolis, "Huckleberry Finn; or, Consequences," 339.
94. Jen, *Mona and the Promised Land*, 239.
95. Ibid., 292.
96. Margolis, "Huckleberry Finn; or, Consequences," 340.

97. As David Theo Goldberg explains, "The modern state has a legacy of turning violence into injury, historical wrong and its memory into legal redress, reconciliation, and reparations. Those states of unspeakable historical experience are metamorphosed at the hands of states and their agents into representable conditions, manageable states of affairs and affairs of state, through their reinscription in(to) the terms of legality" (*The Racial State*, 250).

98. Jen, *Mona and the Promised Land*, 269.
99. Ibid., 299.
100. Ibid., 293.
101. Quoted in Jacobs, "Allegories of Reading Paul de Man," 113.
102. Derrida, *Rogues*, 92.

103. Ibid.
104. Jen, *Mona and the Promised Land*, 236.
105. Ibid., 212.
106. Derrida, "Passions," 20.
107. Derrida, *Specters of Marx*, 23.
108. Ibid., 22.
109. Jen, *Mona and the Promised Land*, 280.
110. Ibid., 281.
111. Indeed, Theresa's status as an ethical guide in this way becomes clear when, upon learning of Mona's role in Alfred's lawsuit and foreseeing the trouble that Mona might face with her parents, she tells Mona, in advice that resonates with Derrida's description of ethicity as hospitality, "One thing very important in life . . . is to know how to make yourself at home," and extends an open invitation to Mona: "You are welcome to come to California anytime. Anytime you like, you can come make yourself at home" (*Mona and the Promised Land*, 247).
112. Derrida, "Psyche," 60.
113. As Derrida argues, this moment of justice must necessarily come too late, and it is a burden that is inherited at birth, as he writes of Hamlet, "given *by* his birth as much as *at* his birth" (*Specters of Marx*, 20). This inheritance, fundamental to the second generation, marks the "righter of wrongs" as one who, "like the right, can only come after the crime, or simply *after*" (ibid., 21). To do justice to the Other, the subject of justice exists "in a necessarily second generation, originarily late and therefore destined to *inherit*" (ibid.).
114. Jen, *Mona and the Promised Land*, 303.
115. Butler, *Bodies that Matter*, 242.

Chapter 3

1. Takagi, *The Retreat from Race*, 58.
2. See Raymund A. Paredes, "Mexican-American Literature," 37; and Muñoz, *Youth, Identity, Power*, 180–82.
3. Arlen, "Notes on the New Journalism."
4. Of course, as Mark Mordue and Scott Sherman each point out, neither the genre nor its literary ambitions are entirely unique or new to this period, since writers such as Stephen Crane, Theodore Dreiser, and George Orwell worked at the intersections of journalism, literature, and political treatise much earlier in the twentieth century (see Mordue, "The Pull of 'New Gravity'"; and Sherman, "'New' Journalism." Moreover, as Michael E. Staub has demonstrated, New Journalism played a significant role in "elaborating an anti-Left agenda," participating in the development of "sophisticated anti-Left strategies [that] were already being tested and refined" during the early 1970s, even as the genre represented itself, at least stylistically, as elemental to 1960s and 1970s counterculture (see Staub, "Black Panthers, New Journalism, and the Rewriting of the Sixties").
5. Ling, *Narrating Nationalisms*, 8.
6. Liu, *The Accidental Asian*, 153–54.
7. Ibid., 154.
8. Richard Rodriguez, *Days of Obligation*, 169.
9. Ibid.

10. Ibid.

11. The most egregious of these errors include the contention that somehow minority histories are not a nation's history, but that the history of an Anglo-America generically is; that teaching one necessarily excludes the other, so that somehow we are leaving behind the seemingly universal narratives of Benjamin Franklin, Andrew Jackson, and Thomas Jefferson (as Rodriguez fears), and the D-Day veterans, by offering recognition to the "particular" stories of racial minorities; and that ethnic studies and minority discourse critics are so intellectually unsophisticated as to be unaware of the "ironies," contradictions, and complexities that inhere in the telling of a nation's history, issues about which hegemonic U.S. history and culture have supposedly been, in contrast, more forthcoming. Rosaura Sánchez, in "Calculated Musings," offers a detailed critique of the historical and ideological elisions that Rodriguez commits in the rhetorical politics of *Days of Obligations*; David Leiwei Li, in "On Ascriptive and Acquisitional Americanness," similarly treats *The Accidental Asian*.

12. As, for example, José F. Aranda Jr. explains about Rodriguez's popularity: "His notoriety among conservatives, whether or not ultimately deserved, is not what helped to erode the myth of Aztlán, as much as it was his eloquent, anguished portrayal of a second-generation immigrant male child" ("Making the Case for New Chicano/a Studies," 142).

13. Artists writing from a broad range of political perspectives, working in any number of genres, and employing a variety of styles complain that such labels are limiting and unfair. As David Leiwei Li explains in detail, such disavowals manifest the conflicting cultural and material loyalties and pressures felt by the minority artist, who has been authorized (in the form of a reading audience) usually by a group other than his or her own to write, but nonetheless assigned by the hegemonic culture to the minority group whose experience the writer treats as his or her subject (*Imagining the Nation*, 177). As Lauren Berlant also explains about the "specific contradiction" that the minority autobiographer inhabits: "Insofar as she is exemplary, she has distinguished herself from the collective stereotype; and at the same time, she is also read as a kind of foreign national, an exotic representative of her alien 'people' who reports to the dominant culture about collective life in the crevices of national existence" (*The Queen of America Goes to Washington City*, 245).

14. Sánchez, "Calculated Musings," 158.

15. Richard Rodriguez, *Days of Obligation*, 70; Liu, *The Accidental Asian*, 73.

16. Lounsberry, "Personal Mythos and the New Journalism," 518.

17. Ibid., 528. Lounsberry, whose essay on New Journalism I cite here, in fact admonishes writers of this genre to more fully acknowledge the "bias in their work" and thus more clearly distinguish for their audience the subjective and objective dimensions in their treatment of particular topics and themes. Others have of course described New Journalism's innovative value to be precisely this blurring of the line between fact and fiction, the subjective and objective, the imaginative and empirical, which challenges its readers to question the epistemological and ideological assumptions that undergird the journalistic production of knowledge. See, for example, David L. Eason, "New Journalism, Metaphor and Culture."

18. In *Constituting Americans*, her influential study of American nation-building in the nineteenth and twentieth centuries, Priscilla Wald argues that the intersections and confluence of personal and national narratives stem from a collective desire to

present a continuous narrative of the past and present. Personhood not only parallels nationhood, but is in fact forged through it, so that national narratives shape personal narratives by marking out the terms of personhood available to the nation's subjects. In moments of generative tension, writers move between a dialectic of "conformity" and "incomprehensibility" in order to challenge the limits to personhood available within national formation. At the same time, Wald argues, formulations and reformulations of personhood that legislate insiders and outsiders produce their own anxieties and haunting specters. When the uncanny elements that have been repressed return to claim a selfhood, the nation needs to reabsorb them, but this reabsorption is always a risky matter, because it threatens to expose the fissures that a national narrative seeks to cover over.

19. Richard Rodriguez, *Hunger of Memory*, 16.
20. Ibid., 31, 36.
21. Ibid., 29.
22. Ibid., 30. He further asserts that "most of those people who called me a *pocho* could have spoken English to me" but refused to because of their stubborn belief that "Spanish was the only language we could use, that Spanish alone permitted our close association" (ibid., 30).
23. Richard Rodriguez, *Days of Obligation*, 54.
24. Ibid.
25. Ibid., 61.
26. Richard Rodriguez, *Hunger of Memory*, 19.
27. Rodriguez's formulation, that "forgetting Spanish" is a necessary precondition of "learning English," of course elides the position of "those people" who can and do move fluently between the two languages. Instead, he resents the movement by political activists to insert what he sees as the private into the public through the use of the familial language and kinship relations (e.g., "brother/sister" by African-Americans, "sisterhood" by feminists) to figure public relations between individuals. For an extended discussion of the "miseducation" inherent to Rodriguez's politics, see Alarcón, "Tropology of Hunger."
28. Staten, "Ethnic Authenticity, Class, and Autobiography," 110.
29. Ibid.
30. Richard Rodriguez, *Hunger of Memory*, 33.
31. Ibid.
32. Ibid., 34.
33. Ibid., 31.
34. Richard Rodriguez, *Days of Obligation*, 65.
35. Ibid.
36. Ibid., 166.
37. Liu, *The Accidental Asian*, 78.
38. Ibid., 35.
39. Ibid., 36.
40. Richard Rodriguez, *Days of Obligation*, 69. He writes: "How much does the Central American refugee have in common with the Mexican from Tijuana? What does the black Puerto Rican in New York have in common with the white Cuban in Miami?" (ibid., 69).
41. Liu, *The Accidental Asian*, 67.

42. Ibid., 73.

43. Certainly George Lipsitz has provided us with an apt name for these gains in his concept of "the possessive investment in whiteness," or, as Ian Haney López describes it, "the tremendous value of Whiteness to Whites," whereby the historical formations of whiteness are embedded in the accumulation of material privileges and gains (*The Possessive Investment in Whiteness*; see also López, *White by Law*, 197–202). Yet another formulation of whiteness is offered by David Theo Goldberg: "In class terms whiteness definitionally signifies social superiority, politically equates with control, economically equals property and privilege" (*The Racial State*, 113).

44. Liu, *The Accidental Asian*, 55. Susan Koshy offers an incisive analysis as to how a transformation in the construction of whiteness "allows for *cultural difference* even as it facilitates *political affiliations* between whites and some nonwhites on certain critical issues" ("Morphing Race into Ethnicity," 186). Koshy makes an important distinction between the different meanings of whiteness. On the one hand, "whiteness as culture" proves less compulsory for minorities under prevailing models of ethnic pluralism. On the other hand, "whiteness as power" remains a powerful force in racial identifications and class aspirations (ibid., 186). See also Viet Nguyen's hypothesis that Asian Americans might be assimilated into, or become aligned with, whiteness (*Race and Resistance*, 168–69). Because these critics have demonstrated that minority subjects might participate in "whiteness as power" without necessarily submitting to "whiteness as culture," I suggest that Liu's and Rodriguez's insistence that both culture *and* power are integral to assimilation casts them as neoconservative (rather than neoliberal) in their formulation of social relations.

45. Christopher, "Rags to Riches to Suicide."

46. Richard Rodriguez, *Hunger of Memory*, 118.

47. Ibid., 113.

48. Christopher, "Rags to Riches to Suicide," 81.

49. Ibid., 80.

50. Here I am synthesizing the impressive body of scholarship that theorizes racial transformation. This includes, to name only a few of the most well-known works in the field, Omi and Winant, *Racial Formations in the United States*; López, *White by Law*; Goldberg, *The Racial State*; Lubiano, *The House that Race Built*; and Crenshaw et al., *Critical Race Theory*.

51. See, for example, Howard Winant's "Racial Dualism at Century's End," on the "racial dualism" in the late twentieth century; and David Theo Goldberg's *The Racial State*, on the distinction between the "naturalist" (i.e., white supremacist) and "historicist" (i.e., liberal racialist) perspectives of race, which ground different historical versions of the "racial state."

52. A number of Asian American scholars—including, for example, Ronald Takaki and Sucheng Chan—have critiqued the assumptions and statistics upon which the model minority myth has been developed for Asian Americans, including the inaccuracies in the image of Asian Americans as extraordinarily wealthy, or the exceptional education and employment opportunities available to them (see Takaki, *Strangers from a Different Shore*, 475–77; and Chan, *Asian Americans*, 169–71). In addition, a number of critics in Asian American studies have also provided ideological critiques of this image (see Dirlik, "Asians on the Rim"; Koshy, "Morphing Race into Ethnicity"; Prashad, *The Karma of Brown Folk*; Nguyen, *Race and Resistance*; and Visweswaran,

"Diaspora by Design"). Angie Chabram-Dernersesian, in "On the Social Construction of Whiteness within Selected Chicana/o Discourses," describes in detail the gendered and nationalist inflections around which Chicana/o discourse produces multiple discourses of whiteness, including the specific figure of the *pocho*, an identity that, she contends, is irreconcilable to dehistoricized multiculturalism.

53. The construct of the model minority and the *pocho* certainly do not function identically within a neoconservative agenda. A fundamental difference between these two representations of assimilation is that, for the most part, the model minority signifies a betrayal of *all* racial minorities by the collectivity of Asian America, whereas the *pocho* is often imagined as a betrayal by the individual of the Mexican American (and sometimes Latina/o) community, not unlike the "Uncle Toms" of African American cultural politics. Nevertheless, significant overlaps and intersections between these images prove revelatory for minority discourse and racial formations more broadly. For example, perceptions that immigrant Latina/os displace blacks in urban labor markets and neoconservative rhetoric that praises Latina/os for "strong family values" and their "good stable nuclear families," in marked contrast to perceptions and rhetoric about African Americans, point to tensions between black and Latina/o communities and to the limits of any identification *between* African Americans and Latina/os (see Suro, "The Next Wave," C-2; Zavella, "Living on the Edge," 371). See also the discussion between Jorge Klor de Alva, Earl Shorris, and Cornell West addressing relations between African Americans and Latinos in U.S. racial formations in "Our Next Race Question."

54. In their seminal work, *Racial Formation in the United States*, Michael Omi and Howard Winant suggest that ethnicity, or the articulation of political interests based on ethnic groups, has historically provided social scientists and policymakers with an explanatory model for race. Based on the assimilation patterns of European immigrant groups from the nineteenth and early twentieth centuries, this paradigm reduces race to ethnicity, suggesting that there is very little difference between European immigrants, on the one hand, and blacks, Latina/os, and Asian Americans, on the other hand.

55. Omi and Winant, *Racial Formations in the United States*, 129.

56. Ibid., 128. See Ruth Hsu's and E. San Juan Jr.'s critiques of this pluralist or multicultural political model, which Hsu explains as "rehabilitative," and San Juan as legitimating of the "hierarchical status quo" because it never disturbs the underlying presumption of the egalitarian state (Hsu, "Will the Model Minority Please Identify Itself?" 37; San Juan, *Racial Formation/Critical Transformations*, 5). As San Juan explains, the debate about ethnicity focuses on the essentially ethnocentric immigrant, on the one hand, and the assimilation of immigrants to hegemonic culture (i.e., the "salad bowl"-versus-"melting pot" debate between liberals and neoconservatives), on the other. Consequently, the prevalent paradigms describe social formation as the result of individual choices by members of groups that remain atomized from one another, rather than understanding such formation as thoroughly structured, constrained, and/or permitted by relational networks of power and privilege, dominance and subordination (*Racial Formation/Critical Transformations*, 12–13).

57. Omatsu, "The 'Four Prisons' and the Movements of Liberation," 43–44.

58. Indeed, Hsu, in "Will the Model Minority Please Identify Itself?" and Aranda, in "Making the Case for New Chicano/a Studies," each explain that the present-day

activist reconstructions of the past must repress synchronic discourses of class and ethnicity to produce a developmental, generational account of social movements. Cultural nationalists and other activist scholars and intellectuals, Hsu argues, define themselves as vigilant, assertively militant, and racially conscious activists against a past that they reconstruct as apolitical. Toward this end, they retroactively and strategically select particular moments from the past (usually those with which a middle-class activist can identify) as forerunners to present-day, oppositional politics. Consequently, they virtually depoliticize the rest of history. Likewise, the history of Chicana/o political activism, Aranda contends, was bound to appeal to the middle and upper classes in order for the movement to succeed, thus rendering it a politics based on ethnic identity rather than on working-class objectives: "For the middle class to be involved, ethnicity and upward mobility had to be foregrounded and stressed. In this way, all classes could claim a united ethnic ethos even if everyone did not suffer the same material and social deprivations" ("Making the Case for New Chicano/a Studies," 135).

59. Nguyen, *Race and Resistance*, 7.

60. Ibid., 145.

61. Nguyen describes an Asian American intellectual class that exhibits "a much higher degree of ideological homogeneity" than Asian America as a whole. The former, he explains, might be characterized as "left-of-center" and "invested in the value of an Asian American identity" (*Race and Resistance*, 13). Nguyen contends that Asian American intellectuals who have an especial investment in the "discourse of the bad subject" fail to account for those "*who only happen to be Asian American* but either do not recognize the importance of such a classification or disagree with that classification to begin with" (ibid., 13). Likewise, in describing what he calls a "new chicano/a studies," Aranda asks after those dimensions of Chicana/o culture and history that do not fit into the nationalist narrative of its subject, from the fact that Chicana/os "are the descendants of colonizers as well as the colonized all the way through to the contemporary value attributed to whiteness and support for neoliberal and neoconservative politics amongst Mexican American communities (many of whose members no longer wish to identify as Chicana/o) today" ("Making the Case for New Chicano/a Studies," 127–28).

62. Ruth Frankenberg argues that constructions of whiteness have varied across space and time and, consequently, the inclusions and exclusions to the category of whiteness have been diverse. Whiteness is a category that points up a political *process* rather than a cultural *essence*, one that marks itself like all racial categories—relationally. Moreover, it is only in its moments of extended dominance that it achieves the universalizing quality of the "unmarked marker" ("Introduction: Local Whitenesses, Localizing Whiteness," 15). See Cynthia Hamilton for an analysis of how "a pecking order" amongst European immigrants in the late nineteenth century consolidated the emergence of the "'middle-class, white' ideal," an ideal that, even while greatly determined by economic processes, is ironically represented as a universal and thus classless one ("Multiculturalism as Political Strategy," 173). A more difficult question—one obviously unanswerable in the present moment—is whether this "passing" on the part of Asian Americans and Latina/os marks the beginning of a fundamental reworking of whiteness itself to *include* these subjects, or if they are instead becoming aligned, but not identified, with it. See Viet Thanh Nguyen for a fuller discussion of this distinction

196 / NOTES

(*Race and Resistance*, 169). My argument here hypothesizes the former, but in either case, such a transformation mitigates the political project that cultural critics invest in non-white identity, because ethnicity, and not race-as-resistance, becomes the primary feature of a group's self-image.

63. In arguing for a more nuanced and effective theory of race relations in the United States, Edward J. W. Park and John S. W. Park have catalogued the various ways in which Asian Americans and Latina/os have been dismissed as "spectators" or categorized either as "white" or "black" in contemporary theories of race. As Park and Park argue, the significance of contemporary discourse seems not so much to be on which side of the black/white divide various critics place Asian Americans and Latina/os, but rather that, "while these groups are present in ever greater numbers, their presence doesn't change American race relations overall" ("A New American Dilemma?" 290).

64. Liu, *The Accidental Asian*, 196–197.

65. As I have argued elsewhere, interracial romance between Asian American male and white female subjects can be productively read as "queering" Asian American masculinity (see "The Most Outrageous Masquerade"). In the case of *The Accidental Asian*, this queerness emerges against the grain of Liu's rhetoric.

66. Richard Rodriguez, *Days of Obligation*, 57.

67. Ibid., 59.

68. Ibid., 76.

69. Ibid., 77.

70. Liu, *The Accidental Asian*, 96–98.

71. Ibid., 128, 138.

72. Ibid., 104–23.

73. The "idea of China" that Liu resists is one that has received much recent critical attention in Asian diaspora studies, that of the "transnational bridges" formed between mainland China and "overseas Chinese." In particular, see Aiwha Ong's description of the historical and material conditions giving rise to these transnational formations of "fraternal network capitalism" and "Greater China" (*Flexible Citizenship*, 7). Ong's work challenges the association of "triumphant Chinese capitalism" with "insurmountable cultural differences," by examining instead the construction of the "cultural logics" at work in these narratives of Chineseness.

74. Sánchez, "Calculated Musings," 162.

75. Chu, *Assimilating Asians*, 72, 54.

76. Liu, *The Accidental Asian*, 23.

77. Ibid., 24.

78. Ibid., 26.

79. Ibid., 30.

80. Ibid.

81. Ibid., 33.

82. Ibid., 152.

83. Ibid., 197.

84. Richard Rodriguez, *Hunger of Memory*, 195.

85. Ibid., 128.

86. Richard Rodriguez, *Days of Obligation*, 52–56.

87. Richard Rodriguez, *Hunger of Memory*, 129.

88. Ibid., 124.
89. Ibid., 125.
90. Ibid., 126.
91. Ibid., 113.
92. Ibid., 134.
93. Ibid., 136.
94. Staten, "Ethnic Authenticity, Class, and Autobiography" 111.
95. Richard Rodriguez, *Hunger of Memory*, 137.
96. Ibid., 139.
97. Richard Rodriguez, *Days of Obligation*, 219.
98. Richard Rodriguez, *Hunger of Memory*, 24.
99. Behdad, *A Forgetful Nation*, 4.
100. Liu, *The Accidental Asian*, 59, 201.
101. Behdad, *A Forgetful Nation*, 5, 172.
102. Richard Rodriguez, *Hunger of Memory*, 84. Again, see Sánchez's "Calculated Musings" for a discussion of the dehistoricizing, dichotomizing essentialism at work in the national characters upon which Rodriguez's rhetoric depends.
103. Richard Rodriguez, *Hunger of Memory*, 77.
104. Ibid., 79.
105. Richard Rodriguez, *Days of Obligation*, 182–83.
106. Ibid., 158.
107. Ibid., 172.
108. Ibid., 159.
109. Richard Rodriguez, *Hunger of Memory*, 98.
110. Richard Rodriguez, *Days of Obligation*, 192.
111. Richard Rodriguez, *Hunger of Memory*, 7.
112. Martin A. Danahay's "Richard Rodriguez's Poetics of Manhood" offers a detailed account of the public performance of masculinity that Rodriguez narrates. However, whereas Danahay suggests that despite some ambivalence in his identifications with his mother in *Hunger of Memory*, Richard's renunciation of privatized "feminine-identified aspects of his identity" is both completed and the necessary process by which he enters into American masculinity, I am arguing that when we approach Rodriguez's works through an ethics of betrayal, not only does the ambivalence of these identifications come to haunt and queer both narratives, but it destabilizes the binaries that Rodriguez's rhetoric tries so stridently to uphold.
113. As Randy Rodríguez writes, "*Hunger of Memory* is about being different even in one's family and community of origin . . . about Rodriguez finding or constructing a gendered and sexual identity more accommodating to his needs and desires for self-expression based on imaginative possibilities available to him" ("Richard Rodriguez Reconsidered," 410).
114. Randy A. Rodríguez, "Richard Rodriguez Reconsidered," 411. This queer aesthetic carries over to, and becomes more explicit in, *Days of Obligation* as well. For example, in the essay "Late Victorians," a portrait of gentrification in San Francisco by its gay male community and the plight of this community under AIDS, Rodriguez acknowledges gay cultural politics that extravagantly remake domestic bourgeois Victorian cultural forms ("sins" against natural law). Normal Tilden argues that, in this essay, Rodriguez stages Catholicism's "profound ambivalence" towards bodies, and

that this ambivalence accords with the alienation Richard experiences from his body in *Hunger of Memory*. "Late Victorians" discovers a sacramental exchange, where God becomes sensory, and ordinary life "when channeled through ritual, could be sacramentalized" ("Word Made Flesh," 446). Tilden suggests that this essay thus comprises a "nativity story," where Rodriguez performs a series of inversions centered around queer life and domestic spaces in order to transform "indefinite, unfocused longing" into a physicality that might then be "perceptible, uncloseted, and, most importantly, redemptive" (ibid., 454).

115. The American self thus aspires to inhabit a body that is, in Lauren Berlant's words, "without history, an abstraction that mimes the abstraction of the American promise that retains power *because* it is unlived" (*The Queen of America Goes to Washington City*, 202).

116. Richard Rodriguez, *Days of Obligation*, 229–30.

117. Behdad, *A Forgetful Nation*, 5.

118. Staten, "Ethnic Authenticity, Class, and Autobiography," 114.

119. Ibid.

120. Ramon Saldívar, Introduction to *The Hammon and the Beans and Other Stories*, vii.

121. Ibid., xxviii.

122. As David W. Noble contends, while some historians throughout the second half of the twentieth century "choose to live with the memory of an 'innocent America,'" such an image has become increasingly difficult to maintain since the 1960s, with the emergence of feminist and minority historiography. Noble also explicitly connects the decline of this unified image of the nation's interior with a parallel decline in the image of the nation as singularly exceptional on a global terrain: "It has become increasingly difficult to look at that culturally diverse landscape and still fail to recognize the power that male Anglo-Protestants exercised from 1789 to the 1940s in monopolizing the academic presentation of the national landscape. The same logic applies to the exercise of power that monopolized the academic presentation of the United States as the only 'America' [where "America" signified the "New World" of democratic liberty]" ("The Anglo-Protestant Monopolization of 'America,'" 268).

123. Américo Paredes, "The Gringo," 56.

124. Ibid.

125. See Charles Bright and Michael Geyer on the Mexican conflict, which, they argue, although it did eventually result in the legal incorporation of Texas and the Southwest territories into the republic, signaled the beginning of the U.S.'s moving away from European traditions of colonialism toward an abstraction of geopolitical power and national self-image ("Where in the World Is America?" 77–79).

126. María Josefina Saldaña-Portillo analyzes the way in which the term "character" in the Treaty of Guadalupe Hidalgo and in mid-nineteenth-century U.S. governmentality indexes the assumption of intertwined racial, moral, and national identities (see "Wavering on the Horizon of Social Being," 140).

127. Américo Paredes, "The Gringo," 55.

128. Goldberg, *The Racial State*, 95.

Chapter 4

1. Richard Rodriguez, *Hunger of Memory*, 178. In "Resisting the Heat," Doris Sommer argues that the refusal to reveal is itself a mechanism for the creation of insider/outsider positions; writers like Rodriguez (who ironically portrays himself as an alienated Mexican American) use such a strategy to affirm their cultural identity by calling attention to an object of knowledge unknowable "from the outside."

2. I use the term "community" in this chapter to index the commonplace notion of an identity-based collectivity that is the subject of political representation and the object of knowledge production in the university. Because I am concerned here primarily with the construction of the intellectual subject of minority discourse, I have not delved into the problem of positing the community itself as an idealized, organic form of utopian social relations through which the cultural politics of representation take place. For an extended discussion of how the rhetoric of community and the discursive articulations of social formations as community are imbricated in capitalism, see Joseph, *Against the Romance of Community*.

3. For studies that explore the national, class, and international politics of the genre of the conventional spy-thriller novel, see Bloom, *Spy Thrillers*; Denning, *Cover Stories*; Sauerberg, *Secret Agents in Fiction*; and Stafford, *The Silent Game*. These analyses, and others like them, focus primarily on the spy genre as a peculiarly British form, and as such, on British spy novels. As Denning maintains, "The spy thriller has been, for most of its history, a British genre, indeed a major cultural export" (*Cover Stories*, 6). It is not my intent to make an argument for *George Washington Gómez* or *Native Speaker* as part of this genre. Indeed, my discussion at the end of the chapter explains the significance of their limited adoption of the generic conventions. These cultural studies of the spy novel, however, elucidate the paradigms that Paredes's and Lee's novels both incorporate and rework.

4. See Andrew Ross's *No Respect* and Stephen Leonard's "A Genealogy of the Politicized Intellectual," which provide genealogies on the concept of the intellectual. See also Stanley Aronowitz's *The Politics of Identity*, which discusses the social position of intellectuals and emergent class formations.

5. Leonard, "A Genealogy of the Politicized Intellectual," 10–11.

6. This is true even if individuals are unwilling to take on the name of "intellectual." Despite their often privileged positions, intellectuals have also been subject to a long history of disparagement and anti-intellectualism, a phenomenon especially evident in American political and cultural history. Thus, political activists, cultural critics, and other elites have often tried to distance themselves from those they see as "true intellectuals"—for example, academicians. This question of defining the role of the intellectual was taken up in the "Forum" section of *PMLA* by leading intellectuals and scholars in literary studies, further emphasizing the extent to which the formation of the intellectual subject occurs within a (self-)critical discursive practice. See, for example, Tzvetan Todorov, who argues that the intellectual "is engaged in an activity of the mind resulting in the production of a work . . . [and] is also concerned about the state of society and participates in public debate" ("Forum," 1121–22). For Todorov, "the intellectual cannot be replaced by the expert: the latter knows facts; the former discusses values. . . . There is a difference in their positions."

7. Said, *Representations of the Intellectual*, 11.

8. Ibid.

9. Interestingly, one pivotal moment to which this particular definition can be traced, the Dreyfus affair of the 1890s and Zola's condemnation of the French government in his famous "J'accuse" article, also invoked the specter of the spy-traitor and pitted racial (in the form of virulent anti-Semitism) and national loyalties against each other.

10. For example, see Margaret Soltan, in the *PMLA* "Forum," who dramatically explains that "attentiveness, passion, and lack of compromise are the attributes that an advanced technical, managerial consumer society confounds. Concentration disperses when the object world thins to images; passion goes when, after sufficient betrayal and confusion, people become affectless and paranoid; conviction falters when everyone self-protectively refuses to make judgment."

11. Ross, *No Respect*, 125.

12. Ibid., 118.

13. Again, for further detail on this debate, see Aronowitz, *The Politics of Identity*.

14. Bourdieu has offered a detailed analysis of how these conditions reproduce social and economic hierarchies. For Bourdieu, social and cultural representations are tied to social power relations, which underwrite "the game" of social practice. In this sense, all intellectuals, i.e., cultural producers, even those without access to material capital or any control over *economic* modes of production, wield power, have "gained position," by accumulating cultural capital. The cultural producer, Bourdieu contends, is a symbolically empowered yet economically dominated subject who positions him- or herself oppositionally by identifying with those who are both economically and culturally dominated (*The Field of Cultural Reproduction*, 44). For Bourdieu, cultural producers (those whom I refer to as intellectuals) who make too easy identifications with the economically disenfranchised fail to recognize that their access to the means of representation distances and differentiates them from these very classes.

15. Bourdieu, *Language and Symbolic Power*, 209.

16. Ibid.

17. Certain parameters circumscribe my discussion of minority intellectuals and ethnic studies. Most importantly, it has been restricted to individuals, whether artists or critics, working within ethnic studies, primarily in an academic setting. Of course, a large number of minorities work in fields other than ethnic studies and the humanities and social sciences from which these academics are drawn—especially, for example, in the natural and physical sciences. Yet, the situation of these individuals, despite their amassing of cultural capital, does not acutely manifest the contradictions of the minority intellectuals that this chapter investigates, insofar as they have not, at least not within their own scholarly production, committed to the work of cultural and political *self*-representation. While minority subjects who work outside of ethnic studies certainly play an important role simply in their presence and visibility on campus, and while many of my arguments might be extended and applied to include these individuals, their own knowledge-production is less straightforwardly tied to the value-critiques or the ethico-political commitments of ethnic studies. Secondly, the intellectuals I consider are themselves people of color. As my argument below suggests, a certain notion of a "true" minority subject generates a concomitant conception of the most "appropriate" type of intellectual in ethnic studies. Accordingly, it becomes difficult for a non-"insider," especially white academics, to "justify" their work in ethnic

studies and defend themselves against charges of orientalism or a racist othering, that is portrayed, as I describe below, in Paredes's "experts." In other words, they are rather "imperfect" spies because they clearly cannot claim a transparent identification with their objects of study. Ultimately, this chapter implicitly argues against such constructions of intellectual authority, contending that the possibilities of betrayal reveal the problems with "authenticity" and transparency on the part of minority intellectuals. Finally, the focus of my argument is the production of knowledge by and about minority subjects, and ethnic studies programs and departments seem to offer the most formalized version of this process. But I mean to include in this category those individuals (like myself) working in traditional academic departments and disciplines whose scholarship nevertheless includes the subjects of race and ethnicity.

18. For historical accounts of these movements and the establishment of ethnic studies programs in Asian American and Chicana/o studies, see Wei, *The Asian American Movement*; and Muñoz, *Youth, Identity, Power*. For further discussions on the historical development of ethnic studies, and shifts and innovations in the field, see Johnnella E. Butler, *Color-Line to Borderlands*.

19. Most minority activists and critics saw the goal of these programs to be multiple; they were intended to raise the consciousness of students in terms of racial and ethnic identities, produce and disseminate historical and cultural knowledge about ethnic minorities in the United States, and provide culturally specific and sensitive services to both minority students and communities (Wei, *The Asian American Movement*, 135).

20. This division between the theoretical abstractness of academic study and practical, community-oriented work is, of course, hardly unique to ethnic studies. It is a version of the opposition between the "ivory tower" and the "real world" that has proven a long-standing cliché of university life. As Bruce Robbins points out, the dual charges of the professionalization of intellectual work and the significant support (especially in the humanities and social sciences) of these professionals for multiculturalism, both of which are attacked by neoconservatives as the subordination of "general human concern" to "special interests," are not so much parallel developments, as intersecting ones ("Comparative Cosmopolitanisms," 246–47). Nevertheless, this charge of alienation is acutely troublesome in the context of minority discourse, insofar as the very formation of ethnic studies programs was seen as organically linked to the material histories of minority communities. For examples of such critiques in Chicano/Latino studies and Asian American studies, see Ignacio M. García's "Juncture in the Road" and Lane Ryo Hirabayashi and Marilyn Alquizola's "Asian American Studies," respectively.

21. Readings's analysis goes a long way toward explaining how the radical critiques made within ethnic studies have managed to persevere. Because it is no longer in the service of reproducing national culture, the university "does not carry with it an automatic political or cultural orientation," whether conservative or radical: "This is one of the reasons why the success of a left wing criticism . . . is turning out to fit so well with institutional protocols. . . . It is not that radical critics are 'sell-outs,' or that their critiques are 'insufficiently radical' and hence recoverable by the institution. Rather, the problem is that the stakes of the University's functioning are no longer essentially ideological, because they are no longer tied to the self-reproduction of the nation-state" (*The University in Ruins*, 14). In fact, for Readings the "culture wars" that

have troubled the university for the past two decades are themselves symptomatic of the lack of any central, unifying teleology that defines the university's role and the meaning of culture more generally: "The University as an institution can deal with all kinds of knowledges, even oppositional ones, so as to make them circulate to the benefit of the system of as a whole" (ibid., 163).

22. See Dominick LaCapra's "The University in Ruins?" for a more detailed critique of Readings's analysis. LaCapra explains that Readings's account of ideology does not parry with models such as that theorized by Slavoj Zizek, wherein "a subject sees through or recognizes the baselessness of an ideological perspective but affirms or follows its injunctions anyway" ("The University in Ruins?" 32–55).

23. Readings, *The University in Ruins*, 145.

24. Ross, *No Respect*, 126.

25. Several anthologies provide a range of compelling narrative and critical essays attesting to the experiences of the marginalized subject in the university context, pedagogical strategies, and the departmental, disciplinary and institutional politics of difference. See, for example, Dews and Law, *This Fine Place So Far From Home*; Mayberry, *Teaching What You're Not*; and Lim and Herrera-Sobek, *Power, Race, and Gender in Academe*.

26. Robbins, "Comparative Cosmopolitanisms," 255.

27. For a careful analysis of the racial dimensions of the conflict symbolized in the dual name, see Saldaña-Portillo, "Wavering on the Horizon of Social Being."

28. Américo Paredes, *George Washington Gómez*, 270.

29. Ibid., 272.

30. Ibid., 292–94.

31. Ibid., 299.

32. Ibid., 300.

33. Ibid., 294.

34. Ibid., 282.

35. Saldaña-Portillo, "Wavering on the Horizon of Social Being," 156.

36. José David Saldívar, *Border Matters*, 42.

37. Saldaña-Portillo, "Wavering on the Horizon of Social Being," 157.

38. Américo Paredes, *George Washington Gómez*, 302.

39. José David Saldívar, *Border Matters*, 44–45.

40. Levinson, Foley, and Holland, *The Cultural Production of the Educated Person*, 1.

41. Ibid.

42. Américo Paredes, *George Washington Gómez*, 302.

43. Ibid.

44. Ramón Saldívar has written of Paredes's works in general: "Given the modernity of their concerns, it is startling to learn that Paredes's literary creations are not contemporary pieces, nor even products of the fifties and sixties. . . . As products of an era and of literary formations different from those currently in vogue, the literary texts belie their postmodern, post-Chicano Movement thematics and publication dates" ("Border Subjects and Transnational Sites," 373).

45. Ramón Saldívar, "The Borderlands of Culture," 273–93. See also Christopher Schedler's "Inscribing Mexican-American Modernism in Américo Paredes' *George Washington Gómez*," which brings our attention to the historical context of the novel

as well. Schedler describes the novel as an inscription of border modernism—a deconstruction of the epic tradition of *corridos* that responds to both the experimental aesthetics of high modernism and the uneven process of social and cultural development in the U. S. borderlands in the twentieth century.

46. González, "Segregation of Mexican Children in a Southern California City," 55–76.

47. Chang-rae Lee, *Native Speaker*, 46.

48. Ibid., 17.

49. Ibid., 18.

50. Ibid., 22.

51. Ibid.

52. Tina Chen provides a thorough analysis of how the multiplicity of performances that Henry enacts comes at the cost of self-coherence, of a "wholeness that is ever deferred, ever impossible to attain" (*Double Agency*, 164).

53. Chang-rae Lee, *Native Speaker*, 140.

54. Chen, *Double Agency*, 176.

55. Chang-rae Lee, *Native Speaker*, 311.

56. Ibid., 279.

57. See Rachel Lee's "Reading Contests and Contesting Reading" on the parable for reading and literacy as disciplinary practices of biopower that *Native Speaker* offers.

58. Chang-rae Lee, *Native Speaker*, 232.

59. Ibid., 235.

60. Ibid., 11.

61. Ibid., 10–12.

62. Liam Corley's "Just Another Ethnic Pol" offers a compelling reading of Lelia's character that troubles the seemingly fixed authority and privilege that critics have ascribed to her.

63. Chang-rae Lee, *Native Speaker*, 211.

64. Ibid., 293.

65. See Daniel Y. Kim's "Do I, Too, Sing America?"—which I cite below —for a discussion of the novel's meditation on how an African American political tradition both enables and delimits Asian American liberal politics. Kim argues that the novel affords African American politics an "exemplary status," but that this ascription exists in tension with Lee's aspiration to "imagine a new political 'syntax,' one that would speak to those Americans who are brown and yellow as well as to those who are black and white" ibid., 241).

66. Chang-rae Lee, *Native Speaker*, 143. See Corley's "Just Another Ethnic Pol," which situates *Native Speaker*'s portrayal of John Kwang within the history of the racial and immigrant politics of New York City.

67. Chang-rae Lee, *Native Speaker*, 319–20.

68. As adults, they both continue to face racist affronts in the most intimate of settings, the family. For example, both authors depict their protagonists as resented by and resentful of their fathers-in-law, white men who enact an othering by articulating their own ethnic chauvinism.

69. Denning, *Cover Stories*, 14.

70. Ibid.

71. Lowe, *Immigrant Acts*, 12.

72. Chang-rae Lee, *Native Speaker*, 139.
73. Ibid., 140.
74. Ibid.
75. Kim, "Do I, Too, Sing America?" 250.
76. Ibid., 521.
77. Américo Paredes, *George Washington Gómez*, 282.
78. In forwarding this argument, I am adopting but also reworking John Guillory's influential account of the culture wars, literary canonicity, and academic situation of the humanities vis-à-vis cultural capital along the lines of Bill Readings's urgent injunction that we must think change from the "difficult space" of "where one is." Following the general theory of cultural capital that Bourdieu explicates, Guillory (like Readings) persuasively argues that the crisis over the canon, dubbed the "culture wars," is actually a problem in the accrual and dissemination of cultural capital or "of access to the means of literary production and consumption" (*Cultural Capital*, ix). As such, the crisis pertains not to the content of the canon itself (and the changes to which the canon is subject) but to the flight of symbolic capital from culture, such that increasingly only a "technobureaucratic class" retains power and status under the auspices of transnational capital. Guillory thus explains that the humanities as a whole have suffered a marked decline in their relevance to national life, and the culture wars amount to a diversion from and displacement of the material practices of political change. Guillory's account provides a much needed and clear-eyed context for understanding the cultural politics of academic debates. However, as Barbara Foley points out, in relegating the university to a space from which "real" politics is diverted, this critique tends to give short shrift to "the importance of what does and can take place in the humanities classroom" ("What's at Stake in the Culture War," 477). Readings distinguishes his account of the university from that of Bourdieu and Guillory by emphasizing that the transnational situatedness of the university forestalls the closure of the national-cultural system in which cultural capital attains its symbolic status and ideological function. According to Readings, in Bourdieu's and Guillory's analyses, the "University necessarily appears as an ideological apparatus of the nation-state rather than a potentially transnational bureaucratic-capitalist enterprise" (*The University in Ruins*, 164). By approaching the university as analogous to the transnational corporation, Readings finds "both limitation and openness": "We are more free than we used to be in our teaching, but we can no longer see what it is that our freedom is freedom from" (ibid.). I certainly do not want to overstate the possibilities for transformation that originate in the humanities—or the ethnic studies—classroom. I do, however, want to suggest that the minority subject of intellectual discourse situated in the university participates in something other than only the diversion of a politics that would somehow be more authentic or more radical elsewhere.
79. Quoted in Derrida, *Adieu to Emmanuel Levinas*, 18.
80. Readings, *The University in Ruins*, 154.
81. Ibid., 160.
82. Ibid., 161.
83. Chang-rae Lee, *Native Speaker*, 348.
84. Ibid., 349.
85. Ibid.
86. Ibid.

NOTES / 205

87. For a helpful discussion of the impact of the scarcity of resources on racial formations, and the competition for such resources by minority groups in the United States, see McCarthy and Dimitriades, "Globalizing Pedagogies."
88. Readings, *The University in Ruins*, 161.
89. McCarthy and Dimitriades, "Globalizing Pedagogies," 187; Popkewitz, "Reform as the Social Administration of the Child," 174.
90. Popkewitz, "Reform as the Social Administration of the Child," 171.
91. Readings, *The University in Ruins*, 162–63.
92. Ibid., 162.
93. Chang-rae Lee, *Native Speaker*, 208.
94. Ibid.
95. Ibid., 207.
96. Ibid., 78, 72.
97. Ibid., 80.
98. Ibid., 334–35.

Chapter 5

1. See Gene Weingarten's "The Passion of Elián," which details the adoration and symbolization of Elián González both in Cuba and in Miami's Cuban exile community. Weingarten explains that Elián's school desk in Havana had been turned into a shrine, and that in Miami many Cubans identified him with baby Jesus. Further, he describes reports that circulated amongst Cuban Americans protesting the possibility of Elián's return to Cuba. According to these stories, Fidel Castro, rumored to be a practitioner of the Afro-Cuban religion of Santería, wished to have Elián returned to Cuba because he believed that the saint Eleggua inhabited Elián's body. It was further rumored that Castro intended to sacrifice Elián. As the author writes, "It does not take an expert in geopolitics to understand that the saga of Elián Gonzalez . . . is not merely about the fate of a little boy whose mother drowned and whose father wants him back. That would be clean, and easy. This is not easy. Or clean."
2. I adopt this formulation of diaspora as the other of the nation-state from Khachig Tölölyan's "The Nation-State and Its Others," which explains that analyses from the diasporic perspective can provide us insight into the way that "real yet imagined communities . . . are fabulated, brought into being, made and unmade, in culture and politics, both on land people call their own and in exile" (3). Homi K. Bhabha, in the introduction to *Nation and Narration*, also very usefully describes the concept of "narrating the nation."
3. Rey Chow, *Ethics after Idealism*, xxii.
4. Ibid.
5. Amy Kaplan concisely describes the threat that "American imperialism" poses to the "American republic": "If the fantasy of American imperialism aspires to a borderless world where it finds its own reflection everywhere, then the fruition of this dream shatters the coherence of national identity, as the boundaries that distinguish it from the outside world promise to collapse" (*Anarchy of Empire in the Making of U.S. Culture*, 16).
6. It is interesting to note that both of these cases evocatively recall the trial and execution of Julius and Ethel Rosenberg for espionage in the 1950s and their impact on Jewish national belonging as it played out through and against the threat of

Communism. The Rosenberg trial provides an important point of reference in the genealogy of American anti-Communism and the terms of loyalty and treason (although, like Wen Ho Lee, the Rosenbergs were never tried for treason, but rather for espionage) in the construction of the national security state. As Virginia Carmichael explains, "The Rosenberg story can be read either, in mythic terms, as a story of the betrayal of the patriarchal father (the nation-state, or perhaps civil society at large) by the children ... or as a story of the patriarchal father's allaying of family guilt, shame, and fear of retribution through the ritual of scapegoating sacrifice" (*Framing History*, xv). As such, the Rosenberg case provides what Carmichael calls a "frame story," within which both the experience of Cuban American nationalism and the investigation and indictment of Wen Ho Lee were articulated. For example, during one of the interrogation sessions Lee underwent, a federal agent pressured him by explicitly alluding to the Rosenberg case, threatening, "Do you know who the Rosenbergs are? . . . The Rosenbergs are the only people that never cooperated with the federal government in an espionage case. You know what happened to them? They electrocuted them, Wen Ho" (Stober and Hoffman, *A Convenient Spy*, 15). As Deborah Dash Moore has written about the impact of the Rosenberg trial, "For second-generation Jews, especially for those born and bred in New York City, the trial of the Rosenbergs became a definitional ceremony in which opposing versions of American Jewish identity competed for ascendancy. At stake was an understanding of what was required of a Jew in America" ("Reconsidering the Rosenbergs," 21–22). While the Rosenbergs might have felt that their Communist loyalties, patriotism to a democratic America, and Jewish heritage were mutually compatible with one another, their trial and execution (an "all Jewish drama" where the defendants, prosecutor, and judge identified as Jewish) were seen by many, including the judge who handed down the sentence, as an act of atonement to the nation: "Thus, the Rosenbergs' execution cleansed American Jewry of the taint of betrayal. Their death represented a symbolic atonement demanded to signify the loyalty of American Jews to the United States and its ideals" (ibid., 33–34; see also Horwitz, "Jews and McCarthyism"). Thus, in the symbolic absolutism regarding Jewish and American identity that pervaded the trial and later public debate, the Rosenberg case provides many of the terms through which national loyalty and treason have since been framed for racial and ethnic minorities. Yet, to the extent that, as I am arguing in this chapter, such bilateralism has been relegated to anachronism in contemporary neoliberal discourse, these terms have also been remarkably rearticulated in the Lee and González cases. Moreover, although suspicion of Jewish American loyalties continues to emerge in nativist rhetoric (illustrated, for example, in the case of Jonathon Pollard), Jewish American identity has also become, as Andrew Ross argues, increasingly assimilated to U.S. national interests, displaced in particular by fears of Muslims and Arab Americans in the United States ("The Work of the State," 291–99).

7. There have been two versions of Brotons's actions. On the one hand, it is stipulated that Brotons's own dream for capitalist freedom, not only or even firstly for herself but for her son, led her to make the heroic voyage. On the other hand, she is blamed for making the decision to leave Cuba in order to accompany her boyfriend, Lazaro Munero. Hardly the self-sacrificing mother in this latter version, she recklessly endangered her son's life for her own illicit passions, or because she was unable to stand up to Munero, who some described as physically and verbally abusive toward her. Likewise, Lee's wife played a central but in many ways unintelligible role in his story. In the

summer of 1998, when the two-year investigation of Lee had produced little evidence against him, the FBI mounted a "false flag" operation, in which an FBI agent pretending to be a foreign operative contacted Lee in order to maneuver him into saying or doing something self-incriminating. While, during the undercover agent's first phone call, Lee initially seemed interested in meeting the undercover agent, he backed out of the meeting, presumably because his wife had cautioned him against it. Furthermore, while Lee did not report the incident to the lab's counterintelligence staff, Sylvia Lee did so, through a friend's husband working at the lab: "The FBI didn't know what to make of the situation. Wen Ho Lee had not reported an obvious approach by a foreign intelligence service, but his wife arguably had—apparently without his knowledge" (Stober and Hoffman, *Convenient Spy*, 159–61). Moreover, Sylvia Lee worked as an informant for the FBI and the CIA from 1985 to 1991. Socializing with delegations of Chinese scientists, she served as a translator and eventually supplied both agencies with intelligence on correspondence, even as agents from the FBI investigated her husband. In fact, her work as an informant jeopardized her position as a data analyst at LANL, as it took her away from her assigned job duties. Her supervisors described her as difficult to work with, partly because they believed that she used her ethnic difference, including language difficulties, as a ruse for getting out of work she found overly menial. When Sylvia Lee committed a major security violation in what appeared to be a retributive gesture, her supervisor, Harold Sullivan, found himself unable to terminate her employment. While the Human Resources division of the lab cited numerous problems, including domestic problems with her husband, for her poor job performance, Sullivan denounced the decision as an example of political correctness: "She was a woman, she was a TEC ['a job defined as requiring minimal experience and involving fairly simple tasks under direct supervision'], she was ethnic, and she had some connection with the laboratory director." Sylvia Lee was never charged with any crimes, but it was clear that the FBI considered her central to their investigation of Lee as a potential spy, in part because of her "aggressive" involvement with visiting Chinese. However, agents involved in Lee's investigation overlooked that she had been recruited by other federal agents for this very purpose (ibid., 69–81).

8. For examples, see Linehan, "Cuba's Exiles Bring New Life to Miami"; and Alexander, "Those Amazing Cuban Émigrés." A Heritage Foundation report, "The Cuban Refugee Problem in Perspective: 1959–1980," which unequivocally celebrated the economic and social successes of Cuban exiles, was presented to the U.S. Congress and recorded in full in the *Congressional Record* as a means to stem anti-Cuban fears following the Mariel boatlift of 1980 (see "The Cuban Success Story"). As might be expected, the *Miami Herald* has also extensively chronicled the social and economic experiences of Cuban exiles and their descendants in the United States over the past four decades. For *analysis* of the representation of Cuban Americans as a model minority, see Boswell and Curtis, *The Cuban-American Experience*; as well as Croucher, *Imagining Miami*.

9. This does not mean, however, that Cuban exiles did not encounter significant hostility as well. Especially in local political and social responses, beginning in the 1960s and lasting well into the 1980s, both African Americans and Anglo-Americans in the Miami area voiced strong concerns, and in numerous cases outright antipathy, in response to the influx of Cubans into the region. These complaints centered on the job displacement and economic burdens that "native" South Floridians feared

would result from Cuban immigration. Cultural xenophobia, especially concerning language issues, also played a significant role (see Croucher, *Imagining Miami*; Masud-Piloto, *From Welcomed Exiles to Illegal Immigrants*; and María Cristina García, *Havana USA*.

10. Palumbo-Liu, *Asian/American*, 156. The bulk of Cuban emigrants from 1959 to the early 1980s (until just after the Mariel boatlift of April 1980) were allowed to enter the United States under the special status afforded to refugees. It is important to note, however, that not all of these emigrants can be said to conform to the status of "refugee" as defined by the 1949 U.N. Convention Relating to the Status of Refugees. As Jesús Arboleya argues, most Cuban emigrants have not been *persecuted* for their political views, and "political nonconformity doesn't determine status as a political refugee" (*Havana<n>Miami*, 10). Furthermore, as Thomas Boswell and James Curtis point out, the reasons for Cuban emigration have changed over time, such that, while in the 1960s most emigrants departed Cuba for political, social, and religious reasons—and received special immigration status upon arriving in the United States—by the 1970s, economic factors became prominent. The 1980 Refugee Act, which drastically limited the number of Cubans permitted to enter the U.S legally, reflected this shift (*The Cuban-American Experience*, 57).

11. I am describing here the *ideological* function of the model minority construct, not its descriptive accuracy. Several studies have suggested that the socioeconomic situation of the majority of Cuban Americans is more tenuous than the model minority image suggests (see Croucher, *Imagining Miami*, 125–26). It is also important to consider the extensive legislative and economic assistance provided in all aspects of Cuban refugee resettlement. Most significantly, the Cuban Adjustment Act, passed in 1966, allowed for Cuban refugees to apply for permanent status if their asylum claim had not been acted upon within a year and a day. In contrast, other groups, such as Haitians, have faced much longer waiting periods and received much less assistance as immigrants.

12. McLaren and Pinkney-Pastrana, "Cuba, Yanquización, and the Cult of Elián González," 206.

13. This characterization grossly oversimplifies the political affinities of those Cuban exiles who arrived during the early 1960s as "wealthy extremists with Fascist leanings who only wanted to recoup the property and social position they had lost as a result of Castro's revolution." According to various surveys from the early 1960s, a majority of Cuban Americans had in fact favored the end of Batista's regime, and somewhere between one-third and one-half of the exiles at one time supported Castro's revolution. Contemporary Cuban American testimonies also eloquently record that exiles held a spectrum of political views toward the Castro government in the early days of the Cuban revolution (Boswell and Curtis, *The Cuban-American Experience*, 170). See also *ReMembering Cuba*, edited by Andrea O'Reilly Herrera, which offers a wide range of autobiographical essays, many of which address this issue.

14. Hua, "A Daughter's Struggle," D1.

15. In a September 26 Editors' Note, the *Times* both defended but also, remarkably, described some of the flaws in its coverage of the Wen Ho Lee case, beginning in March 1999 when it first reported that the PRC had made advances in its nuclear weapons program via access to U.S. defense secrets and that the FBI had concentrated its investigation on a Chinese American scientist: "Looking back, we also found some

things we wish we had done differently in the course of the coverage to give Dr. Lee the full benefit of the doubt. In those months, we could have pushed harder to uncover weaknesses in the F.B.I. case against Dr. Lee. Our coverage would have been strengthened had we moved faster to assess the scientific, technical and investigative assumptions that led the F.B.I. and the Department of Energy to connect Dr. Lee to what is still widely acknowledged to have been a major security breach.... Passages of some articles also posed a problem of tone. In place of a tone of journalistic detachment from our sources, we occasionally used language that adopted the sense of alarm that was contained in official reports and was being voiced to us by investigators, members of Congress and administration officials with knowledge of the case.... There are articles we should have assigned but did not. We never prepared a full-scale profile of Dr. Lee, which might have humanized him and provided some balance. Some other stories we wish we had assigned in those early months include a more thorough look at the political context of the Chinese weapons debate, in which Republicans were eager to score points against the White House on China; an examination of how Dr. Lee's handling of classified information compared with the usual practices in the laboratories; a closer look at Notra Trulock, the intelligence official at the Department of Energy who sounded some of the loudest alarms about Chinese espionage; and an exploration of the various suspects and leads that federal investigators passed up in favor of Dr. Lee" (see "The *Times* and Wen Ho Lee").

16. See, for example, Adams, "No Insulation from Racial Discrimination." The Coalition Against Racial Scapegoating was organized as a result of the Lee case. The coalition, which began with the interest of a number of Asian American organizations, such as the National Asian Pacific American Bar Association and the Committee of 100, eventually appealed to a broad array of minority and civil rights advocacy groups, including the ACLU of Northern California, the National Lawyers Guild, the NAACP, the Mexican American Legal Defense Fund, and the Anti-Defamation League (see Hua, "A Daughter's Struggle; Fighting to Free Her Father, Charged with Violating National Security," D1; see also Sterngold, "Asian Americans Outraged about Arrest of Scientist").

17. William Wong, "DOE, FBI, Wen Ho Lee and the 'China Card,'" A17. For a detailed list of the evidence that the FBI and Department of Energy investigations engaged in racial profiling, see "Update: The Wen Ho Lee Case."

18. Davila, "What It Feels Like Being on 'Outside,'" B1. Lee's arrest followed the fundraising scandals for President Bill Clinton's and Vice President Al Gore's 1996 election campaigns that focused on two Asian Americans, John Huang and Charlie Yahn-lin Trie. Huang and Trie, both naturalized U.S. citizens, were accused of raising money from illegal foreign sources, fueling suspicions of a plot by foreign Chinese to gain influence over U.S. politics. Many Asian American critics saw the actions of Bill Richardson and Janet Reno in the Lee case as an attempt to counter Republican criticism that the Clinton administration had been "soft" on China. For a discussion of the racial politics in the campaign finance scandal, see Volpp, "Obnoxious to Their Very Nature."

19. For extended discussions of Miami's multiracial history, including the numerous conflicts between Anglo-American, Cuban American, Afro-Caribbean, and African American residents, see Sheila Croucher's *Imagining Miami*, as well as Alejandro Portes and Alex Stepick's *City on the Edge*. This is not to suggest that there were *no*

attempts made to articulate Elián's case—and that of the Cuban exiles—rhetorically in the terms of minoritarian discourse. For example, see Augustin Tamargo ("La honra en el estrado"), who urges the federal appeals court to make an "honorable" decision in the González case, using Martin Luther King Jr.'s activism and Lyndon Johnson's signing of the Civil Rights Act as examples of such "honor," and the Japanese internment as an instance of "dishonor."

20. As Tamargo writes about the Cuban "sufferers in exile": "Cubans will remain, many Cubans, as witnesses to that hour of return, which historically is bound to arrive. Even if there are not many, it does not matter. To step on the native soil, upon the rubble of despotism, only one exile is enough, he who shouts out on that day, 'Cuba, we will not fail you!'" ("Los enfermos del exilio" [translation by Christopher Sánchez]; see also Sánchez-Boudy, "El exilio histórico"). The religious interpretation of Elián's story unfolded for the most part according to the symbols and iconography of Cuban Catholicism, and often in opposition to Santería, with the racist demonization of the Afro-Cuban tradition only thinly, if at all, veiled. Elián's rescue by fishermen recalls the recovery of the image of La Virgin de la Caridad del Cobre, the patron saint of Cuba. Protestors also drew out the Christ allegory further, with signs in Spanish that demanded, "Do not deliver Elián to the Romans," and "Elián is Christ. Reno is Lucifer. Castro is Satan." Clergy also explained that "Jesus was saved by his mother and foster father who took him away from Herod's murderous grasp, just as Elián was saved by his mother and stepfather who took him away from Castro to make him safe." As one priest bluntly explained, "These religious connections to Elián are a way for people to channel their grief and anger over 41 years of revolution. This child is a way for them to envision resurrection for Cuba" (Laughlin, "Prayer Vigil Lifts Elián Fervor to New High," 1B; see also "Como Herodes en madrugada," in which José Sánchez-Boudy compares the early morning raid on Lázaro Gonzáles's home with Herod's seizing of Jesus). Because of the pervasiveness of Santería in both Cuban and Cuban American culture, it was never entirely or exclusively demonized. Rather, appeals were made to Santería saints to protect Elián as well. Cuban Americans involved with Santería cast Elián as a "son" of Eleggua, "who has a boyish mischievous manifestation not unlike Elián." They were also often likely to cite the story regarding Castro's belief that Elián was either favored or inhabited by Eleggua and destined to bring about the demise of Castro's regime (see Carter, "Santería Ceremony Held to Guard Boy"). For further detail on the rumors regarding Castro's belief that Elián was an incarnation of Eleggua, see Infante, "El niño prodigo."

21. Arboleya, Havana<n>Miami, 31–32.

22. For an example of such a critique of "Castro appeasing" in the case of Elián González, see Horowitz, "Los dos Cuba de Elián González."

23. Tamargo, "Los enfermos del exilio" (translation by Christopher Sánchez).

24. The more extreme versions of this rhetoric in the González case accused the American press of being influenced or infiltrated by Cuban Communism and thus never able to report the truth of Castro's regime: "The American press has demonstrated that it is subsidized by the murderer of more than 140,000 Cubans, Fidel Castro Ruiz, by its constant attacks against the combatant Cubans in exile, and by their silence regarding the misery, corruption, deaths, and imprisonments that occur daily on the enslaved Cuban island" (Iglesias, "El vir del castrismo en la prensa norteamericana" [translation by Christopher Sánchez]).

25. Clendenning, "Free Speech a One-Sided Notion on Elián's Street." Gene Weingarten further explains: "The leaders of Cuban Miami rose to power and held it by marshaling the passion of a single political ideology: Communism is evil; Castro is the enemy, and he must be punished through relentless economic sanctions until he is overthrown. It has been said that the mayoralty of Miami is the only municipal position in America that requires a foreign policy" ("The Passion of Elián").

26. It is also important to consider, as Sheila Croucher contends, that an interest in U.S. domestic politics and issues beyond Cuba, Castro, and Communism on the part of Cuban Americans (especially second-generation, U.S.-born Cuban Americans) does not necessarily mean that exile politics have been altogether displaced. Rather, Cuban American deployment of a more traditional immigrant narrative of Americanization "does not simply represent a desire or willingness among Cubans to assimilate into the American mainstream.... An increased focus on the 'new land' does not signal a disinterest in the 'homeland.' Instead, the shift away from exile politics is more accurately interpreted as an alternative discursive strategy consistent with an altered set of social, political and economic circumstances" (*Imagining Miami*, 135).

27. Julio Estorino ("Los tres niños y el milagro posible") contends that Cuban Americans can "avoid the irreverence of comparing [Elián] with Christ, by turning instead to the human model of Jose Martí" (translation by Christopher Sánchez). Moreover, writing on the anniversary of the birth of Cuba's national hero, Estorino insists on the need for unity amongst Cubans: "Today we must again ask all those who squander their energies in fratricidal and stupid enmity against those who they consider their ideological or political adversaries in the ranks of the exile or of the internal dissidence, that they stop for a moment this twenty-eighth of January and reconsider their course in light of the ideal and the commonality of practical experience."

28. Elián's arrival in the United States as a "virtual orphan" recalls the mass emigration of children in the early 1960s as part of the Operation Peter Pan, emigration sparked by rumors that the revolutionary government of Cuba would be eliminating parental rights. An estimated fourteen thousand children arrived in the United States as part of Operation Peter Pan (for detailed discussions of the operation, see Conde, *Operation Pedro Pan*; and Triay, *Fleeing Castro*). One Cuban American commentator, Ramon Ferreira, writes "¿Quién es el padre de Moisés?" (Who is the father of Moses?). Ferreira further presses the question of the child's role in the community by arguing that for those destined to be great leaders, the identity, and the claims, of the father are insignificant. History recalls only the great leader himself, and in Elián, the author locates the possibility of another such preordained history (see also Ferreira, "Elián: Derecho o maniobra política?").

29. Male, "Es Elián un angel?" (translation by Christopher Sánchez).

30. Leitsinger, "Elián's Fla. Home Opens as a Shrine," A10. Others have also likened the conditions on the island under Castro's government and of exile displacement to the Holocaust. See, for example, Nestor Diaz de Villegas ("Elián y el sistema americano") and Bob Hohler ("As Rage Dies Down, Little Havana Experiences Sense of Loss"). See also "Una decisión desacertada," in which José Sánchez-Boudy portrays the decision to return Elián to Cuba as the infliction of "a wound in the collective soul of a people" that "will never disappear even with the passing of centuries" (translation by Christopher Sánchez).

31. For example, see "Elián: El hijo de los delfines."

32. Indeed, in Cuba, Elián had been likened to a "new Che" (see Laughlin, "Prayer Vigil Lifts Elián Fervor to New High"). As one Havana resident predicted Elián's position in Cuban society upon the child's return: "He is going to be written into Cuban history. He is going to have to live up to the image of himself with Fidel's arm around him—when that happens—forever"; another added, "The party is going to be telling us that this is one of the triumphs of the revolution" ("Havana Residents Wait, Wondering What's Next").

33. Horowitz, *The Conscience of Worms and the Cowardice of Lions*, 71.

34. See, for example, Markovits, "The Enemy Makes the Man."

35. Ortíz, "*Café, Culpa*, and *Capital*," 77.

36. In 1974 the *Miami News* reported that, despite increasing numbers of Cuban exiles who were becoming U.S. citizens, many regarded naturalization as a "convenience" rather than a committed choice, and many others refrained altogether from naturalizing, as they considered this (or thought others would see it as) an act of betrayal to their country (Cruz, "Some Cubans Feel U.S. Citizenship Just 'Convenience'"). In 1990, amidst optimism that events in Eastern Europe forebode the end of Communism in Cuba, a survey of Cuban adults in Dade County found that one of every five claimed he or she would return to Cuba if Castro's government were to fail (Ramos,"1 in 5 Dade Cubans Would Go Back"). While this number had fallen greatly since the 1970s, that 20 percent of the population lived with the hope of returning, coupled with the survey's finding that 54 percent of Cuban Americans favored a U.S. invasion of Cuba, is in keeping with the sense that non-Latinos have that the Cuban community's national loyalties remain divided. This perception in turn influenced much of the coverage and discourse surrounding the Elián González case.

37. Sarah Banet-Weiser, in "Elián González and 'The Purpose of America,'" charts the various "frames" (e.g., media, religious, etc.) through which the Elián narrative gained meaning for both Cuban Americans as well as a broader U.S. public and emphasizes the contradictions between the different framings of this story. In particular, she describes the fraught relationship between ideals of democratic liberalism and "family values," especially as these revolved around the much vaunted "innocence" of the child. However, Banet-Weiser significantly overlooks the extent to which non-Latinos in the United States disagreed with the Cuban exile community's demands regarding González. Thus, the implication that the case straightforwardly and nostalgically returned *both* Cuban Americans *and* the American public to a sense of national identity mired in conservative Cold War politics critically overlooks, as I am arguing in this chapter, the extent to which the American imaginary posited such an identity as anachronistic.

38. Hertzberg, "A Tale of Two Cubas," 33. For a summary article on the presentation of Miami as a "banana republic," see Laughlin, "Elián Case Puts Miami 'Republic' in Spotlight."

39. A national Gallup poll, conducted in February 2000, found that 67 percent of Americans supported the return of Elián to his father in Cuba, which marked a steady increase of support of the federal government's position since December 1999, when public opinion was more evenly split between allowing him to stay and returning him to Cuba (Rosenberg, "National Polls Steadily Support Return of Elián," 3B). An April 2000 poll of Miami-Dade County residents found deep divisions based on race and ethnicity, where 92 percent of blacks and 76 percent of non-Hispanic whites favored

the child's return to Cuba, in contrast to 83 percent of Cuban Americans who believed he should remain in the United States (Viglucci and Marrero, "Poll Reveals Widening Split over Elián," 1A). Interestingly, the poll also found that the majority (55 percent) of other non-Cuban Latinos agreed with the majority of Cuban Americans (ibid.). As one news story explained, "The least sympathetic [to the Cuban Americans position on the Elián case] was Miami's black community, whose own long-standing civil rights issues don't command equal attention from Cuban-American political leaders. American and Haitian-born blacks can only dream of the political clout and media-drawing powers of the Cuban Americans" (Douthat, "Miami's Cuban Community Strengthens Its Position"). Perhaps one of the most striking pieces of evidence that the opposition to the mainline Cuban American position in the Elián case displaced racial antagonisms between blacks and whites with a strongly nationalist discourse is the participation of African Americans in "pro-American" protests alongside "self-described rednecks." "Walking alongside whites waving the Confederate flag, a symbol she detests," one black woman explained her presence at such an event by stating: "This is a greater cause than the Confederate flag" (Dorschner and Ocaña, "Deep Anguish over Elián Splitting the Community"). Cuban Americans certainly did not help their own cause here when they insisted on presenting themselves as model minorities in the face of such hostility: "We've been around here for 41 years and have learned how the system works. . . . Other groups can do the same thing we do" (Douthat, "Miami's Cuban Community").

40. In March 2000 Alex Penelas stated that he would refuse to allow county police to aid federal agents if they attempted to remove Elián from his Miami relatives' home, and that Attorney General Reno and President Clinton would be to blame if any violence ensued from such a course of action. A poll showed that 90 percent of blacks and 80 percent of white non-Hispanics disapproved of these statements. Penelas later argued that his statements had been misconstrued, and that police would indeed be available to maintain order and protect agents (see Viglucci and Marrero, "Poll Reveals Widening Split over Elián").

41. Douthat, "Miami's Cuban Community." Moreover, Cuban Americans were perceived by non-Latinos as "using Elián for purely political reasons while ignoring the father's rights to claim his own child." *Time* magazine construed the conflicts surrounding the Elián case in terms of "We"—that is to say, of a reasonable, paternal America *and* its Cuban others: "We sympathize with his father, who wants Elián returned home to Cuba. But then we remember that Elián's mother drowned trying to get him to freedom. And we're disgusted with both Castro and the anti-Castro zealots in Miami who are shamelessly using Elián and his father as fresh draftees in their tiresome feud" (Ramo, "The Odyssey of Elián González," 60; see also Steinback, "Cuban Exiles in Need of Allies").

42. Veiga, "Elián Saga United Cuban Exiles, But Hurt Image, Political Clout"; see also Katel, "Buscan reparar la afectada imagen de los cubanoamericanos."

43. Veiga, "Elián Saga United Cuban Exiles, But Hurt Image, Political Clout."

44. Welsome, "Spies Lies & Portable Tapes."

45. Stober and Hoffman, *A Convenient Spy*, 312.

46. Herrington, "Is Wen Ho Lee a Tarnished Martyr?"

47. For example, many activists called attention to the fact that CIA director John Deutch was not prosecuted for the security breaches that he committed, which were

similar in nature to Lee's. For a comparison of Deutch's and Lee's security violations, see Peng, "The Tragic Case of Wen Ho Lee."

48. The possibility of Lee's guilt further explains why many local Chinese Americans living in Los Alamos distanced themselves altogether from Lee. Some recalled that during the Cold War, Taiwanese intelligence agencies branded critics of the Kuomintang in the United States as Communist sympathizers. Moreover, because federal agents cited, as reasons for their suspicion of Lee, his socializing with PRC officials when they visited LANL and when he visited Beijing—a common practice amongst many Chinese American scientists—many also worried about being fingered as well (Stober and Hoffman, *A Convenient Spy*, 206).

49. Clark, "Unsealed Documents Shed Light on Wen Ho Lee Plea Deal Talks."

50. Frank H. Wu also posits the possibility of Lee's guilt, although toward a different but important end. Wu argues, with respect to legal strategy and principle, that a defense of Lee must subordinate entirely as a premise the likelihood of Lee's guilt or innocence to that of his civil rights. Indeed, Wu suggests, the defense must be willing even to concede the probability of guilt in order to get to the principle of racial profiling. As Wu contends, against the utilitarianism of "rational discrimination," "if an anti-discrimination principle has any meaning at all, it must be at its most effective when it is least attractive" ("Profiling Principle," 53).

51. For Wen Ho Lee's explanation of his actions, see his *My Country versus Me*. For a discussion of the questions that remain unanswered in his account, see Holt, "It Takes Two Books to Untangle Story of Accused Spy."

52. Stober and Hoffman, *A Convenient Spy*, 310.

53. Dolinsky, "A Chinese Spy Mystery Remains Just That," WB1.

54. Stober and Hoffman, *A Convenient Spy*, 316–17.

55. Ibid., 262–65.

56. Ibid., 259.

57. Ibid., 245.

58. Carmichael, *Framing History*, 11.

59. Stober and Hoffman, *A Convenient Spy*, 72.

60. Ibid., 77.

61. Ibid., 92.

62. To argue that the development of the security state has been imbricated in the disciplinary and epistemological formation of the physical sciences is not, however, to imply that this was an inevitable state of affairs, nor that this mutual dependency went uncontested by all or even most scientists. As Jessica Wang explains in impressive detail, during the postwar period between 1945 and 1950 the relationship between the military, the government, and the sciences was a highly contested one. Many of the scientific elite, who espoused what Wang calls a "progressive left politics," promoted civilian oversight and international cooperation over research in nuclear energy and weapons, in order to prevent the proliferation of an arms race. Further, many strongly objected to the underlying assumptions that shaped the Atomic Energy Act, arguing that the scientific knowledge could not be conceived of as a "secret" over which the state needed to maintain a monopoly. One theoretical physicist who became a Senate adviser predicted: "Having created an air of suspicion and mistrust, there will be persons among us who think other nations can know nothing except what is learned by espionage. So, when other countries make atom bombs, these persons will cry 'treason'

at our scientists, or they will find it inconceivable that another country could make a bomb in any other way except by aid from Americans" (Wang, *American Science in an Age of Anxiety*, 17–25). The warning was prescient for the Lee case, four decades later, where it remains yet unclear whether advances in the PRC nuclear capability were even in fact a result of espionage at all, or rather of independent advances made by Chinese scientists over the past decade.

63. Yin, "The Lee Case Shakes Asian Americans' Faith in Justice System," M1.

64. Wen Ho Lee, *My Country versus Me*, 19.

65. Ibid., 25.

66. For a historical overview of the military-scientific-industrial complex through which the national security state was organized, and of the revitalization of Cold War militarism and science under the conditions of globalization, see McLauchlan and Hooks, "Last of the Dinosaurs?"

67. Koo, "The Impact of the Wen Ho Lee Case on Asian Americans," 29. This comparison became especially pointed when it was referenced the PRC in particular. In other words, the critique charged that in the name of national security—security of democratic freedom and rights from the likes of the PRC—the United States enacted the same repressive measures as are common in (or commonly attributed to) the PRC.

68. Brown, *States of Injury*, 134.

69. Ibid.

70. Cheah, "Posit(ion)ing Human Rights in the Current Global Conjuncture," 34.

71. For a further elaboration of this concept of "right(s) by reason," see Dimock, *Residues of Justice*.

72. Cheah, "Posit(ion)ing Human Rights in the Current Global Conjuncture," 34.

73. Koshy, "From Cold War to Trade War," 22.

74. Cheah, "Posit(ion)ing Human Rights in the Current Global Conjuncture," 33.

75. Ibid.

76. Ibid. Cheah categorizes the different positions taken with respect to human rights into three predominant "voices": (1) the institutional voice of economically hegemonic, constitutional democracies in the North and the West, (2) the voice of Asian—and other rapidly developing national—governments, and (3) human rights NGOs in the South. As Susan Koshy further notes: "Unlike the earlier stage where the opposition was between capitalist and socialist ideologies, the current confrontation is between two forms of capitalism," authoritarian, or "communitarian" capitalism, on the one hand, and liberal capitalism, on the other hand ("From Cold War to Trade War," 13). All three voices are quite critical of one another for what they deem to be the others' ideologically impure positions with respect to political and economic realities. Nevertheless, Cheah argues, they *share* a normative framework grounded in a concept of human dignity that transcends particularistic and historical contingencies, in the value that they place on rational form over material history, and in the transformative force they ascribe to rational form over institutional structures. If the first and second voices are clearly caught in a "miasmic complicity between domestic oppression and international exploitation," Cheah believes that the third voice of human rights, NGOs, appeals to a global civil society, or public sphere, which is equally conditioned by the investments and interests of global capitalism ("Posit(ion)ing Human Rights in the Current Global Conjuncture," 26).

77. Cheah, "Posit(ion)ing Human Rights in the Current Global Conjuncture," 28.
78. Ibid., 35.
79. As Jack Donnelly describes it: "Many Americans thus believe and perpetuate the quaint fiction that human rights problems exist only in places that must be reached by crossing large bodies of waters. Other countries have human rights problems. The US, however, suffers from police brutality, civil rights problems, homelessness or a health-care crisis—none of which are considered human rights violations" (quoted in Koshy, "From Cold War to Trade War," 23).
80. In the specific case of Elián González, for example, numerous observers saw in Elián's performance at school an indication of the robust general educational system and rates of literacy in Cuba, which we might productively understand in terms of second-generation rights.
81. Chow, "Leading Questions," 195–96. Kandice Chuh and Karen Shimakawa further describe the configuration of China in liberal discourse: "China thus easily becomes a market that needs opening in order that (American) democracy may prevail. It is important to note here the distinction between China-as-government and China-as-people central to this imagining. China-as-government is the bad other: the force of Communist repression through violation of human rights" (*Orientations*, 3).
82. This "departure" also, of course, finds its material body in the Chinese diaspora, which has been documented in detail. For especially useful discussions of overseas Chinese and modes of Chineseness under transnational capitalism, see Ong, *Flexible Citizenship*; and Ong and Nonini, *Ungrounded Empires*.
83. Chow, "Leading Questions," 206.
84. Derrida, *Specters of Marx*, 39.
85. Ibid., 99.
86. Ong, *Flexible Citizenship*, 32–36.

Epilogue

1. Morris, "Theses on the Questions of War," 150.
2. As Rosalind Morris explains, the war against terror breaks with the hot and cold battles of the Cold War precisely because it is "not just a return to war, but a return to holy war," against a "politicized and militarized Islamic entity whose nature is precisely *not national*" ("Theses on the Questions of War," 153). The attacks constitute not only an attack on America, but "an attack on the principle of nationhood, of which America claims to be the exemplary instance" (ibid., 153). Rearticulating extant formations of nation, diaspora, religion, and class, the present war might seem to resuscitate the rhetoric and postures of the Cold War, but it nonetheless "constitutes something of a break with Cold War policy" and the social and political realities of bilateralism (ibid., 152). Noam Chomsky dubs this realignment of the United States and its allies and clients "Intcom," distinguishing this formation from the "international community" in whose name the United States purports to act. Chomsky explains that, unlike the symbolic Intcom, the literal counterpart that is the international community has been mostly subject by the U.S. to defiance at best, and at worst, to a string of antidemocratic *realpolitik* crimes. In contrast, where Intcom is concerned, the U.S. authorizes by force the legitimacy of its status, so that "it is a logical impossibility for the United States to defy the international community" ("The Crimes of 'Intcom,'" 34).

3. For a prescient analysis of the way in which the state "works" to "consolidate some new shift in the definition of the U.S. nation-state" during the 1994 trial of the suspects in the *first* World Trade Center bombing in 1993, see Andrew Ross's "The Work of the State." In this essay, Ross compares the trial of Ramzi Yousef and his associates to that of Ethel and Julius Rosenberg in order to consider "history's nomination process," by which a story emerges as the "official explanation" of an event and "begins its journey into the congealed state of common sense" (299).

4. Pease, "*The Patriot* Acts," 42.

5. Milbank, "Sovereignty, Empire, Capital, and Terror," 310.

6. Derrida, "Force of Law."

7. As David Noble argues, the emergence of a historical narrative of the separation of the "New World" from the "Old World" in the nineteenth century assumed the American Revolution as pivotal in the development of forms of sovereignty. In the progressive narrative of national formation, the United States represents "the perfect separation of liberty from power," such that European destiny was not ultimately located in the "spaces" of northwestern Europe, but, rather, the promised land of the West, "where liberty would find her final home, was that space in North America populated by the descendants of English Protestants—the space destined to be the national landscape of the United States" ("The Anglo-Protestant Monopolization of 'America,'" 261). For a discussion on the global implications of this concept of the United States as a "global nation," see Bright and Geyer, "Where in the World Is America?"

8. James Yee, *For God and Country*, 15.

9. Ibid., ix.

10. Ibid., 25.

11. Ibid., 33.

12. Ibid., 40.

13. Ibid., 136.

14. Mamdani, *Good Muslim, Bad Muslim*. As Mamdani explains, after September 11, "unless proved to be 'good,' every Muslim was presumed to be 'bad.' All Muslims were now under obligation to prove their credentials by joining in a war against 'bad Muslims'" (ibid., 15).

15. James Yee, *For God and Country*, 48–49.

16. Ibid., 132.

17. Ibid., 141.

18. Ibid., 147.

19. Ibid., 187.

20. Ibid., 186.

21. Ibid., 126.

22. Ibid., 218.

23. Ibid., 200.

24. Ibid., 213, 216.

25. Ibid., 101.

26. The history of the protections guaranteed by Title III of the Omnibus Crime Control and Safe Streets Act of 1968 and the Foreign Intelligence Surveillance Act (FISA) of 1978, with which the Patriot Act is concerned, is already a thoroughly racialized one, and that racialization both continues into and is rearticulated in the discursive constitution of the suspected terrorist. For example, the protections afforded

by Title III and FISA came as a result of a Senate select committee's findings that U.S. intelligence agencies routinely and extensively violated U.S. privacy interests in the name of national security during the Vietnam and Cold Wars, illegally spying on thousands of American citizens during the 1960s and 1970s as part of Operation Chaos (Rackow, "How the USA PATRIOT ACT Will Permit Governmental Infringement upon the Privacy of Americans in the Name of 'Intelligence' Investigations," 1666). As has been well documented, black nationalists and civil rights leaders were amongst the primary objects of these invasive practices. Even more fundamentally significant, the judicial interpretation and application of the Fourth Amendment protection against unreasonable search and seizure to ensure privacy, rather than merely more limited property rights, devolves from a much longer history where the privacy *and* property rights of (white) Americans has been formulated against the exclusion of racialized others (ibid., 1656).

27. Heymann, "Civil Liberties and Human Rights in the Aftermath of September 11," 453.

28. James Yee, *For God and Country*, 145.

29. Ibid., 221.

30. If the history of the right to privacy and its protection *in* the United States has been thoroughly racialized, the production of a global imaginary of America and its pre- and postcolonial others has of course also been thoroughly gendered. This has been most obvious, as numerous postcolonial feminists have demonstrated, in the touting of the cause of "Woman" to justify the war in Afghanistan. It is salient too in the hyper-masculine patriotism that responds to the September 11 attacks as a crime of passion, casting the nation as "the enraged, loyal, humiliated husband killing his wife's lover upon discovering him in the marital bed" (Ahmad, "Homeland Insecurities," 108). Less obvious, but more insidious in and constitutive of colonial domination, are the gendered practices of regulation, surveillance, and torture that were part and parcel of colonial rule. In this "awful patriarchal complicity," as Rosalind Morris describes it, between colonized male subjects and colonial powers, colonizers secured domination by humiliating, assaulting, and violating colonized women in order to undermine the patriarchal privileges of colonized men: "Where colonial domination has worked through this mechanism, it produces an inexorable link between terrorism and gender. Our current belief that the war on terrorism is the war to liberate women is a misrecognition of this historical fact, whose origins are to be found less in any indigenous oppression of women ... than in the histories of colonialism to which the United States is heir" ("Theses on the Questions of War," 164–65).

Bibliography

Adams, Pam. "No Insulation from Racial Discrimination." Copley News Service. 27 September 2000. http://academic.lexisnexis.com/.
Ahmad, Muneer. "Homeland Insecurities: Racial Violence the Day after September 11." *Social Text* 20, no. 3 (2002): 101–15.
Ahmed, Sara. *Differences that Matter: Feminist Theory and Postmodernism*. Cambridge: Cambridge University Press, 1998.
———. "Home and Away: Narratives of Migration and Estrangement." *International Journal of Cultural Studies* 2, no. 3 (1999): 329–47.
———. *Strange Encounters: Embodied Others in Post-Coloniality*. London: Routledge, 2000.
Alarcón, Norma. "Tropology of Hunger: The 'Miseducation' of Richard Rodriguez." In *The Ethnic Canon: Histories and Interventions*, edited by David Palumbo-Liu, 140–52. Minneapolis: University of Minnesota Press, 1995.
Alexander, Tom. "Those Amazing Cuban Émigrés." *Fortune*, October 1966, 144–49.
Ancheta, Angelo N. *Race, Rights, and the Asian American Experience*. New York: Rutgers University Press, 1988.
Appadurai, Arjun. "Disjuncture and Difference in the Global Cultural Economy." *Theory, Culture, and Society* 7 (July 1990): 295–310.
———. "Heart of Whiteness." *Callaloo* 16, no. 4 (1993): 796–807.
Aranda, José F., Jr. "Making the Case for New Chicano/a Studies: Recovering Our Alienated Selves." *Arizona Quarterly* 58, no. 1 (2002): 127–58.
Arboleya, Jesús. *Havana–Miami: The U.S.–Cuba Migration Conflict*. Translated by Mary Todd. Melbourne: Ocean Press, 1996.

Arlen, Michael J. "Notes on the New Journalism." *Atlantic Monthly,* May 1972. http://www.theatlantic.com/issues/72may/newjournalism-p1.htm.
Aronowitz, Stanley. *The Politics of Identity: Class, Culture, Social Movements.* New York: Routledge, 1992.
Attridge, Derek. "Innovation, Literature, Ethics: Relating to the Other." *PMLA* 114, no. 1 (1999): 20–31.
———. "Introduction: Derrida and the Questioning of Literature." In *Acts of Literature,* by Jacques Derrida, 1–29. New York: Routledge, 1992.
Baker, Susan Gonzalez. "Demographic Trends in the Chicana/o Population: Policy Implications for the Twenty-First Century." In *Chicanas/Chicanos at the Crossroads: Social, Economic and Political Change,* edited by David R. Maciel and Isidro D. Ortiz. Tucson: University of Arizona Press, 1996, 5–24.
Banet-Weiser, Sarah. "Elián González and 'The Purpose of America': Nation, Family, and the Child-Citizen." *American Quarterly* 55, no. 2 (2003): 149–78.
Batker, Carol J. *Reforming Fictions: Native, African, and Jewish American Women's Literature and Journalism in the Progressive Era.* New York: Columbia University Press, 2000.
Behdad, Ali. *A Forgetful Nation: On Immigration and Cultural Identity in the United States.* Durham, NC: Duke University Press, 2005.
Bergo, Bettina G. "Inscribing the 'Sites' of Desire in Levinas." In *Philosophy and Desire,* edited by Hugh J. Silverman, 63–82. New York: Routledge, 2000.
Berlant, Lauren. *The Queen of America Goes to Washington City: Essays on Sex and Citizenship.* Durham, NC: Duke University Press, 1997.
Bhabha, Homi K. "Introduction: Narrating the Nation." In *Nation and Narration,* edited by Homi K. Bhabha, 1–7. London: Routledge, 1990.
———. *The Location of Culture.* London: Routledge, 1994.
Bloom, Clive, ed. *Spy Thrillers: From Buchan to Le Carré.* New York: St. Martin's Press, 1990.
Bonilla, Frank, et al., eds. *Borderless Borders: U.S. Latinos, Latin Americans, and the Paradox of Interdependence.* Philadelphia: Temple University Press, 1998.
Boswell, Thomas D., and James R. Curtis. *The Cuban-American Experience: Culture, Images, and Perspectives.* Totawa, NJ: Rowman & Allanheld, 1984.
Bourdieu, Pierre. *The Field of Cultural Reproduction.* Edited by Randal Johnson. New York: Columbia University Press, 1993.
———. *Language and Symbolic Power.* Edited by John B. Thompson. Translated by Gino Raymond and Matthew Adamson. Cambridge, MA: Harvard University Press, 1991.
Bow, Leslie. *Betrayal and Other Acts of Subversion: Feminism, Sexual Politics, Asian American Women's Literature.* Princeton, NJ: Princeton University Press, 2001.

Brah, Avtar. *Cartographies of Diaspora: Contesting Identities.* London: Routledge, 1996.
Bright, Charles, and Michael Geyer. "Where in the World Is America?: The History of the United States in the Global Age." In *Rethinking American History in a Global Age*, edited by Thomas Bender, 63–99. Berkeley: University of California Press, 2002.
Brock, Lisa. "Introduction: Between Race and Empire." In *Between Race and Empire: African-Americans and Cubans before the Revolution*, edited by Lisa Brock and Digna Castañeda, 1–32. Philadelphia: Temple University Press, 1998.
Brown, Wendy. *States of Injury: Power and Freedom in Late Modernity.* Princeton, NJ: Princeton University Press, 1995.
Butler, Johnnella E., ed. *Color-Line to Borderlands: The Matrix of American Ethnic Studies.* Seattle: University of Washington Press, 2001.
Butler, Judith. *Bodies that Matter: On the Discursive Limits of "Sex."* New York: Routledge, 1993.
———. "Ethical Ambivalence." In *The Turn to Ethics*. Edited by Marjorie Garbor, Beatrice Hanssen, and Rebecca L. Walkowitz, 15–28. New York: Routledge, 2000.
———. *The Psychic Life of Power: Theories in Subjection.* Stanford, CA: Stanford University Press, 1997.
Camarota, Steven A. "Immigrants in the United States—2002: A Snapshot of America's Foreign-Born Population." Center for Immigration Studies *Backgrounder* (Washington, DC), November 2002.
Carmichael, Virginia. *Framing History: The Rosenberg Story and the Cold War.* Minneapolis: University of Minnesota Press, 1993.
Carter, Tom. "Santería Ceremony Held To Guard Boy." *Washington Times*, 3 April 2000, A10. http://academic.lexisnexis.com/.
Chabram-Dernersesian, Angie. "On the Social Construction of Whiteness within Selected Chicana/o Discourses." In *Displacing Whiteness: Essays in Social and Cultural Criticism*, edited by Ruth Frankenberg, 107–64. Durham, NC: Duke University Press, 1997.
Chan, Sucheng. *Asian Americans: An Interpretative History.* Boston: Twayne, 1991.
Cheah, Pheng. "Posit(ion)ing Human Rights in the Current Global Conjuncture." In *Transnational Asia Pacific: Gender, Culture, and the Public Sphere*, edited by Shirley Geok-lin Lim, Larry E. Smith, and Wimal Dissanayake, 11–42. Urbana: University of Illinois Press, 1999.
Chen, Tina. *Double Agency: Acts of Impersonation in Asian American Literature and Culture.* Stanford, CA: Stanford University Press, 2005.
Chin, Frank. *"The Chickencoop Chinaman"; and, "The Year of the Dragon": Two Plays.* Seattle: University of Washington Press, 1981.

Chomsky, Noam. "The Crimes of 'Intcom.'" *Foreign Policy* (October 2002): 34–35.

Chow, Rey. *Ethics after Idealism: Theory—Culture—Ethnicity—Reading*. Bloomington: Indiana University Press, 1998.

———. "Leading Questions." In *Orientations: Mapping Studies in the Asian Diaspora*, edited by Kandice Chuh and Karen Shimakawa, 189–212. Durham, NC: Duke University Press, 2001.

Christopher, Renny. "Rags to Riches to Suicide: Unhappy Narratives of Upward Mobility: *Martin Eden*, *Bread Givers*, *Delia's Song*, and *Hunger of Memory*." *College Literature* 29 (2002): 79–108.

Chu, Patricia P. *Assimilating Asians: Gendered Strategies of Authorship in Asian America*. Durham, NC: Duke University Press, 2000.

Chuh, Kandice. "Hierarchies of Color: Legal and Literary Logics of Whiteness." Paper presented at the annual meeting of the Association for Asian American Studies, Philadelphia, PA, April 1999.

———. *Imagine Otherwise: On Asian Americanist Critique*. Durham, NC: Duke University Press, 2003.

———. "Transnationalism and Its Pasts." *Public Culture* 9, no. 1 (1996): 93–112.

Chuh, Kandice, and Karen Shimakawa, eds. *Orientations: Mapping Studies in the Asian Diaspora*. Durham, NC: Duke University Press, 2001.

Clark, Heather. "Unsealed Documents Shed Light on Wen Ho Lee Plea Deal Talks." Associated Press State and Local Wire, 5 October 2001. http://academic.lexisnexis.com/.

Clendenning, Alan. "Free Speech a One-Sided Notion on Elián's Street." Associated Press State and Local Wire, April 21, 2000. http://academic.lexisnexis.com/.

Conde, Yvonne M. *Operation Pedro Pan: The Untold Exodus of 14,048 Cuban Children*. New York: Routledge, 1999.

Corley, Liam. "'Just Another Ethnic Pol': Literary Citizenship in Chang-rae Lee's *Native Speaker*." In *Transnational Asian American Literature: Sites and Transits*, edited by Shirley Geok-lin Lim, Larry E. Smith, and Wimal Dissanayake, 55–74. Philadelphia: Temple University Press, 2006.

Crenshaw, Kimberlé, et al., eds. *Critical Race Theory: The Key Writings that Formed the Movement*. New York: New Press, 1995

Critchley, Simon. *The Ethics of Deconstruction: Derrida and Levinas*. Oxford: Blackwell, 1992.

———. *Ethics—Politics—Subjectivity: Essays on Derrida, Levinas, and Contemporary French Thought*. London: Verso, 1998.

Croucher, Sheila. *Imagining Miami: Ethnic Politics in a Postmodern World*. Charlottesville: University of Virginia Press, 1997.

Cruz, Humberto. "Some Cubans Feel U.S. Citizenship Just 'Convenience.'" *Miami News*, 1 July 1974.

"The Cuban Success Story: Let Us Tell It." *Congressional Record*, 96th Cong., 2nd sess. (4 August 1980).

Danahay, Martin A. "Richard Rodriguez's Poetics of Manhood." In *Fictions of Masculinity: Crossing Cultures, Crossing Sexualities*, edited by Peter F. Murphy, 290–307. New York: New York University Press, 1994.

Davila, Florangela. "What It Feels Like Being on 'Outside': Asian Americans Gather For Meeting." *Seattle Times*, 26 July 2001, B1. http://academic.lexisnexis.com/.

Denning, Michael. *Cover Stories: Narrative and Ideology in the British Spy Thriller*. New York: Routledge, 1987.

Derrida, Jacques. *Acts of Literature*. Edited by Derek Attridge. New York: Routledge, 1992.

———. *Adieu to Emmanuel Levinas*. Translated by Pascale-Anne Brault and Michael Naas. Stanford, CA: Stanford University Press, 1999.

———. "Autoimmunity: Real and Symbolic Suicides." In *Philosophy in a Time of Terror: Dialogues with Jürgen Habermas and Jacques Derrida*, edited by Giovanna Borradori, 85–136. Chicago: University of Chicago Press, 2003.

———. "Force of Law: The 'Mystical Foundation' of Authority." In *Deconstruction and the Possibility of Justice*, edited by Drucilla Cornell. New York: Routledge, 1992.

———. *The Gift of Death*. Translated by David Wills. Chicago: University of Chicago Press, 1995.

———. *On Cosmopolitanism and Forgiveness*. London: Routledge, 2001.

———. "Passions: 'An Oblique Offering.'" In *Derrida: A Critical Reader*, edited by David Wood, 5–35. Oxford: Blackwell, 1992.

———. *Politics of Friendship*. Translated by George Collins. London: Verso, 1997.

———. "Psyche: The Inventions of the Other." In *Reading de Man Reading*, edited by Lindsay Waters and Wlad Godzich, 25–65. Minneapolis: University of Minnesota Press, 1989.

———. *Rogues: Two Essays on Reason*. Translated by Pacale-Anne Brault and Michael Naas. Stanford, CA: Stanford University Press, 2005.

———. *Specters of Marx: The State of the Debt, the Work of Mourning, and the New International*. Translated by Peggy Kamuf. New York: Routledge, 1994.

Dews, C. L. Barney, and Carolyn Leste Law, eds. *This Fine Place So Far From Home: Voices of Academics from the Working Class*. Philadelphia: Temple University Press, 1995.

Diaz de Villegas, Nestor. "Elián y el sistema americano." *El Nuevo Herald*, 18 April 2000.

Dimock, Wai Chee. *Residues of Justice: Literature, Law, Philosophy*. Berkeley: University of California Press, 1996.

Dirlik, Arif. "Asians on the Rim: Transnational Capital and Local Community in the Making of Contemporary Asian America." *Amerasia Journal* 22, no. 3 (1996): 1–24.

Dolinsky, Lewis. "A Chinese Spy Mystery Remains Just That." *San Francisco Chronicle*, 18 March 2001, WB1. http://academic.lexisnexis.com/.

Dorschner, John, and Damarys Ocaña. "Deep Anguish over Elián Splitting the Community." *Miami Herald*, 7 May 2000, 1A.

Douthat, Bill. "Miami's Cuban Community Strengthens Its Position." Cox News Service, 15 April 2000. http://academic.lexisnexis.com/.

Eason, David L. "New Journalism, Metaphor and Culture." *Journal of Popular Culture* 15, no. 4 (1982): 142–49.

"Elián: El hijo de los delfines." *La Voz Libre*, 21 January 2000.

Eng, David L. "Out Here and Over There: Queerness and Diaspora in Asian American Studies." *Social Text* 15, no. 3-4 (1997): 31–52.

Estorino, Julio. "Los tres niños y el milagro posible." *Diario Las Américas*, 28 January 2000 (translated by Christopher Sánchez).

Ferreira, Ramon. "Elián: Derecho o maniobra política?" *El Nuevo Herald*, 16 June 2000.

———. "¿Quién es el padre de moisés?" *El Nuevo Herald*, 28 March 2000, 10A.

Flores, William V. "Citizens vs. Citizenry: Undocumented Immigrants and Latino Cultural Citizenship." In *Latino Cultural Citizenship: Claiming Identity, Space, and Rights*, edited by William V. Flores and Rina Benmayor, 255–78. Boston: Beacon Press, 1997.

Foley, Barbara. "What's at Stake in the Culture War." *New England Quarterly* 68, no. 3 (1995): 459–79.

Fox, Claire E. "Comparative Literary Studies of the Americas." *American Literature* 76, no. 4 (2004): 871–86.

Frankenberg, Ruth. "Introduction: Local Whitenesses, Localizing Whiteness." In *Displacing Whiteness: Essays in Social and Cultural Criticism*, edited by Ruth Frankenberg, 1–34. Durham, NC: Duke University Press, 1997.

Fregoso, Rosa Linda. *meXicana Encounters: The Making of Social Identities on the Borderlands*. Berkeley: University of California Press, 2003.

Friedman, Susan Stanford. *Mappings: Feminism and the Cultural Geographies of Encounter*. Princeton, NJ: Princeton University Press, 1998.

Furman, Andrew. "Immigrant Dreams and Civic Promises: (Con-)Testing Identity in Early Jewish American Literature and Gish Jen's *Mona in the Promised Land*." *MELUS* 25 (Spring 2000): 209–26.

García, Ignacio M. "Juncture in the Road: Chicano Studies Since 'El Plan de Santa Barbara.'" In *Chicanas/Chicanos at the Crossroads: Social, Economic, and Political Change*, edited by David Maciel and Isidro D. Ortiz, 181–203. Tucson: University of Arizona Press, 1996.

García, María Cristina. *Havana USA: Cuban Exiles and Cuban Americans in South Florida, 1959–1994*. Berkeley: University of California Press, 1996.

Goldberg, David Theo. *The Racial State*. Oxford: Blackwell, 2002.

Gómez-Quiñones, Juan, and David R. Maciel. "'What Goes Around, Comes Around': Political Practice and Cultural Response in the Internationalization of Mexican Labor, 1890–1997." In *Culture across Borders: Mexican Immigration and Popular Cultures*, edited by David R. Maciel and María Herrera-Sobek, 27–65. Tucson: University of Arizona Press, 1998.

González, Gilbert G. "Segregation of Mexican Children in a Southern California City: The Legacy of Expansionism and the American Southwest." *Western Historical Quarterly* 16, no. 1 (1985): 55–76.

Grewal, Inderpal. *Transnational America: Feminisms, Diasporas, Neoliberalisms*. Durham, NC: Duke University Press, 2005.

Gruesz, Kirsten Silva. "Utopía Latina: *The Ordinary Seaman* in Extraordinary Times." *Modern Fiction Studies* 49, no. 1 (2003): 54–83.

Guillory, John. *Cultural Capital: The Problem of Literary Canon Formation*. Chicago: University of Chicago Press, 1994.

Hamilton, Cynthia. "Multiculturalism as Political Strategy." In *Mapping Multiculturalism*, edited by Avery F. Gordon and Christopher Newfield, 167–77. Minneapolis: University of Minnesota Press, 1996.

Harasym, Sarah. *Levinas and Lacan: The Missed Encounter*. Albany: State University of New York Press, 1998.

Hartman, Saidiya V. *Scenes of Subjection: Terror, Slavery, and Self-Making in Nineteenth-Century America*. New York: Oxford University Press, 1997.

Hellwig, David J. "The African-American Press and the United States Involvement in Cuba, 1902–1912." In *Between Race and Empire: African-Americans and Cubans before the Revolution*, edited by Lisa Brock and Digna Castañeda, 70–84. Philadelphia: Temple University Press, 1998.

Herrera, Andrea O'Reilly, ed. *ReMembering Cuba: Legacy of a Diaspora*. Austin: University of Texas Press, 2001.

Herrington, Stuart. "Is Wen Ho Lee a Tarnished Martyr?" *San Diego Union-Tribune*, 6 October 2000. http://academic.lexisnexis.com/.

Hertzberg, Hendrik. "A Tale of Two Cubas." *The New Yorker*, 17 April 2000, 33. http://academic.lexisnexis.com/.

Heymann, Philip B. "Civil Liberties and Human Rights in the Aftermath of September 11." *Harvard Journal of Law & Public Policy* 25, no. 2 (2002): 441–56.

Hirabayashi, Lane Ryo, and Marilyn Alquizola. "Asian American Studies: Reevaluating for the 1990s." In *The State of Asian America: Activism and Resistance in the 1990s*, edited by Karin Aguilar-San Juan, 351–64. Boston: South End Press, 1994.

Hohler, Bob. "As Rage Dies Down, Little Havana Experiences Sense of Loss." *Boston Globe*, 24 April 2000.

Holt, Pat. "It Takes Two Books to Untangle Story of Accused Spy." *Pittsburgh Post-Gazette*, 3 March 2002, E-9. http://academic.lexisnexis.com/.

Horowitz, Irving Louis. *The Conscience of Worms and the Cowardice of Lions:*

Cuban Politics and Culture in an American Context. New Brunswick, NJ: Transaction Publishers, 1993.

———. "Los dos Cuba de Elián González." *El Nuevo Herald,* 16 April 2000, 127.

Horwitz, Morton J. "Jews and McCarthyism: A View from the Bronx." In *Secret Agents: The Rosenberg Case, McCarthyism, and Fifties America,* edited by Marjorie Garber and Rebecca L. Walkowitz, 257–63. New York: Routledge, 1995.

Hsu, Ruth Y. "'Will the Model Minority Please Identify Itself?': American Ethnic Identity and Its Discontents." *Diaspora* 5, no. 1 1996): 37–63.

Hua, Vanessa. "A Daughter's Struggle; Fighting to Free Her Father, Charged with Violating National Security." *San Francisco Examiner,* 11 June 2000, D1. http://academic.lexisnexis.com/.

Iglesias, Aurelio Torrente. "El vir del castrismo en la prensa norteamericana." *Diario Las Américas,* 20 April 2000 (translated by Christopher Sánchez).

Infante, Guillermo Cabrera. "El niño prodigo." *El Nuevo Herald,* 24 February 2000, 17A.

Jacobs, Carol. "Allegories of Reading Paul de Man." In *Reading de Man Reading,* edited by Lindsay Waters and Wlad Godzich, 105–20. Minneapolis: University of Minnesota Press, 1989.

JanMohammed, Abdul, and David Lloyd. *The Nature and Context of Minority Discourse.* New York: Oxford University Press, 1990.

Jen, Gish. *Mona and the Promised Land.* New York: Alfred Knopf, 1996.

———. *Typical American.* New York: Plume, 1991.

Joseph, Miranda. *Against the Romance of Community.* Minneapolis: University of Minnesota Press, 2002.

Juffer, Jane. "In Search of the Latino Public Sphere: Everywhere and Nowhere." *Neaplanta: Views from the South* 4, no. 2 (2003): 263–68.

———. "The Limits of Culture: Latino Studies, Diversity Management, and the Corporate University." *Neaplanta: Views from the South* 2, no. 2 (2002): 265–93.

Kalra, Virinder S., Raminder Kaur, and John Hutnyk. *Diaspora & Hybridity.* London: Sage Publications, 2005.

Kang, Laura Hyun Yi. *Compositional Subjects: Enfiguring Asian/American Women.* Durham, NC: Duke University Press, 2002.

Kaplan, Amy. *Anarchy of Empire in the Making of U.S. Culture.* Cambridge, MA: Harvard University Press, 2002.

———. "The Birth of an Empire." *PMLA* 114, no. 5 (1999): 1068–79.

———. "Romancing the Empire: The Embodiment of American Masculinity in the Popular Historical Novel of the 1890s." In *Postcolonial Theory and the United States: Race, Ethnicity, and Literature,* edited by Amritjitt Singh and Peter Schmidt, 220–43. Jackson: University of Mississippi Press, 2000.

Kaplan, Amy, and Donald E. Pease, eds. *Cultures of United States Imperialism.* Durham, NC: Duke University Press, 1993.

Katel, Peter. "Buscan reparar la afectada imagen de los cubanoamericanos." *El Nuevo Herald*, 27 April 2000, 4A.

Kim, Daniel Y. "Do I, Too, Sing America?: Vernacular Representations and Chang-rae Lee's *Native Speaker*." *Journal of Asian American Studies* 6, no. 3 (2003): 231–60.

———. "The Strange Love of Frank Chin." In *Q & A: Queer in Asian America*, edited by David L. Eng and Alice Y. Hom, 270–303. Philadelphia: Temple University Press, 1998.

Kim, Elaine, and Lisa Lowe, eds. "New Formations, New Questions: Asian American Studies." Special issue, *positions: east asia culture critique* 5 (1997): 325–669.

Klor de Alva, Jorge, Earl Shorris, and Cornel West. "Our Next Race Question: The Uneasiness between Blacks and Latinos." In *The Latino Studies Reader: Culture, Economy, and Society*, edited by Antonia Darder and Rodolfo D. Torres, 180–89. Malden, MA: Blackwell, 1998.

Koo, George. "The Impact of the Wen Ho Lee Case on Asian Americans." *Chinese American Forum*, April 2001, 29.

Koshy, Susan. "The Fiction of Asian American Literature." *Yale Journal of Criticism* 9, no. 2 (1996): 315–46.

———. "From Cold War to Trade War: Neocolonialism and Human Rights." *Social Text* 17, no. 1 (1999): 1–32.

———. "Morphing Race into Ethnicity: Asian Americans and Critical Transformations of Whiteness." *boundary 2* 28, no. 1 (2001): 153–94.

Kraidy, Marwan M. *Hybridity, or the Cultural Logic of Globalization*. Philadelphia: Temple University Press, 2005.

Lacan, Jacques. *Feminine Sexuality: Jacques Lacan and the École Freudienne*. Edited by Juliet Mitchell and Jacqueline Rose. Translated by Jacqueline Rose. New York: W. W. Norton, 1982.

LaCapra, Dominick. "The University in Ruins?" *Critical Inquiry* 25, no. 1 (1998): 32–55.

Laclau, Ernesto, and Chantal Mouffe. *Hegemony and Socialist Strategy: Towards a Radical Democracy*. London: Verso, 1985.

Laughlin, Meg. "Elián Case Puts Miami 'Republic' in Spotlight." *Miami Herald*, 2 April 2000, 1A.

———. "Prayer Vigil Lifts Elián Fervor to New High." *Miami Herald*, 31 March 2000, 1B.

Lee, Chang-rae. *Native Speaker*. New York: Riverhead Books, 1995.

Lee, Rachel C. "Reading Contests and Contesting Reading: Chang-rae Lee's *Native Speaker*." *MELUS* 29, no. 3-4 (2004): 341–52.

Lee, Wen Ho, with Helen Zia. *My Country versus Me: The First-Hand Account by the Los Alamos Scientist Who Was Falsely Accused of Being a Spy*. New York: Hyperion, 2001.

Leitsinger, Miranda. "Elián's Fla. Home Opens as a Shrine." *The Record,* 22 October 2001, A10. http://academic.lexisnexis.com/.

Leonard, Stephen T. "A Genealogy of the Politicized Intellectual." In *Intellectuals and Public Life: Between Radicalism and Reform,* edited by Leon Fink, Stephen T. Leonard, and Donald M. Reid, 1–25. Ithaca, NY: Cornell University Press, 1996.

Levinas, Emmanuel. "Ethics as First Philosophy" (1984). Translated by Seán Hand and Michael Temple. In *The Levinas Reader,* edited by Seán Hand, 75–87. Oxford: Blackwell, 1989.

———. *Existence and Existents* (1978). Translated by Alphonso Lingis. Dordrecht: Kluwer Academic, 1995.

———. *Otherwise Than Being* (1974). Translated by Alphonso Lingis. Dordrecht: Kluwer Academic, 1991.

———. *Time and the Other* (1947). Translated by Richard A. Cohen. Pittsburgh: Duquesne University Press, 1987.

Levinson, Bradley A., Douglas E. Foley, and Dorothy C. Holland, eds. *The Cultural Production of the Educated Person: Critical Ethnographies of Schooling and Local Practice.* Albany: State University of New York Press, 1996.

Li, David Leiwei. *Imagining the Nation: Asian American Literature and Cultural Consent.* Stanford, CA: Stanford University Press, 1998.

———. "On Ascriptive and Acquisitional Americanness: *The Accidental Asian* and the Illogic of Assimilation." *Contemporary Literature* 45, no. 1 (2004): 106–34.

———. "The Production of Chinese American Tradition: Displacing American Orientalist Discourse." In *Reading the Literatures of Asian America,* edited by Shirley Geok-lin Lim and Amy Ling, 319–31. Philadelphia: Temple University Press, 1992.

Lim, Shirley Geok-lin Lim, et al. *Transnational Asian American Literature: Sites and Transits.* Philadelphia: Temple University Press, 2006.

Lim, Shirley Geok-lin, and María Herrera-Sobek, eds. *Power, Race, and Gender in Academe: Strangers in the Tower?* New York: Modern Language Association, 2000.

Lim, Shirley Geok-lin, and Amy Ling, eds. *Reading the Literatures of Asian America.* Philadelphia: Temple University Press, 1992.

Lin, Erika T. "Mona on the Phone: The Performative Body and Racial Identity in *Mona in the Promised Land.*" *MELUS* 28, no. 2 (2003): 47–57.

Linehan, Edward J. "Cuba's Exiles Bring New Life to Miami." *National Geographic Magazine,* July 1973, 68–95.

Ling, Jinqi. *Narrating Nationalisms: Ideology and Form in Asian American Literature.* New York: Oxford University Press, 1998.

Lipsitz, George. *The Possessive Investment in Whiteness: How White People Profit from Identity Politics.* Philadelphia: Temple University Press, 1998.

Liu, Eric. *The Accidental Asian: Notes of a Native Speaker.* New York: Vintage Books, 1998.

López, Ian F. Haney. *White by Law: The Legal Construction of Race.* New York: New York University Press, 1996.

Lounsberry, Barbara. "Personal Mythos and the New Journalism: Gay Talese's Fathers and Sons." *Georgia Review* 37, no. 3 (1983): 517–29.

Lowe, Lisa. *Immigrant Acts: On Asian American Cultural Politics.* Durham, NC: Duke University Press, 1996.

———. "The International within the National: American Studies and Asian American Critique." *Cultural Critique* 40 (Autumn 1998): 29–47.

Lowe, Lisa, and David Lloyd, eds. *The Politics of Culture in the Shadow of Capital.* Durham, NC: Duke University Press, 1997.

Lubiano, Wahneema, ed. *The House that Race Built: Black Americans, U. S. Terrain.* New York: Pantheon, 1997.

Lye, Colleen. *America's Asia: Racial Form and American Literature, 1893–1945.* Princeton, NJ: Princeton University Press, 2005.

Male, Belkin Cuza. "Es Elián un angel?" *El Nuevo Herald*, 28 January 2000 (translated by Christopher Sánchez).

Mamdani, Mahmood. *Good Muslim, Bad Muslim: America, the Cold War, and the Roots of Terror.* New York: Pantheon, 2004.

Margolis, Stacey. "Huckleberry Finn; or, Consequences." *PMLA* 116, no. 2 (2001): 329–44.

Markovits, Elizabeth Katharyn. "The Enemy Makes the Man: U. S. Foreign Policy, Cuban Nationalism, and Regime Survival." *Problems of Post-Communism* 48, no. 6 (2001): 31–42.

Masud-Piloto, Felix. *From Welcomed Exiles to Illegal Immigrants: Cuban Migration to the U. S., 1959–1995.* Lanham, MD: Rowman & Littlefield, 1996.

Mayberry, Katherine J., ed. *Teaching What You're Not: Identity Politics in Higher Education.* New York: New York University Press, 1996.

McCann, Sean. "Connecting Links: The Anti-Progressivism of Sui Sin Far." *Yale Journal of Criticism* 12, no. 2 (1999): 73–88.

McCarthy, Cameron, and Greg Dimitriades. "Globalizing Pedagogies: Power, Resentment, and the Re-Narration of Difference." In *Globalization and Education: Critical Perspectives*, edited by Nicholas C. Burbules and Carlos Alberto Torres, 187–204. New York: Routledge, 2000.

McDonald, Dorothy Ritsuko. Introduction to *"The Chickencoop Chinaman"; and, "The Year of the Dragon": Two Plays*, by Frank Chin. Seattle: University of Washington Press, 1981.

McLaren, Peter, and Jill Pinkney-Pastrana. "Cuba, Yanquización, and the Cult of Elián González: A View From the 'Enlightened' States." *International Journal of Qualitative Studies in Education* 14, no. 2 (2001): 201–19.

McLauchlan, Gregory, and Gregory Hooks. "Last of the Dinosaurs? Big Weapons, Big Science, and the American State from Hiroshima to the End of the Cold War." *Sociological Quarterly* 36, no. 4 (1995): 749–76.

Meier, Matt S., and Feliciano Ribera. *Mexican Americans / American Mexicans: From Conquistadors to Chicanos*. 2nd ed. New York: Hill and Wang, 1993.

Michaels, Walter Benn. *Our America: Nativism, Modernism, and Pluralism*. Durham, NC: Duke University Press, 1997.

Milbank, John. "Sovereignty, Empire, Capital, and Terror." In *Dissent from the Homeland: Essays after September 11*, edited by Stanley Hauerwas and Frank Lentricchia, 305–24. Durham, NC: Duke University Press, 2002.

Miller, J. Hillis. *On Literature*. London: Routledge, 2002.

Moore, Deborah Dash. "Reconsidering the Rosenbergs: Symbol and Substance in Second Generation American Jewish Consciousness." *Journal of American Ethnic History* 8 (Fall 1988): 21–37.

Moraga, Cherríe. *Loving in the War Years: Lo que nunca pasó por sus labios*. Boston: South End Press, 1983.

Mordue, Mark. "The Pull of 'New Gravity.'" *The Nation*, 6 May 2002. http://www.ebscohost.com/thisTopic.php?marketID=1&topicID=3.

Morris, Rosalind C. "Theses on the Questions of War: History, Media, Terror." *Social Text 72* 20, no. 3 (2002): 149–75.

Muñoz, Carlos, Jr. *Youth, Identity, Power: The Chicano Movement*. London: Verso, 1989.

Nash, Phil Tajitsu. "Washington Journal: Elián Gonzalez and the Context of History." *Asian Week*, 3 May 2000, 12.

Ngai, Mae. *Impossible Subjects: Illegal Aliens and the Making of Modern America*. Princeton, NJ: Princeton University Press, 1994.

Nguyen, Viet Thanh. *Race and Resistance: Literature and Politics in Asian America*. Oxford: Oxford University Press, 2002.

Noble, David W. "The Anglo-Protestant Monopolization of 'America.'" In *José Martí's "Our America": From National to Hemispheric Cultural Studies*, edited by Jeffrey Belnap and Raúl Fernández, 253–74. Durham, NC: Duke University Press, 1998.

Oboler, Suzanne. *Ethnic Labels, Latino Lives: Identity and the Politics of (Re)Presentation in the United States*. Minneapolis: University of Minnesota Press, 1995.

Omatsu, Glenn. "The 'Four Prisons' and the Movements of Liberation: Asian American Activism from the 1960s to the 1990s." In *The State of Asian America: Activism and Resistance in the 1990s*, edited by Karin Aguilar-San Juan, 19–69. Boston: South End Press, 1994.

Omi, Michael, and Howard Winant. *Racial Formations in the United States: From the 1960s to the 1990s*. 2nd ed. New York: Routledge, 1994.

Ong, Aiwha. *Flexible Citizenship: The Cultural Logics of Transnationality*. Durham, NC: Duke University Press, 1999.

Ong, Aihwa, and Donald M. Nonini, eds. *Ungrounded Empires: The Cultural Politics of Modern Chinese Transnationalism*. New York: Routledge, 1997.

Ortíz, Ricardo L. "*Café, Culpa*, and *Capital*: Nostalgic Addictions of Cuban Exile." *Yale Journal of Criticism* 10, no. 1 (1997): 63–84.

Palumbo-Liu, David. *Asian/American: Historical Crossings of a Racial Frontier*. Stanford, CA: Stanford University Press, 1999.

Paredes, Américo. *George Washington Gómez: A Mexicotexan Novel*. Houston: Arte Público Press, 1990.

———. "The Gringo." In *The Hammon and the Beans and Other Stories*, 43–56. Houston: Arte Público Press, 1994.

Paredes, Raymund A. "Mexican-American Literature: An Overview." In *Recovering the U.S. Hispanic Literary Heritage*, edited by Ramón Gutiérrez and Genaro Padilla, 31–51. Houston: Arte Público Press, 1993.

Parikh, Crystal. "'The Most Outrageous Masquerade': Queering Asian American Masculinity." *Modern Fiction Studies* 48, no. 4 (2002): 858–98.

Park, Edward J. W., and John S. W. Park. "A New American Dilemma?: Asian Americans and Latinos in Race Theorizing." *Journal of Asian American Studies* 2, no. 3 (1999): 289–309.

Pease, Donald E. "The Patriot Acts." *boundary 2* 29, no. 2 (2002): 29–43.

Peng, Tzy C. "The Tragic Case of Wen Ho Lee." *Chinese American Forum*, October 2000, 26.

Poblete, Juan, ed. *Critical Latin American and Latino Studies*. Minneapolis: University of Minnesota Press, 2003.

Popkewitz, Thomas S. "Reform as the Social Administration of the Child: Globalization of Knowledge and Power." In *Globalization and Education: Critical Perspectives*, edited by Nicholas C. Burbules and Carlos Alberto Torres, 157–86. New York: Routledge, 2000.

Portes, Alejandro, and Alex Stepick. *City on the Edge: The Transformation of Miami*. Berkeley: University of California Press, 1993.

Prashad, Vijay. *The Karma of Brown Folk*. Minneapolis: University of Minnesota Press, 2000.

Rackow, Sharon H. "How the USA PATRIOT ACT Will Permit Governmental Infringement upon the Privacy of Americans in the Name of 'Intelligence' Investigations." *University of Pennsylvania Law Review* 150, no. 5 (2002): 1651–96.

Ramirez, Deborah A. "It's Not Just Black and White Anymore." In *The Latino/a Condition: A Critical Reader*, edited by Richard Delgado and Jean Stefancic, 478–87. New York: New York University Press, 1998.

Ramo, Joshua Cooper. "The Odyssey of Elián González: A Big Battle for a Little Boy." *Time*, 17 January 2000, 58–67.

Ramos, Ronnie. "1 in 5 Dade Cubans Would Go Back." *Miami Herald*, 20 February 1990, 1.

Readings, Bill. *The University in Ruins.* Cambridge, MA: Harvard University Press, 1996.

Robbins, Bruce. "Comparative Cosmopolitanisms." In *Cosmopolitics: Thinking and Feeling beyond the Nation,* edited by Pheng Cheah and Bruce Robbins, 246–64. Minneapolis: University of Minnesota Press, 1998.

Rodríguez, Randy A. "Richard Rodriguez Reconsidered: Queering the Sissy (Ethnic) Subject." *Texas Studies in Literature and Language* 40, no. 4 1998): 396–423.

Rodriguez, Richard. *Days of Obligation: An Argument with My Mexican Father.* New York: Penguin, 1992.

———. *Hunger of Memory: The Education of Richard Rodriguez.* Boston: David R. Godine, 1982.

Romero, Mary, Pierrette Hondagneu-Sotelo, and Vilma Ortiz, eds. *Challenging Fronteras: Structuring Latina and Latino Lives in the U. S.* London: Routledge, 1997.

Rorty, Richard. "Justice as a Larger Loyalty." In *Cosmopolitics: Thinking and Feeling beyond the Nation,* edited by Pheng Cheah and Bruce Robbins, 45–58. Minneapolis: University of Minnesota Press, 1998.

Rosenberg, Carol. "National Polls Steadily Support Return of Elián." *Miami Herald,* 23 February 2000, 3B.

Ross, Andrew. *No Respect: Intellectuals and Popular Culture.* New York: Routledge, 1989.

———. "The Work of the State." In *Secret Agents: The Rosenberg Case, McCarthyism, and Fifties America,* edited by Marjorie Garber and Rebecca L. Walkowitz, 291–99. New York: Routledge, 1995.

Rowe, John Carlos. *Post-Nationalist American Studies.* Berkeley: University of California Press, 2000.

Said, Edward. *Representations of the Intellectual: The 1993 Reith Lectures.* New York: Pantheon, 1994.

Saldaña-Portillo, María Josefina. "Wavering on the Horizon of Social Being: The Treaty of Guadalupe-Hidalgo and the Legacy of Its Racial Character in Américo Paredes's *George Washington Gómez.*" *Radical History Review* 89 (Spring 2004): 135–64.

Saldívar, José David. *Border Matters: Remapping American Cultural Studies.* Berkeley: University of California Press, 1997.

———. *The Dialectics of Our America: Genealogy, Cultural Critique, and Literary History.* Durham, NC: Duke University Press, 1991.

Saldívar, Ramon. "The Borderlands of Culture: Américo Paredes's *George Washington Gómez* and Chicano Literature at the End of the Twentieth Century." *American Literary History* 25, no. 2 (1993): 272–93.

———. "Border Subjects and Transnational Sites: Américo Paredes's *The Hammon and the Beans* and Other Stories." In *Subjects and Citizens: Nation, Race, and Gender from Oroonoko to Anita Hill,* edited by Michael Moon and Cathy Davidson, 373–94. Durham, NC: Duke University Press, 1995.

———. Introduction to *The Hammon and the Beans and Other Stories,* by Américo Paredes. Houston: Arte Publico Press, 1994.
Sánchez, Rosaura. "Calculated Musings: Richard Rodríguez's Metaphysics of Difference." In *The Ethnic Canon: Histories and Interventions,* edited by David Palumbo-Liu, 153–73. Minneapolis: University of Minnesota Press, 1995.
Sánchez-Boudy, José. "Como Herodes en madrugada." *Diario Las Americas,* 25 April 2000.
———. "El exilio histórico: Compendio de una Cuba eterna." *Diario Las Americas,* 3 January 1990.
———. "Una decisión desacertada." *Diario Las Américas,* 22 August 2000.
San Juan, E., Jr. *Racial Formation/Critical Transformations: Articulations of Power in Ethnic and Racial Studies in the United States.* New Jersey: Humanities Press, 1992.
Sauerberg, Lars Ole. *Secret Agents in Fiction: Ian Fleming, John Le Carré and Len Deighton.* London: Macmillan, 1984.
Schedler, Christopher. "Inscribing Mexican-American Modernism in Américo Paredes' *George Washington Gómez.*" *Texas Studies in Literature and Language* 42, no. 2 (2000): 154–76.
Schroeder, Brian. "The (Non)Logic of Desire and War: Hegel and Levinas." In *Philosophy and Desire,* edited by Hugh J. Silverman, 45–62. New York: Routledge, 2000.
Sherman, Scott. "'New' Journalism." *Columbia Journalism Review* 40, no. 4 (2001): 59. http://www.ebscohost.com/thisTopic.php?marketID=1&topicID=3.
Singh, Amritjit, and Peter Schmidt, eds. *Postcolonial Theory and the United States: Race, Ethnicity, and Literature.* Jackson: University of Mississippi Press, 2000.
Soltan, Margaret. "Forum" (letters to the editor). *PMLA* 112, no. 5 (1997): 1131–32.
Sommer, Doris. "Resisting the Heat: Menchu, Morrison, and Incompetent Readers." In *Cultures of United States Imperialism,* edited by Amy Kaplan and Donald Pease, 407–32. Durham, NC: Duke University Press, 1993.
Spillers, Hortense. "Introduction: Who Cuts the Border? Some Readings on 'America.'" In *Comparative American Identities: Race, Sex, and Nationality in the Modern Text,* edited by Hortense Spillers, 1–25. New York: Routledge, 1991.
Stafford, David. *The Silent Game: The Real World of Imaginary Spies.* Athens: University of Georgia Press, 1991.
Staten, Henry. "Ethnic Authenticity, Class, and Autobiography: The Case of *Hunger of Memory.*" *PMLA* 113, no. 1 (1998): 103–16.
Staub, Michael E. "Black Panthers, New Journalism, and the Rewriting of the Sixties." *Representations* 57, no. 1 (1997): 52–72.
Steinback, Robert. "Cuban Exiles in Need of Allies." *Miami Herald,* 6 January 2000, 1B.

Sterngold, James. "Asian Americans Outraged about Arrest of Scientist." *Austin American-Statesman*, 13 December 1999, A11. http://academic.lexisnexis.com/.

Stober, Dan, and Ian Hoffman. *A Convenient Spy: Wen Ho Lee and the Politics of Nuclear Espionage*. New York: Simon and Schuster, 2001.

Suro, Roberto. "The Next Wave: How Immigration Blurs the Race Discussion." *Washington Post*, 19 July 1998.

Takagi, Dana Y. *The Retreat from Race: Asian-American Admissions and Racial Politics*. New Brunswick, NJ: Rutgers University Press, 1992.

Takaki, Ronald. *Strangers from a Different Shore*. Boston: Little, Brown, 1989.

Tamargo, Augustin. "La honra en el estrado." *El Nuevo Herald*, 4 June 2000, 30A.

———. "Los enfermos del exilio." *El Nuevo Herald*, 1 October 1989.

"The *Times* and Wen Ho Lee." *New York Times*, 26 September 2000, A2. http://academic.lexisnexis.com/.

Tilden, Norma. "Word Made Flesh: Richard Rodriguez's 'Late Victorians' as Nativity Story." *Texas Studies in Language and Literature* 40, no. 4 (1998): 442–59.

Todorov, Tzvetan. "Forum" (letters to the editor). *PMLA* 112, no. 5 (1997): 1121–22.

Tölölyan, Khachig. "The Nation-State and Its Others: In Lieu of a Preface." *Diaspora* 1, no. 1 (1991): 3–7.

Triay, Victor Andres. *Fleeing Castro: Operation Pedro Pan and the Cuban Children's Program*. Gainesville: University of Florida Press, 1998.

United States. Department of Commerce. Bureau of the Census. *Profiles of General Demographic Characteristics 2000: 2000 Census of Population and Housing: United States*. 2 vols. Washington, DC: U.S. Dept. of Commerce, Economics and Statistics Administration, U.S. Census Bureau, 2001.

"Update: The Wen Ho Lee Case." *Chinese American Forum*, July 2000, 40.

Veiga, Alex. "Elián Saga United Cuban Exiles, but Hurt Image, Political Clout." Associated Press State and Local Wire, 28 June 2000. http://academic.lexisnexis.com/.

Viglucci, Andres, and Diana Marrero. "Poll Reveals Widening Split over Elián." *Miami Herald*, 9 April 2000, 1A.

Villareals, José Antonio. *Pocho* (1959). New York: Anchor, 1994.

Visweswaran, Kamala. "Betrayal: An Analysis in Three Acts." In *Scattered Hegemonies: Postmodernity and Transnational Feminist Practices*, edited by Inderpal Grewal and Caren Kaplan, 90–109. Minneapolis: University of Minnesota Press, 1996.

———. "Diaspora by Design: Flexible Citizenship and South Asians in U.S. Racial Formations." *Diaspora* 6, no. 1 (1997): 5–29.

Volpp, Leti. "'Obnoxious to Their Very Nature': Asian Americans and Constitutional Citizenship." *Asian Law Journal* 8, no. 1 (2001): 71–87.

Wald, Priscilla. *Constituting Americans: Cultural Anxiety and Narrative Form.* Durham, NC: Duke University Press, 1995.

Wang, Jessica. *American Science in an Age of Anxiety: Scientists, Anticommunism, and the Cold War.* Chapel Hill: University of North Carolina Press, 1999.

Wei, William. *The Asian American Movement.* Philadelphia: Temple University Press, 1993.

Weiner, Mark. S. "Teutonic Constitutionalism: The Role of Ethno-Juridical Discourse in the Spanish-American War." In *Foreign in a Domestic Sense: Puerto Rico, American Expansion, and the Constitution,* edited by Christina Duffy Burnett and Burke Marshall. Durham, NC: Duke University Press, 2001.

Weingarten, Gene. "The Passion of Elián: Spirited Away from a Dictator's Land, a Child Surfaces among Those Who See in Him Their Salvation." *Washington Post,* 7 April 2000, C1. http://academic.lexisnexis.com/.

Welsome, Eileen. "Spies Lies & Portable Tapes." *Denver Westword,* 20 April 2000. http://academic.lexisnexis.com/.

Winant, Howard. "Racial Dualism at Century's End." In *The House that Race Built: Black Americans, U. S. Terrain,* edited by Wahneema Lubiano, 87–115. New York: Pantheon, 1997.

Wong, Sau-ling C. "Denationalization Reconsidered: Asian American Cultural Criticism at a Theoretical Crossroads." In *Postcolonial Theory and the United States: Race, Ethnicity, and Literature,* edited by Amritjit Singh and Peter Schmidt, 122–48. Jackson: University of Mississippi Press, 2000.

Wong, William. "DOE, FBI, Wen Ho Lee, and the 'China Card.'" *Seattle Post-Intelligencer.* 10 May 2000: A17. http://academic.lexisnexis.com/.

Wu, Frank H. "Profiling Principle: The Prosecution of Wen Ho Lee and the Defense of Asian Americans." *UCLA Asian Pacific American Law Journal* 7 (Spring 2001): 52–56.

Yamamoto, Traise. "An Apology to Althea Connor: Private Memory, Public Racialization, and Making a Language." *Journal of Asian American Studies* 5, no. 1 (2002): 13–30.

Yee, Albert H. "Elián Gonzalez and Wen Ho Lee: No Racial Profiling?" *The Asian Reporter,* 14 February 2000, 7.

Yee, James. *For God and Country: Faith and Patriotism under Fire.* New York: Public Affairs, 2005.

Yin, Xiao-huang. "The Lee Case Shakes Asian Americans' Faith in Justice System." *Los Angeles Times.* 24 September 2000, M1. http://academic.lexisnexis.com/.

Zavella, Patricia. "Living on the Edge: Everyday Lives of Poor Chicano/Mexicano Families." In *Mapping Multiculturalism,* edited by Avery F. Gordon and Christopher Newfield, 362–86. Minneapolis: University of Minnesota Press, 1996.

Index

Accidental Asian, The. See under Liu, Eric
African American(s), black Americans, 17, 21, 51–52, 75, 77, 139, 144, 181n86; history, 80, 181n86; incorporation of, as citizens, 17–18, 177n66, 179n74, 181n85; as "majority minority," 31, 184n12; politics, 77, 192n27, 194nn53, 54, 203n65; relations with Asians and Latinos, 35, 107, 116, 138–39, 144–45, 181n86, 194n53, 207–8n9, 209–10n19, 212–13n39, 213n40; representations of, 34, 42–43, 51, 73, 74; segregation of, 17, 21. *See also* blackness
alien(s), citizens, 17–22, 23 121, 181n86; the "forever foreign," 39; national, 17–19, 21, 75, 86–87, 115, 117, 119, 164, 178–79n72, 179n73; others, 14, 16, 29, 121, 128, 176nn55, 56, 181n13. *See also under* Asian(s)
alienation, of Asians and Latinos, 16, 20, 80, 119, 145, 179–80n74, 181n85, 185n23, 199n1; of the body, 197–98n114; cultural and political, 100, 103, 201n20; as effect of modernity, 21, 181n86; socioeconomic, 78
alien land laws, 19
allegory, of the arrival of the subject, 61; of desire, 48, 128; of ethical responsibility, 38, 128; of intellectual work, 23, 97–98, 100, 104, 119 120–23, 130; as literary form, 122–23

American exceptionalism, 20, 36, 93, 136, 146, 180nn79, 80, 198n122
American Indians. *See* Native Americans
Arar, Maher, 163–64, 170
Asian(s), alien or other, 16–21, 119, 179–80n74, 181n86; diaspora, 70, 196n73; exclusion,16, 17, 19–20, 33, 179–80n74, 180n81, 181n86; immigrants, 19–21, 83, 179–80n74, 181–82n86, 184n17, 194n54. *See also under* alienation; black/white binary
Asian American(s), category of, 3, 24, 64–65, 195n61; history, 69, 85, 92, 179n74; identity or subjectivity, 22, 32, 33–49, 55–62, 76–78, 183n4, 185n23, 185–86n24, 186n36, 195n61; literature, 22, 27; men, 81, 196n65; politics, 77, 80, 107, 136–39, 149–50, 153, 154, 203n65, 209nn16, 18; population, 31, 184n12; in the sciences, 152–53; studies (*see under* ethnic studies); women, 35, 38, 127, 186n34, 187–88n59. *See also under* African American(s), relations with Asians and Latinos; Chinese (Americans); Cold War politics; Filipino (Americans); Japanese (Americans); Korean (Americans); model minority
assimilation, as alienation, 71; as betrayal, 22, 67, 74, 81, 92, 194n53; education

as mode for, 90, 109, 114–17, 126; limits of, 73, 103; to the nation, 2, 17–23, 30, 32, 65–69, 71–96, 107, 109, 120–27, 141, 162, 166, 185n19, 188n66, 194nn54, 56, 206n6; as socioeconomic access, 64; into whiteness, 23, 76–77, 95, 193n44. *See also* model minority; neoconservative politics

benevolent assimilation, 180n81
betrayal, acts and instances of, 22–30, 40, 44–47, 71, 76, 95–99, 109–17, 129–34, 150–51, 175–76n49, 182–83n95, 200–201n17, 205–6n6; definition of, 1–2, 3, 10–11, 12, 60, 63, 138–39, 160, 161; of the minority subject, 15–16, 21, 22, 27, 28, 66–109, 138–47, 167, 170, 194n53, 200–201n17, 212n36; narratives of, 21, 27; parables of, 25, 28, 67, 123; politics of, 11, 13, 15, 62, 68; self-betrayal, 1, 2, 3, 10, 114, 115, 123. *See also* ethics of betrayal
bildungsroman, 50, 65, 104, 118, 120. *See also* developmental narrative
black Americans. *See* African Americans
blackness, 35, 42, 63, 73, 75, 76, 95, 178n68, 181n86; black English, 73–74; separatism, 75. *See also* black/white binary
black/white binary, 20, 23, 63; Asians and Latinos in, 18, 21, 34–35, 37, 39, 42, 73, 75–76, 77, 95, 139, 177n66, 196n63, 203n65, 212–13n39. *See also* blackness; whiteness
Bourdieu, Pierre, 100, 103, 104, 200n14, 204n78
Brotons, Elizabeth, 132, 135, 206–7n7

Castro, Fidel, 23, 136–37, 140–45, 205n1, 210n22,nn25, 26, 212n32, 213n41; revolutionary government of, 130, 141–43, 208n13, 210,nn20, 24, 211nn28, 30, 212n36
Catholicism, 88–90, 180n80, 197n114, 210n20
Chicana/o (s), 19, 86, 109, 110, 178n69, 193–94n52, 195n61; category of, 64, 195n61; history, 110, 195n61; identity or subjectivity, 110; literature, 110; nationalism (*see under* nationalism); studies (*see under* ethnic studies)
The Chickencoop Chinaman. See Chin, Frank

Chin, Frank, *The Chickencoop Chinaman*, 22, 33–38, 39, 46, 61, 63, 185n24, 186n36, 188n68
Chinese (Americans), activism and politics in Wen Ho Lee case, 134–39, 152, 214n48; Exclusion Act, 179–80n79; Chinatown, 82–83; diaspora, 83–84, 146, 158, 196n73, 209n18, 216n82; representations of, 23, 29, 34–35, 40–44, 52– 57, 84, 127–65, 165, 185n23, 208n15. *See also under* Communism
citizenship, bars to, 18–20; citizen as normative subject, 21, 30, 104, 184n17; "generic," 65, 70, 75; promise of equal protection and freedom for citizens, 16, 64–65, 149, 178–79n72, 181n85; racialized, 17–19, 80, 163–64, 177–78n67, 181n85, 181–82n86; and sovereignty, 161, 163, 176n59; and whiteness, 80
civil rights discourse and politics, as counter-discourse, 16, 138; and human rights, 154–59, 216n79; in the juridical arena, 54; national limits of, 32, 80, 145, 153, 154, 178n72; post-Civil Rights era and politics, 53, 77, 78, 110; reforms resulting from, 31, 164
class, and education, 74, 88, 108, 110, 124; global formation of, 31–32, 184n16; intellectuals as a, 98–100, 195n61, 199n4, 200n14, 204n78; as marker of minoritarian subjectivity, 63, 74; middle-, 71, 74, 80, 86, 110, 181–82n86, 194–95n58, 195n62; national boundaries of, 181–82n86; and race, 74–81, 94, 193nn43, 44, 194–95n58, 195n62
Cold War politics, and Asian Americans, 136, 150; bilateralism, 152; intelligence, 151; and Cuba(ns), 137, 140–44, 212n37; post- (*see* New World Order); refugees, 31, 39, 208nn10, 11; and September 11, 160, 162, 216n2
Communism, anti-, 152, 205–6n6; in China, 144, 154, 158, 216n81; in Cuba, 142, 144, 158, 210n24, 211n25, 212n36, 214n48; specter of, in New World Order, 24, 134, 136, 144, 158
community, 199n2; divide between university and, 23, 101–4, 122, 201nn19, 20; future terrain of, 63; loyalty to, 96, 98; traitor to, 96, 106, 108, 120

INDEX / 239

Cuban (Americans), diasporic nationalism, 140–43, 144, 205–6n6; and the Elián González case, 23, 129–47, 205n1, 210nn20, 22, 24, 211nn25, 27, 28, 30, 212nn32, 37, 212–13n39, 213nn40, 41; exiles 136–37, 140–42, 154, 207n8, 207–8nn9, 10, 13, 209–10n19, 211n26, 212n36. *See also under* Cold War politics; Communism; model minority
cultural capital, 27, 32, 99, 108, 123, 200n14, 200n17, 204n78
cultural nationalism. *See under* nationalism

Days of Obligation. See Rodriguez, Richard.
deconstruction, 9, 63, 155, 174n23, 188n68. *See also* Derrida, Jacques
democracy, access, 29, "actual," 8–9; democratic politics, 9; ethnic studies and, 29; liberal (*see* liberal discourse and politics); the others of, 163, "to come," 8–10, 27, 59, 63, 92, 122, 123, 175nn32, 42; U.S. image of itself as (*see under* nation, national self-image)
Derrida, Jacques, 3, 6–10, 13, 26, 28, 36, 46, 50, 57–63, 129, 130, 155, 158, 160, 162, 174n17, 175nn26, 32, 37, 42, 186n31, 190nn111, 113. *See also* deconstruction
desire, agency of, 125; ambivalence of, 92; for democracy and justice, 9; ethical, 7, 188–89n68; racial, 186n33; sexual, 38, 45–51, 59–60, 85. *See also under* diaspora, diasporic desire
developmental narrative, 38, 127; of Asian (American) selfhood, 39, 43, 58; of the nation, 131, 140, 153, 191–92n18. *See also* bildungsroman
diaspora, diasporic desire, 24, 42, 128–49, 150, 153, 159; diasporic difference or otherness, 12, 22, 33–37, 42, 56, 61–63, 92, 185n21; diasporic loyalty, 16, 32–33, 42, 61, 82, 87, 91; studies and methodology, 22, 29–33, 37, 183nn1, 4, 17, 184n17, 196n73, 205n2. *See also under* Asian(s); Chinese (Americans)
difference, social, 2, 13–14, 40, 111, 120, 179n73. *See also under* diaspora, diasporic difference
Dreyfus affair, 200n9
DuBois, W. E. B., 181n86

education, 65, 68, 69, 78, 88, 90, 104–18, 123–26, 165, 192n27, 216n80. *See also* pedagogy. *See also under* assimilation
empire. *See* imperialism
ethico-politics, 6–10, 22, 27, 32–33, 37–38, 53, 118, 130; agency, 130 ,156
ethics, ethical critique or inquiry, 1–6, 10, 15–16, 26; ethical obligation or responsibility, 7, 10, 13, 14, 49, 62, 92, 97, 98, 122–28; as first philosophy, 4, 6, 7; as hospitality (*see* hospitality); post-Enlightenment, 4–15, 188–89n68. *See also* Levinas, Emmanuel
ethics of betrayal, 3, 10–13, 61–63
ethnic enclaves, 82, 187n51
ethnic studies, 13, 101, 103, 125–26, 200–201n17, 201n18, 201–2n21; Asian American studies, 25, 28, 137, 152, 193n52, 201nn18, 20; Chicana/o and Latina/o studies, 25, 28, 92, 195n61, 201n20; division from minority communities, 23, 97–98, 101, 104, 122, 201n20; paradigm shifts in, 22, 29–30; politics of, 68, 80, 97. *See also under* democracy
ethnicity paradigm, 79

fathers, 34, 37, 65, 70, 71, 81–87, 91–92, 142, 147, 203n68, 211n28
femininity, 35–38, 82–83, 88, 89, 127, 135, 174n17, 184n17, 188n68, 197n112, 218n30
Filipino (Americans), 18, 112, 177n65, 179–80n74, 180n81
feminism, 4, 11, 38 110, 176n51, 186n34, 187–88n59, 192n27, 198n122, 218n30
For God and Country. See Yee, James
foreclosure, 5, 12, 22, 33–37, 46, 56, 87
futurity, 3, 5, 8–10, 11, 13, 47, 50, 56 59, 61, 62–63, 71. *See also under* democracy; justice

George Washington Gómez. See Paredes, Américo
globalization, 30–33, 131, 134, 183n6, 184n16; and human rights, 154–57, 159, 162, 215n76. *See also* transnationalism
González, Elián, 23, 129, 131–35, 137–47, 153–59, 205n1, 206–7n7, 209 -10n19, 210nn20, 24, 216n80. *See also under* Cuban (Americans)
"The Gringo." *See* Paredes, Américo

240 / INDEX

Guantánamo Bay, 161, 165–70

Heidegger, Martin, 5–6, 8,n174n17
Hispanics. *See under* Latina/o(s)
hospitality, 15, 174n17, 179n73, 190n111
Huckleberry Finn, 50–54
human rights, 24, 129, 154–59, 163, 167, 169, 170, 171, 215n76, 216nn79, 81. *See also under* civil rights discourse and politics
Hunger of Memory. See Rodriguez, Richard
hybridity, 39, 48, 55, 56, 61, 104, 188n66

immigration, 179n73; 1965–reforms, 31, 183–84n11; incorporation of European immigrants, 17; policy, 17–20. *See also under* Asian(s), exclusion, immigrants; Latina/o(s); Mexican (Americans)
imperialism, 17–20, 93–95, 177nn64, 66, 177–78n67, 179n74, 180nn80, 81, 205n5; American expansionism, 17–18, 20, 93–95, 157, 163, 179n47, 181n86
indigenous peoples. *See* Native Americans
Insular Cases, 18
intellectual(s), 23, 25, 98–103, 118–28, 194–95n58, 195n61, 199nn2, 4, 6, 200n14, 200–201n17; as intelligence agent, 23, 95, 97–98, 109, 118, 119, 151; production, 23, 97, 119, 122, 124, 201n20, 204n78. *See also under* class
irony, 47, 48, 50, 53, 56–57, 62, 90, 143, 154, 162, 169, 199n1

Japanese (Americans), 19, 34, 40–41, 44, 74, 76, 178n2, 179–80n74; internment, 19, 138, 178–79n72, 181n86, 209–10n19
Jen, Gish, *Mona in the Promised Land*, 22, 33, 38, 39–63, 128, 187n51, 187n6, 188–89n68; *Typical American*, 39, 55, 58, 59, 60
Jewish (Americans) identity, 39– 43, 52, 84–85, 205–6n6
justice, 3, 6–10, 13, 48, 58, 62, 155–56; political and social, 1, 2, 29, 54–55, 59, 78, 92, 138; "to come," 8–10, 59, 175n26, 190n113

knowledge production, 97–108, 111, 118–26, 151–52, 200–201n17, 214–15n62
Korean (Americans), 76, 111, 115, 121, 127

Lacanian psychoanalysis, 188–89n68
Latina/o(s), as category, 3, 14, 24; immigrants, 19, 21, 184n12; population, 16, 31, 184n12; racialization of, 19, 177–78n67; studies (*see under* ethnic studies); Hispanics, 65, 66, 77, 79. *See also under* African American(s), relations with Asians and Latinos; alienation; black/white binary; Chicana/o(s); Cuban (Americans); Mexican (Americans); Puerto Rican(s)
Lee, Chang-rae, *Native Speaker*, 2, 10, 23, 97–98, 100, 104, 110–22, 123, 124–28, 199n3, 203nn52, 57, 65, 66 68
Lee, Sylvia, 135, 206–7n7
Lee, Wen Ho, 23, 129, 130–35, 136–39, 145–54, 170, 205–6n6, 206–7n7, 208–9n15, 209nn17, 18, 213–14n47, 214nn48, 50, 51, 214–15n62, 215n67. *See also* Lee, Sylvia
Levinas, Emmanuel, 4–5, 6, 13–14, 49, 123, 173–74n7, 176n55, 188–89n68
liberal discourse and politics, 16–23, 37, 38, 49, 54, 61, 63, 154–57, 164–70, 173n3, 187–88n59; limits of, 81; neoliberalism, 21, 66–67, 101, 58, 183n6, 195n61, 205–6n6
literature, acts of, 26–28, 182n92, 182–83n95; literary canons, 24, 204n78; literary reading, 26–27, 123; literary vision of politics, 122; U.S. emergent or ethnic, 24, 32, 70, 110, 119, 123, 187–88n59. *See also* allegory; parable
Liu, Eric, 67, 68, 80, 96; *The Accidental Asian*, 22, 66, 68–71, 76–78, 81, 82–85, 87, 88, 91–92, 95, 121, 193n44, 196nn65, 73
loyalty, 11–12, 24, 27–28, 62, 130; "larger," 2; to the nation, 16, 23–28, 31, 96–98, 146, 164, 169

masculinity, 38, 66, 71, 81, 84, 87, 88, 90, 196n65, 197n112, 218n30; machismo, 85; manhood, 33, 38, 70, 72, 81–91
melancholy, 33, 47, 58, 84, 188n62
Mexican (Americans), 19, 177–78n67; deporations of, 19, 110, 178n69; and education, 110; immigration, 17, 70, 85–86, 110, 178n68, 184n12; representations of, 65, 71–72, 75, 86–92, 93–95, 105–9. *See also* Chicana/o(s)
Miami, 209–10n19
minority discourse, 3,11–16, 21, 30–37, 96, 109, 130–31, 173n3, 185n19; conditions of production for, 97–98, 101–2, 123, 201n20; limits of, 1, 16, 32, 128, 170;

INDEX / 241

neoconservative critique of, 70, 77, 78–80 (*see also* neoconservative politics); as oppositional, 63–64, 184n17; subjects of (*see* minority subjects). *See also* civil rights discourse and politics
minority politics, 4, 21, 42–43, 76, 77, 96, 130, 209n16
minority subjects, 2–4, 15, 16, 21–30, 130, 173n3, 181n86; founding of, 33, 37, 161
model minority, 22, 24, 65–67, 78–81, 134–39, 152, 181–82n86, 187n51, 193–94n52, 194n. 53; Cuban Americans as, 136–37, 139, 143–45, 207n8, 208n11, 212–13n39; middleman minority, 187n51. *See also under* neoconservative politics, minority neoconservatism
modernity, 18–21, 134, 157, 178n68, 181n86; "alternative modernities," 159, 163
modernism, 20, 123, 134, 143, 144, 166, 176n59, 177n64, 202–3n45
Mona in the Promised Land. See under Jen, Gish
mother(hood)s, 38, 46, 47–48, 71–72, 78, 82–83, 85–87, 135, 141, 186n34, 188n68, 197n112, 206n7; secrets of, 36–37, 59–61
multiculturalism, 25, 41, 69, 78, 87, 101, 125, 126, 140, 185n24, 188n66, 193–94n52, 194n56, 201n20; pluralism, 17, 21, 79, 176n59, 182n87, 193n44
Muslims. *See under* religion, Islam

nation, 185n19; as formation, 191–92n18; "national becoming," 41; national self-image, 16–20, 24, 93, 109, 131–34, 141–43, 146, 163–67, 180nn78, 81, 181n85, 198nn122, 125; nativism, 21, 80, 83, 179n73, 205–6n6. *See also under* developmental narrative; security, national and state
nationalism, Asian American, 36; black, 30, 64–65, 217–18n26; Chicano 30, 64, 75, 90, 110, 193–94n52, 194–95n58, 202n44; cultural, 30, 33, 64–65, 79, 80, 101, 109–11, 121, 194–95n58. *See also under* nation, national self-image, nativism
Native Americans, 69, 87, 90, 105, 107, 177n66, 177–78n67, 178n68, 180n80, 181n85
Native Speaker. See Lee, Chang-rae
negation, 87, 81, 114

neoconservative politics, 21, 32, 68, 69, 78–81, 167, 185n19, 193n44, 194n53, 201n20; minority neoconservatism, 2, 66–71, 75, 79, 84, 90–92, 100, 107, 12, 181n86, 194n53, 195n61 (*see also* model minority). *See also under* minority discourse
New Journalism, 66–67, 92, 121, 190n4, 191n17
New World Order, 24, 111, 131, 133, 134, 136, 140, 144, 153–64

Operation Peter Pan, 211n28
otherness, 4–15, 26–27, 38, 48–50, 58, 61, 170–71, 173n3; embodied other, the, 15, 18–19, 21, 29, 115, 128, 176nn51, 55, 56; loss of the other, 47, 62; obligation or responsibility to the other, 2–16, 27, 36, 48–49, 67, 102, 119, 126, 165, 190n113; "other others," 6–7, 15, 22, 23, 25, 62, 123, 126–27, 161, 170, 173n3. *See also under* aliens, alien others; Asian(s), alien or other; diaspora, diasporic difference or otherness; race, racial others

Padilla, José, 163–64, 170
panethnicity, 24–25, 33, 63, 76–77, 182n87, 186n33
parable, 1, 24, 27, 28, 118, 123
Paredes, Américo, 92; *George Washington Gómez*, 23, 97, 98, 100, 104–10, 111, 114, 117, 118–22, 123–25, 199n3, 200–201n17, 202nn27, 44, 202–3n45, 203n68; "The Gringo," 22–23, 68, 92–95, 107
pedagogy, 27–28, 102, 123, 125, 126, 130, 20n25. *See also* education
Plessy v. Ferguson, 17, 18
pluralism. *See under* multiculturalism
pocho, 22, 65, 66, 67, 71–72, 78–82, 181–82n86, 193–94n52, 194n53; *Pocho* (*see* Villareals, José Antonio). *See also under* neoconservative politics, minority neoconservatism
politics, 6–10, 15, 56, 62, 130–31, 174nn17, 23, 175n42; cultural, 188n66; of representation, 16, 25, 27, 30, 64, 108, 109–11, 153, 199n2, 200–201n17. *See also under* African American(s); *under* Asian American(s); *under* betrayal; *under* Chinese (Americans), activism and politics in Wen Ho Lee case; civil

rights discourse and politics; Cold War politics; *under* democracy, democratic politics; *under* ethnic studies, politics of; liberal discourse and politics; *under* literature, literary vision of; minority politics; neoconservative politics
postmodernity, 11, 129, 131, 134, 157, 159, 162
progressive narrative. *See* developmental narrative
professionals, 23, 32, 67, 70, 77, 95, 96, 98–100, 101–4, 109–12, 115, 119, 120, 121–28, 149, 150, 151, 166, 168, 201n20
Progressive Era reforms, 17
prolepsis, 50, 57–58
Puerto Rican(s), 18, 19, 20, 179–80n74, 192n40

queerness, 22, 37, 85, 90, 91, 92, 96, 184n17, 196n65, 197n112, 197–98n114

race, 78–81, 194n54; color line, 12, 20, 65; racial collectivity or unity, 33, 79, 80, 101, 109; racial formation, 121, 193n50; racial identity, 25, 32, 63–64, 80, 101–3, 126; racial others, 21, 53, 63, 87, 92, 119, 126, 164, 177n64, 179–80n180, 183n5, 217–18,n26. *See also* panethnicity; racism
racism, 17, 20, 53, 75, 77, 79, 80, 95, 108, 139, 179n74, 200–201n17, 203n68; racial profiling, 131, 135, 138, 147, 149, 153, 164, 170, 209n17, 214n50; racial violence, 52, 75, 80
religion, 6, 14, 24, 40, 42, 71, 79, 96, 98, 129, 136, 161–66, 170, 216n2; Islam, 205–206,n6, 216n2, 217n14. *See also* Catholicism
Rodriguez, Richard. 67, 68, 70–71, 78, 80, 81, 88, 90–92, 95, 96, 121, 193n44; *Days of Obligation*, 2, 66, 68, 69, 72, 75, 77, 81–91, 191n11, 192nn27, 40, 197n114; *Hunger of Memory*, 22, 66, 68, 71–77, 81–92, 96, 191n12, 192nn22, 27, 197nn102, 112, 113, 197–98n114, 199 n.1
Roman Catholic Church. *See* Catholicism
Rosenberg, Ethel and Julius, 205–6n6, 217n3

scapegoating, 23, 129, 138, 147, 149, 205–6n6
science, 132, 150–53, 177n64, 200n17, 214–15n62, 215n66

security, national and state, 106, 132, 137, 147, 150, 151–53, 163, 167, 169, 205–6n6, 208–9n15, 213–14n47, 214–15n62, 215nn66, 67, 217–18n26
September 11 attacks, 24, 142, 160–63, 165, 170, 186n37, 217n14, 218n30. *See also* terrorism; war on terror
Spanish-American War, 17, 20, 177n66
spies, 23, 95–98, 104–21, 132, 141, 147, 149, 150–51, 160, 168, 200n9, 206–7n7; espionage, 23, 129–30, 132, 149, 165, 167, 205–6n6, 214–15n62; spy novels, 199n3, 118, 119, 120. *See also under* intellectuals, as intelligence agent
symbolic capital. *See* cultural capital

terrorisism, 24, 160–70, 179n73, 217n26, 218n30. *See also* September 11 attacks
torture, 157, 163, 164, 218n35
traitors, 1, 2, 10–13, 23, 47, 68, 76, 95–98,109, 111,113,119, 142, 160, 162, 166, 167, 182–83n95, 188n62, 200n9
transnationalism, 24, 25, 30–33, 97, 101, 113, 131, 134, 159, 162–64, 180n78, 183n6, 184n16, 196n73, 204n78, 216n82. *See also* globalization
treason, 23, 111, 130, 136, 147, 164, 170, 180n80, 205–6n2, 214–15n62
"to come." *See* futurity
Typical American. *See under* Jen, Gish

university, the, 23, 96, 101–3, 109, 123, 126, 199n2, 201n20, 201–2n21, 202n25, 204n78
U.S.-Mexico War, 17, 19, 106, 198n125; Treaty of Guadalupe Hidalgo, 19, 177–78n67, 178nn67, 68, 198n126

Villareals, José Antonio, *Pocho*, 65

war or terror, 2, 161–64, 165, 169, 170, 216n2, 218n30
whiteness, 41, 42, 65, 74, 76–78, 80, 84, 92–95, 111, 115, 118, 193nn43, 44, 193–94n52, 195n61, 195–96n62; white authority, 34, 185–86n25. *See also* black/white binary; *under* assimilation; *under* citizenship

Yee, James, *For God and Country*, 110, 165–70